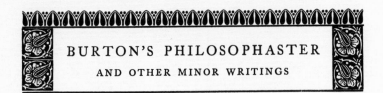

# BURTON'S PHILOSOPHASTER
### AND OTHER MINOR WRITINGS

PORTRAIT OF BURTON AT BRASENOSE COLLEGE

# ROBERT BURTON'S

# Philosophaster

WITH
AN ENGLISH TRANSLATION
OF THE SAME. TOGETHER
WITH HIS OTHER MINOR
WRITINGS IN PROSE
AND VERSE

*The translation, introductions,*
*and notes by*
PAUL JORDAN-SMITH

1931
STANFORD UNIVERSITY PRESS
STANFORD UNIVERSITY, CALIFORNIA

LONDON: HUMPHREY MILFORD
OXFORD UNIVERSITY PRESS

STANFORD UNIVERSITY PRESS
STANFORD UNIVERSITY, CALIFORNIA

LONDON: HUMPHREY MILFORD
OXFORD UNIVERSITY PRESS

———

THE MARUZEN COMPANY
TOKYO, OSAKA, KYOTO, SENDAI

THE BAKER & TAYLOR COMPANY
55 FIFTH AVENUE, NEW YORK

———

*To*

A GREAT BURTONIAN
AND SCHOLAR
Professor Edward Bensly
IN GRATITUDE

| Burton's Life | | Contemporary Events |
|---|---|---|
| 1577 | Burton born, February 8 | Drake circumnavigated the globe<br>William Harvey born, 1578<br>North's *Plutarch*, 1579<br>Timothy Bright's *Treatise on Melancholy*, 1586 |
| 1593 | Entered Brasenose College, Oxford | Sir Richard Hawkins' *Voyage to the South Seas*<br>Gerarde's *Herbal*, 1597<br>Lord Bacon's *Essays*, 1597 |
| 1599 | Elected student at Christ Church, Oxford | Death of Spenser |
| 1602 | Given degree of B.A. (June 30) | |
| 1605 | Given degree of M.A. (June 9) | *Don Quixote*, 1605 |
| 1606 | *Philosophaster* first written | Dekker's *Seven Deadlie Sinnes*<br>Shakespeare's tragedies, 1600–1607 |
| 1614 | Given degree of B.D. | John Barclay's *Icon Animorum* |
| 1615 | Clerk of the Market, Oxford, for year beginning October 10 | |
| 1616 | Made Vicar of St. Thomas Church | Death of Shakespeare |
| 1617 | *Philosophaster* acted (February 16) | |
| | | Thirty Years' War, 1618<br>Raleigh executed, 1618<br>Landing of the Pilgrims, 1620<br>Bacon's *Novum Organum*, 1620 |
| 1621 | *The Anatomy of Melancholy* published | |
| | | First English newspaper, 1622 |
| 1624 | Made Rector of Walesby; resigned, 1631<br>Second edition of *The Anatomy* | |

|  |  |  |
|---|---|---|
|  |  | Charles I's accession, 1625 |
| 1628 | Third edition of *The Anatomy* | Harvey's book on the circulation of the blood |
|  |  | Milton's *Ode on the Nativity*, 1629 |
| 1632 | Fourth edition of *The Anatomy* |  |
|  |  | Galileo appeared before the Inquisition, 1633 |
|  |  | Harvard College founded, 1636 |
| 1638 | Fifth edition of *The Anatomy* | Milton's *Lycidas*, 1638 |
| 1640 | Death of Burton, January 25 |  |
| 1651–52 | Sixth edition of *The Anatomy* |  |

# BIBLIOGRAPHIC CHECK-LIST
# OF BURTON'S WRITINGS

*The Anatomy of Melancholy:*

First edition, 1621, quarto
Second edition, 1624, folio
Third edition, 1628, folio
Fourth edition, 1632, folio
Fifth edition, 1638, folio
Sixth edition, 1651–1652, folio
Seventh edition, 1660, folio
Eighth edition, 1676, folio
Ninth edition, 1800, two volumes, octavo

*Philosophaster:*

Only printed edition:
Philosophaster, Comœdia; Poemata adhuc spar-
sim edita, nunc in unum collecta. Edited by
W. E. Buckley, Roxburghe Club. Hertford,
1862, quarto.

Poemata:

The poems appeared in various Oxford anthologies.

Preface to Rider's *Dictionarie,* editions of 1612 and 1617.

**NOTE**

A complete bibliography is soon to be issued by
Stanford University Press under the title
*Bibliographia Burtoniana*

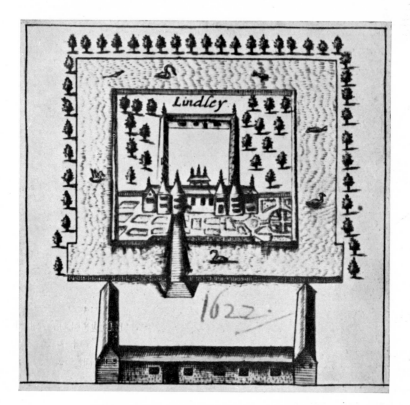

LINDLEY HALL, BURTON'S BOYHOOD HOME

## PREFACE

B Y MOST accounts it is set forth that Robert Burton was a man of but one book. He is forever identified with *The Anatomy of Melancholy,* and those who have come to love that vast compendium of wit and wisdom will feel sure that it is quite enough for one man to have produced. But, as a strict matter of fact, each of the six editions of that work, issued from 1621 until 1651, might be called, to employ the language of bibliophiles, a genuine First Edition; for on each successive appearance of *The Anatomy* he added new material, until the original quarto grew at last into the tall folio of 1651–52. Thus, by the time of his death, what with the sheaf of revisions and notes that he left behind for Cripps, his publisher, he was, on one score alone, the author of six books. That fact, however, is well enough known to good Burtonians.

The rather meager details of his life, preserved by his brother William, and by Anthony Wood,[1] Bishop White Kennet, Thomas Hearne, and John Nichols, are likewise familiar to students, though it may be well to record them here to refresh the reader's mind.

Robert Burton was born on February 8, 1577, at Lindley Hall, in Leicestershire, which, if we but glance at the picture given in William Burton's *Description of Leicestershire,*[2] was a rather noble and imposing home, the life-long habitation of his father, Ralph, and his mother, Dorothy (Faunt). Lindley Hall was situated on that long and curious Roman road called

[1] See Appendix, where Wood's account is given in full.
[2] Picture reproduced opposite.

ix

Watling Street, and it provided a comfortable background for
the nine children that were there gathered about Ralph's knees.
Robert was the fourth of these, and his relations with his
family seem to have been, judging by frequent references in
*The Anatomy* and by his will, more than ordinarily happy.
His elementary schooling at Nuneaton in Warwickshire and
at Sutton-Coldfield left no tender memories, for he speaks of
the martyrdom of children at school, who "think no slavery in
the world (as once I did myself) like to that of a grammar
scholler."[3] In 1593 Robert followed his brother William to
Brasenose College, Oxford, and six years later was elected student at Christ Church College, where he was graduated B.A.
in 1602. For a man so obviously able as Burton, nine years
seems a long period of probation. In 1602 Burton was twen-
ty-five years of age, and it was usual for men at that time to
receive graduation between the ages of sixteen and nineteen.
Mr. Arthur Fox has suggested (in his *Book of Bachelors*) that
Burton may have been ill during a part of this time and living
at home. In the absence of data it would be hazardous to make
a guess.

However that may be, Robert's University life, after 1602,
seems to have proceeded quite normally: he received his M.A.
in 1605 and his B.D. in 1614, and to the end of his days was
tutor and librarian at Christ Church. In addition to his scho-
lastic duties, Burton held three livings: he was made vicar at
St. Thomas in Oxford in 1616; between 1624 and 1631 he
was non-resident Rector of Walesby, his curate being Thomas
Benson;[4] and about 1630 Lord George Berkeley presented
him the rectory of Seagrave in Leicestershire. That Burton
participated in the social life of the University is attested by his

[3] *Anatomy*, Part I, Sec. 2, Mem. 4, Sub. 2.

[4] Information secured April, 1930, from Reverend J. W. Davis,
Rector of Walesby.

frequent contributions of verse to various anthologies for thirty-
five years, and by his play, which was produced by the students
of his college. He seems also to have been pleasantly known
about the town, and, according to the late George Parker of
the Bodleian Library, he was made Clerk of the Market for
Oxford in the year 1615.

Most of these facts, as observed before, are quite familiar.
Nevertheless, apart from *The Anatomy*, his work has remained
buried in obscurity. There were, for example, nineteen short
poems which appeared in as many now forgotten volumes issued
between 1603 and 1638. His Latin comedy, *Philosophaster*,
written in 1606 and produced at Oxford in 1617, four years
prior to the publication of *The Anatomy*, has received little
better than footnote immortality, remaining unprinted until
1862, over two hundred years after its author's death. Even
its belated publication has done little to advance a wide knowledge of Burton's work except among a few British scholars, for
it was printed only privately for a society of antiquarians and
in its original Latin. The edition was limited to but sixty-five
copies and Sir William Osler in his bibliographic notes[5] says he
spent over twelve years searching for a copy of this scarce
volume.

Readers of *The Anatomy* will recall seeing the marginal
note in that famous chapter on "The Love of Learning,"[6]
in which Burton makes reference to his play, a note which occurs in all editions from the very first. Apart from that brief
mention, giving merely the title of the play and the date of its
public performance, *Philosophaster* dropped out of knowledge
until 1861, when, in *Blackwood's Magazine* for September[7]
it was briefly mentioned, though the writer assumed the manu-

---

[5] *Bibliotheca Osleriana*, Oxford, 1929, page 419.

[6] Part I, Sec. II, Mem. 2, Sub. 5.

[7] Page 323. The article is unsigned.

script to have been lost. Then Mr. W. E. Buckley came forward with Burton's own manuscript, and, in 1862, published the first printed edition. His account of the manuscript and its history requires repeating:

The MS. belonged to the Author himself, having his name on the cover and at the end of the Play, and, in spite of some mistakes, which look like those of one copying from dictation, as suggested by Mr. Mansel, it is, no doubt, all in Burton's own hand. In his *Anatomy of Melancholy*, he complains of having no amanuensis, and it does not seem likely that he would have employed one for so short a work as this Comedy. It has the appearance of having been prepared by its Author for publication.

The Editor purchased it in 1846 from the late Mr. W. Pickering, the bookseller, who had bought it in April, 1843, at the sale by Messrs. Sotheby and Wilkinson, of the Library of Jeremiah Milles, D.D., formerly Dean of Exeter, and President of the Society of Antiquaries, whose bookplate is pasted inside the cover. Dean Milles died in 1784, and it is conjectured that the MS. had belonged to Thomas Milles, D.D., Bishop of Waterford and Lismore, previously Canon of Christ Church, and Regius Professor of Greek at Oxford in 1706–7. One reason for this supposition is that the Christian names of the actors of the Play in 1617 have been added in pencil in a hand about this date by some one who had access to the Register of Christ Church. He, most probably, became possessed of this MS. at Oxford; for though Burton bequeathed his printed books mainly to the Bodleian Library, yet he left his MSS. to his executors; and within half a century after his death they would, in the common course of things, have passed into other hands.[8]

Burton presented a second manuscript of the play to his brother William, author of the *Description of Leicestershire* (1622), and this copy found its way at last into the library of Lord Mostyn, from which, I have heard, it has since passed into American hands.

The author took care to note, on his manuscript, that the play was begun in 1606 (when the first draft was probably

---

[8] From the Preface of *Philosophaster*, 1862, pp. x–xi.

completed), then revised and corrected in 1615. It has been
suggested that this care was taken to insure against any possible
charge of plagiary from such plays as Ben Jonson's *Alchemist*
(produced in 1610; published in 1612) and Thomas Tomkis'
*Albumazar* (produced in 1614; published in 1615), both of
which dealt with the escapades of pretended alchemists and
their unfortunate victims. There is, however, but little sim-
ilarity between these, other than their common object of satire.
Those looking for sources of Burton's play will do better to
turn their attention to that section entitled "The Alchemist,"
in the *Colloquies of Erasmus,* from which, it is more than
likely, one or two hints were taken.[9] But, as in the case of
*The Anatomy,* Burton had the genius for making these rich
bits, which he had acquired through vast reading, into an original and organic whole.

We find, for example, that he has borrowed (perhaps
echoed would be the truer word) from Plautus, Terence, Ovid,
Ausonius, Juvenal, Cicero, Seneca, Virgil, Horace, Quintilian,
Porphyrius, the Latin editions of Plato, and Palingenius'
*Zodiac of Life;* and it is more than likely that he took a tip
from the satires of Bishop Joseph Hall. Professor Bensly points
out certain resemblances also to Jovius Pontanus, such as the
trick of listing the characters at the beginning of each scene.[10]

Those who are curious to note the comparison and contrast
between the work of Jonson and that of Burton should read
first the speeches of Sir Epicure Mammon,[11] and then the
soliloquy of Polupistos.[12] Both men have expended large sums

[9] See note 1 to Act IV.

[10] These borrowings are indicated in the notes at the end of the
English translation. For nearly a third of these notes I am indebted
to Professor Bensly.

[11] Act II, scene i, of *The Alchemist.*

[12] Act IV, scene i, of *Philosophaster.*

of real gold upon a wily alchemist; both have been promised a vast fortune; both, counting chickens before the hatching, make permanent plans for future glory. But Polupistos is the nobler man. He looks forward to building a bridge from Calais to Dover, to razing forests, draining marshes, and building institutions for the comfort and culture of mankind. He is a Utopian of the sort one might expect to meet after reading the Introduction to *The Anatomy of Melancholy.* He has vanity, he is foolish; but it is the noble folly of an idealist and a dreamer.

Sir Epicure Mammon, as his name suggests, is of the flesh-pots. He intends to gratify his senses:

> I do mean to have a list of wives and concubines
> Equal with Solomon.....
> I will have all my beds blown up, not stuft:
> Down is too hard.....
>                     Where I spy
> A wealthy citizen, or a rich lawyer,
> Have a sublime pure wife, unto that fellow
> I 'll send a thousand pound to make her mine.
> . . . . . . . . . . . . . . . . . . . . . . . . . . . . . . . . . . . .
>
> My meat shall all come in in Indian shells,
> Dishes of agate set in gold, and studded
> With emeralds, sapphires, hyacinths, and rubies.
> . . . . I myself will have
> The beards of barbels served instead of salads;
> Oiled mushrooms, and the swelling unctuous paps
> Of a fat pregnant sow, newly cut off,
> Drest with an exquisite and poignant sauce;
> For which I 'll say unto my cook, "There 's gold:
> Go forth, and be a knight."

*Philosophaster* is not a great drama, but it will hold its own with the great average of entertaining comedies that were produced during the first half of the seventeenth century. Burton was not a dramatist, but his humor, satire, and rich humanism have given life to an otherwise poorly constructed work. He did not know how to bring action to his stage, and his solution of the tangle of affairs at Osuna in the last act would have amused his great Stratford contemporary.

But *Philosophaster*, if not a veritable masterpiece, is delightful reading. It deserves translation. Indeed, it would require but a few strokes of the pen to convert it into a satire of modern times. The Burtonian will find the play instructive as well as amusing. He will discover, scattered through the five acts, the ideas and even some of the salty sentences that some years later were incorporated into *The Anatomy*. That satiric introduction, "Democritus Junior to the Reader," got some of them: the subsection devoted to "The Weeping Muses" got more. One feels that from the outset of his career Burton had his keen eye on institutional abuses at Oxford and that these things filled him with a righteous indignation. It would seem that even then men could buy degrees as well as livings with gold coin; that honest scholars were not always preferred; and that fakirs were, sometimes, quite successful. But, in his play, one is led to behold the ultimate triumph of honesty and truth.

All of Burton's minor writings are herein, for the first time, brought together. First, his Poemata. In the sixteenth and seventeenth centuries Oxford University issued a number of small volumes of commemorative verse in honor of various notables, and to eighteen of these Burton contributed. His contributions were collected by Mr. Buckley and printed together with his edition of *Philosophaster* under the impression that he had given to the world all the minor writings of his author. But that indefatigable Burtonian, Professor Edward Bensly, in later years, discovered that to the 1617 edition of Rider's *Dictionarie*, edited by Francis Holyoke, Burton had contributed some elegiac Latin verses;[13] there also is a Latin preface that had hitherto been overlooked. The Buckley collection and the Bensly discoveries have been included in the present volume.

Burton's poetry is not of the best—and in saying so I am conscious of understatement. Therefore I believe that, while his Poemata will prove of great interest to the student, there is little to be gained by turning them into English. Perhaps I should say that there are two exceptions to be made (Nos. V and VIII), one a tribute to Sir Thomas Bodley, of whom Burton spoke with such affection in his *magnum opus;* the other a verse in praise of Sir Henry Savile, whose mathematical and astronomical gifts to the University were greatly appreciated by Burton. But, while these tempt the translator, it is thought wiser, for the sake of consistency, to leave them in their original Latin.

Robert Burton's will has often been reprinted, but to the end that the student may have all of his minor writings in convenient form it is again reprinted here.

PAUL JORDAN-SMITH

"EREWHON,"
LOS ANGELES, CALIFORNIA
April 15, 1930

[13] Professor Falconer Madan (*Oxford Books* [Oxford, 1912], Vol. II, p. 66) points out that the verses appeared first in the edition of 1612. Professor Madan was the first to note Burton's Preface to the same work.

# TABLE OF CONTENTS

xvii

THE Latin *Philosophaster* is from the printed text edited by the late William Edward Buckley and issued by the Roxburghe Club in 1862. Mr. Buckley prepared his text from Robert Burton's own manuscript. That manuscript has not been compared, I think, with William Burton's copy, which was formerly in Lord Mostyn's Library. Since both of these manuscripts are in Robert Burton's autograph they should, properly, have been compared; but, although it is rumored that both have now found places in American libraries,[1] it has not been possible at this time to see them. One may be reasonably sure, however, that the Roxburghe text, apart from a misspelling here and a comma there, is the best text now in existence, for Robert Burton's manuscript contained his own latest corrections. The accompanying translation is the first into English.

Burton's Latin is not the easiest: it abounds in both idiom and epigram; it is packed full of allusions to ideas, proverbs, and men familiar enough to the University men of his time but occult to ours. Since those days when Burton hearkened to profane bargemen by Folly Bridge, the currents of language have swept away much that might have enabled us to enjoy his humor to the full.

---

[1] See *Oxford Bibliographical Society Proceedings and Papers*, Volume I, Part III, page 86, where it is related that Mr. Buckley's manuscript is in America, and that Lord Mostyn's Library was sold in 1920. The Buckley manuscript was purchased by Mr. W. A. White of New York; Quarich bought the Mostyn manuscript.

I have long waited in the hope that one more competent would undertake this work of translation, believing that Burton's eternal hold upon human interest might perforce compel some Oxford Don, saturated with the lore of that fascinating period, to read his fellow to the modern world. Failing that, I have at last succumbed to impatience and attempted to do the interpretation myself. For interpretation, rather than a literal rendering, has been my constant aim: and, to preserve the spirit of Democritus, Junior, I have, where it seemed fitting, used those expressions that are familiar to the readers of *The Anatomy of Melancholy*.

Consistency has been deliberately disregarded, and I trust that those who may be familiar with the Latin text may not be too pained thereby. The original is in verse, as Burton's note to the Argument will indicate, but, for the sake of greater clarity I have chosen to resort to prose except where the poetaster, Amphimacer, and the love-lorn Antonius have made the use of doggerel verse inevitable. The songs, as a matter of course, have been turned into what I hope is characteristic Burtonese "poetry."

So, without further apology, I leave the matter to the gentle reader and the scholarly critic. I have so often sneered at the blunders of poor translators that it is only fitting for me here to lay myself open to the diatribes of my contemporaries. Let them rave, as Burton would say. The only sadness I shall feel is that for my shortcomings I may not apologize to the gracious Author whose shade I may have grievously wronged.

I have to thank the officials of the New York Public Library for their courtesy in permitting me to use their copy of *Philosophaster* in this work.

For their valiant and valued assistance in translation I am greatly indebted to Mrs. A. H. Vinton, Mr. E. H. Coles, Dr.

Thomas Cooper, Professor Carleton Vernahil, and Sarah Bixby Smith. If I have disregarded—somewhat reluctantly—many of their suggestions, it has been because their classical training has not always seemed suited to interpreting the facete spirit and droll manner of Robert Burton.

Finally, and more than all, I have to thank that courteous scholar and ardent Burtonian, Professor Edward Bensly, for his patience in reading this translation in manuscript, for correcting many of my errors, for enriching the text with a number of valuable notes, and for tracing most of the Burton borrowings to their sources.

Such errors as may remain are my own. As Burton once wrote,[2]

> On me! On me! Here am I who did the deed,
> Turn your tongues 'gainst me, O scoffers,
> You naught approved: mine the faulty screed.

P. J.-S.

[2] In the "Conclusion of the Author to the Reader," Edition of 1621, translated in Dell–Jordan-Smith Edition of 1927, page 976.

# PHILOSOPHASTER

*A Comedy done in Latin*

*by*

ROBERT BURTON

*Author of*
*The Anatomy of Melancholy*

*Now done into English for the first time*

*by*

PAUL JORDAN-SMITH

# PHILOSOPHASTER

## COMOEDIA NOVA

Scripta
*Anno Domini,* 1606,

Alterata, renovata, perfecta
*Anno Domini,* 1615,

Acta demum et publice exhibita Academicis

In Aula Ædis Chrifti
*et*
A Studiofis Ædis Chrifti Oxon. Alumnis
*Anno* 1617

Februarii die decimo fexto
*Die Lunæ*

Ad horam fextam pomeridianam.

———

### Auctore Roberto Burton,

Sacræ Theologiæ Baccalaureo
Atque Ædis Chrifti Oxon. Alumno.
1617.

———

Ofuna Scena, oppidum Andalufiæ,
In Hifpania Bœtica.

# PHILOSOPHASTER

A NEW COMEDY

Written in 1606

Altered, Revised & Completed
in 1615

At length acted & shewn for the University

In the Hall of Christ Church
&
By the Students of Christ Church, Oxon

February 16, 1617

on Monday
in the afternoon
at the sixth
hour

*By*

Robert Burton, S.T.B.
*"Democritus, Jr."*

Desiderius, Osunæ Dux, Osunam Andalusiæ urbeculam de novo inſtituit Academiam, latifundiis et privilegiis abundè locupletatam: promulgatione factâ per omnem Europam, ut si qui ſtudiosi novam hanc Academiam ſtudendi causâ visitarent, eos se donaturum, non tam privilegiis, sed et salario se digno, cæterisque necessariis. Ad quam promulgationem undiquaque philosophorum fit concursus, tum et philosophaſtrorum, lenarum, et meretricum. Huc etiam appulerunt duo peregrinantes philosophi, Polumathes, et Philobiblos, ut sapientem consulerent, qui poſt moram aliquot mensium in Osunâ mores omnium pseudophilosophorum propalant et sugillant, ob quam causam tandem ab ipso duce, corruptam Academiam repurgaturo, multis modis honorantur. Oppidani interim consultatione habitâ de novâ hâc erectâ Academiâ concludunt futuram in rem suam et suis suffragiis approbant. Ad præscriptum itaque diem omnes omnium ordinum philosophi et ſtudiosi poſt convivium, quod in Lapitharum desinit, liberè admittuntur. De bonis hic non agitur.

Philosophaſtri præ cæteris egregii, et qui totam ferè fabulam agunt, hi sunt.

Desiderius, the Duke of Osuna, a small town of Andalusia, establisheth an University, bestowing thereupon sundry privileges & great estates, and proclaimeth it abroad, throughout all Europe, inviting students to the new University, and offering them not only the advantages of the school but salaries and such other things as might be needful. In response to this invitation philosophers came from all sides, and amongst them also philosophasters, bawds, and whores. Thither also came two wandering scholars, POLUMATHES & PHILOBIBLOS, bent on questioning the wise men; these, after tarrying for many months in Osuna, did both expose and laugh to scorn the methods and practices of the sham-philosophers, for which reason the Duke himself, at length, did most thoroughly re-fashion the now corrupted college, and conferred high honors upon them.

Meanwhiles the townsfolk, after considering the nature of this new-found University, vote their approval of it. On a certain day, therefore, after a banquet, which ended like that of the Lapithæ,[1]* philosophers and students of all sorts were freely admitted. We deal not here with the honest sort.

Philosophasters are preferred above all others, and this fact giveth occasion to well-nigh all of this story. The Philosophasters are:

---

* For this and subsequent notes other than those of Burton, see the section immediately following the play, pages 229–236.

POLUPRAGMATICUS, Jesuita, cum ÆQUIVOCO servo suo, qui varias formas induit, politicum, aulicum, Theologum, magum, quo habitu indutus POLUPISTUM quendam e rure nobilem mirâ verborum grandiloquentiâ deludit; STEPHANIONI verò alteri nobili, cujus filium Antonium erudiendum susceperat, iisdem artibus imponit.

LODOVICUS PANTOMETER, præ se ferens Mathematicum, veteratorem agit suis præstigiis, unde vulgus circumveniens.

PANTOMAGUS, Alcumista, medicus, rudi etiam vulgo miserrimè abutitur suis pharmacis ridiculis, nugarum artifex egregius, tum et POLUPISTUM nobilem, Chimistam se simulans, variis technis circumscribit, aurum se posse dicens conficere; cujus verbis ille inescatus aureos sibi montes pollicetur, multaque regali quâdam magnificentiâ perficienda proponit, sed pro auro (quod aiunt) carbones invenit, post rem familiarem decoctam secundò jam delusus abiit.

SIMON ACUTUS, sophistam agit verbis factisque, post varias easque absurdas confabulationes hoc demum in votis habet, ut a Jesuita edoctus sicut ille charus singulis et celebris evadat, et ob hæc nova quædam dogmata et paradoxa liberius effingit.

AMPHIMACER, Poetaster, rhythmos quosdam in amicæ gratiam ridiculè componit, quosvis obvios eodem tenore salutans.

POLUPRAGMATICUS, a Jesuit (with EQUIVOCUS, his servant), who assumed divers rôles—politician, courtier, theologian,
magician. In the laſt-named guise, and with vaſt outpouring
of eloquence, he cozened and defrauded one POLUPISTOS, a
country nobleman. He undertook, in sooth, the education of
ANTONIUS, son to STEPHANIO, another nobleman, in these
same arts.

LODOVICUS PANTOMETER, a self-professed mathematician,
practiceth his knavish tricks amongſt the common people everywhere.

PANTOMAGUS, alchemiſt & physician, likewise misuseth
the ignorant and vulgar folk wretchedly with his mock-medic-
aments, a passing-good jeſter; and then to POLUPISTOS, the
nobleman, he pretendeth that he is an alchemiſt; deceiving him
with sundry trickeries, he boaſteth that he is able to make gold;
having beguiled him by his speeches, he promiseth unto him
mountains of gold, & setteth forth many things as having already been done with kingly magnificence, but in the ſtead of
gold (as they say), he found charcoals; after the household
hath been made bankrupt, and twice deceived, he taketh his
leave.

SIMON ACUTUS dealeth out sophiſtry in word and deed;
behind his sundry & trifling speeches he hath a single aim, that,
taking, as it were, a cue from the Jesuits, he appear to every
man both acceptable and renowned, and to this end he freely
expresseth certain new dogmas & paradoxes.

AMPHIMACER, a poetaſter, composeth certain silly rhymes
in praise of his miſtress, saluting any he may chance to meet in
the same fashion.

THEANUS, Theologaster, postquam Rhetorem egisset, or-
dines init, et fit collegii sui subpræfectus, ibi per annos aliquot
tanquam fucus consenescens, suasu tandem PEDANI pauperis
olim alumni sui rus abit, quovismodo sacerdotium captaturus.


PEDANUS, Grammatista, quum per annum et alterum pauper alumnus in Academiâ vixisset, pueris edocendis ruri operam
elocat, politicis, criticisque se demum stolidè immiscens, duo
Simoniacè init sacerdotia, et ad Academiam decoro habitu
reversus, barbâque venerandâ conspicuus, Irenarchæ dignitatem
apud suos, et inter Academicos Doctoratus gradum ambit,
Sacellanum Ducis præ se ferens.


ANTONIUS, tyro, STEPHANIONIS filius (ab ÆQUIVOCO
Jesuitæ servo corruptus mendaciorum fabro peritissimo, singulis
imponente, et herum et medicum circumveniente), pictis
chartis, aleæ, compotationi, venerique totum se devovet, hoc
solum in votis habens quo artificio pecuniam emungat a patre,
et ut amicæ placeat, quam cantilenis, Musicâ, et donis ambiens
paulo post gravidam fecit, lenæ vetulæ consiliis adjutus et ille-
cebris inescatus, quæ lotricem se fingens et sutricem, plures
egregiâ formâ puellas tanquam filias nacta, poetam, medicum,
ANTONIUM, cæterosque illactans, suburbanis hortis lupanar
exercuit.

THEANUS, a theologaſter, whereas he represented a rhetorician, took Orders and became sub-prefeſt of his college,
where he spent his years even as a drone-bee; at length, through
the persuasion of his one-time poor pupil, Pedanus, he gets himself to the country. By hook or crook he's about to lay hold on
a Living.


PEDANUS, a grammarian; year after year the poor alumnus
dwelt at the University; he hireth out teaching boys in the
countryside; at length, ſtupidly meddling with politics and
criticism, through Simoniacal praſtices he obtaineth two Livings, and returneth unto the University clad in fitting garments,
wagging a venerable beard, moving amongſt them with the
dignity of a Juſtice; he seeketh a Doctor's degree among the
University men, bearing ever in mind, as a goal, the Duke's
chaplaincy.


ANTONIUS, a fresh-man, the son of STEPHANIO (having
been corrupted by EQUIVOCUS, the Jesuit's servant, a man
skilled in the art of lying, deceiving everyone, and cozening
both his maſter and the physician), devoted himself entirely
to cards, dice, drinking, and wenching; desiring only this, that
by fraud he may extort money from his father and so may
pleasure his miſtress, whom, a little later, soliciting her favors
by music, songs, and presents, he hath made great with child,
egged on by the suggeſtions, and baited by the allurements of
an old bawd, posing as a laundress and sewing-woman, who,
having taken in shapely wenches as though they were her
daughters, keepeth a brothel in a suburban garden, luring
therein a poet, a physician, ANTONIUS, and others.

Dein poſt varios errores propter frequentes impoſturas et
multiplices abusus, multæ eæque variæ ad ducem semel et simul
deferuntur querimoniæ, in philosophaſtros hosce sibi invicem
ob lætiorem fortunam interea congratulantes, multique sup-
plices libelli e rure et urbe. STEPHANIO queritur ob filium de-
perditum quem Jesuitæ fidei commendârat, POLUPISTOS se bis
delusum a mago et medico, oppidani ob cives verberatos, res
suffuratas, etc. ANTONIUS querelam defert de ÆQUIVOCO: ob
alias res queruntur alii.

Hisce tam diversis diversorum querimoniis incensus et irri-
tatus Dux, exilium ſtudiosorum et Academiæ subversionem
minitatur, et sanè subvertisset illicò, si POLUMATHES et PHILO-
BIBLOS jam tum opportunè non intervenissent, quorum suasu
sententia revocata eſt, et eorum consilium sequutus philosophaſtros et delatores ad tribunal suum siſtit. Philosophaſtri, et
lena unà cum meretricibus filiabus, diversorum criminum ac-
cusantur, idque coram ab iis quos prius eluserant, a POLUMATHE
deteguntur omnes, et pro varietate criminum varie mulctantur.

POLUPISTOS aurum suum reſtitutum habet, sed et inter
sutrices CAMÆNAM unicam filiam suam invenit et agnoscit,
quam jam diu crediderat demortuam, sed a lenâ olim ereptam,
et ab ANTONIO gravidam factam, ANTONIO eidem unico
STEPHANIONIS filio, læto parentum consensu, nuptum dat.
Atque hunc in modum pœnis persolutis, consopitis querelis, re-
busque demum compositis, reſtaurâtâ nimirum Academiâ, novis
decretis sancitis, POLUMATHE et PHILOBIBLO procuratoribus
a Duce conſtitutis, pacatus Dux, reconciliata plebs, placati
delinitique omnes in gratiam redeunt, et hymnum canentes in
laudem philosophiæ, æquis animis discedunt.

Furthermore, after sundry deceptions, by reason of frequent impostures and manifold abuses, divers complaints and many petitions from both city and country are, all at once, brought to the Duke, against the Philosophasters, who, meantime, were congratulating themselves on their pleasant fortune. STEPHANIO lamenteth by reason of his depraved son, whom he had entrusted to the keeping of the Jesuit; POLUPISTOS, for that he himself was twice defrauded by a physician and a maker of magic; townsmen for their beaten fellows, for stolen property, &c. ANTONIUS bringeth accusation against EQUIVOCUS; other men complain of other concerns.

Therefore, the Duke, incensed by these sundry complaints, threateneth the exile of the students and the overthrow of the University; and he would have destroyed it at once had not POLUMATHES & PHILOBIBLOS intervened, and by persuasion caused him to revoke the decree; following their advice he summoneth Philosophasters and accusers to his Tribunal. The Philosophasters, the bawd, and both her whorish daughters are accused of various offenses, and in the very presence of those whom they had deceived all are uncovered by POLUMATHES, and for their several misdemeanors are severally punished.

POLUPISTOS hath his gold restored unto him, and furthermore, amongst the seamstresses, he discovereth his daughter, CAMENA, whom he had long believed dead but who had been stolen away by the bawd and got with child by ANTONIUS; and to the same ANTONIUS, only son of STEPHANIO, with the joyful consent of parents, she is given in marriage. And by thus inflicting punishments, laying complaints, and settling all these affairs, soundly restoring the University, POLUMATHES & PHILOBIBLOS, as administrators, appointed by the Duke, establish new decrees; the Duke is pacified, the commoners made friendly, all are appeased, and in profound gratitude they rise, and, singing a hymn in praise of Philosophy, they quietly depart.

Versus per totum sunt Comici Iambici, Senarii, Septenarii, Octonarii, vel Iambi mixti, qui singulis in locis pedes habent indifferentes, excepto ultimo ubi semper Iambus. Noſtrates, enim, veteres, exteri, neoterici, quos vidi, audivi, legi, comici, id unum agunt et plerumque sunt aucupati, ut in Iambum versus continuo desineret.*

"Comici enim, quia populi plausum venantur,
"communem magis loquendi consuetudinem quam
"carminum anxias rationes et pedum constitutionem
"observant, quarè omnibus promiscuè utuntur."†
Idem ego feci per totam hanc comœdiam.

---

* Matthæus Gwinne Præfat. ad suum Vertumnum. "Et iſthoc "ego nomine dum dedi operam, *Pes citus—et certus* ubique ut cur- "reret, conſtaret undique, utcunque *Plautus, Terentius,* noſtrates, "exteri, neoterici, veteres, quos vidi, audivi, legi, Comici, et fluerent "licentius, et canerent immodulatius, id unum plerumque aucupati, "ut in iambum vel scazonta versus continuo desineret, nec tamen "nimis diligens eſt visus mihi,

"  '*Nec ſtultus labor hic ineptiarum.*'
                                 —*Mart.* l. 2, ep. 86, 10."
(*Vertumnus,* Londini, 1607. Epiſtola Dedicatoria, p. 5).

† Rodolphus Gualter, Tigurinus, *de syllabarum et carminum ratione,* lib. 2, cap. 18, p. 80. Ed. Colon. 1574.

ON THE whole the verse is in the Iambic of Comedy, Hexameter, Heptameter, Octameter, or mixed Iambic, which in some places hath varied feet, save that the laſt is ever in Iambus. For our own writers, our anceſtors, foreigners, and neotericks whom I have seen, heard, and read, writers of Comedy, have done the same, and are for the moſt part watchful that their verse should always end in an Iambus.*

"For as writers of Comedy are in pursuit of popular applause, they observe, moſt part, the ordinary usages of speech rather than the rigid rules of poetry & the laws of prosody, wherefore they are used indiscriminately of all."†

'T is thus throughout that I wrote this Comedy.

---

\* Matthew Gwinne, in the Preface to his *Vertumnus*:[2] "And I, "therefore, in accord with the very same authority, have taken pains, "using *The tripping foot—& sure*, so that it should move quickly "everywhere, should be consiſtent everywhere, even as Plautus, Ter-"ence, our own writers, foreigners, neotericks, veterans, whom I have "seen, heard, and read, the writers of Comedy, both that they may "compose more freely and sing more immodulately, being at the same "time, moſt part, watchful that the line should always be finished by "an Iambus or a scazon, however this contention is not of too great "concern to me.

" 'Tis sheer folly to waſte labor on trifles.'

—*Martial*, Bk. ii, Ep. 86, l. 10."

† Rudolph Gualter, Zürich, *On the Order of Syllables and Songs*, Book ii, chap. xviii, p. 80. Ed. Colon, 1574.

DESIDERIUS, *Osunæ Dux*

EUBULUS
CRATINUS } *Ducis Consiliarii*

POLUMATHES
PHILOBIBLOS } *Duo peregrinantes Philosophi*

SORDIDUS
CORNUTUS } *Oppidani, et cives Osunenses*
RUBICUNDUS

POLUPRAGMATICUS, *Jesuita, Magus, etc.*
ÆQUIVOCUS, *Jesuitæ servus*
LODOVICUS PANTOMETER, *Mathematicus*
PANTOMAGUS, *Medicus, Chimista*
SIMON ACUTUS, *Sophista*            } *Philosophastri*
THEANUS, *Theologaster*
PEDANUS, *Grammatista*
AMPHIMACER, *Poetaster*
ANTONIUS, *Tiro, Stephanionis filius*
STEPHANIO, *Nobilis e rure*
POLUPISTOS, *Nobilis e rure*
DROMO, *Polupisti servus*
STAPHYLA, *Anus et lena*

CAMÆNA
TARENTILLA } *Lenæ filiæ, et sutrices habitæ*

LICTOR
PROMUS            TIBICINES
SERVUS            ANCILLA
PATIENTES        PUER, &c.

14

DESIDERIUS, Duke of Osuna

EUBULUS  
CRATINUS } Members of the Duke's Council

POLUMATHES  
PHILOBIBLOS } Two wandering scholars

SORDIDUS  
CORNUTUS } Townspeople, and citizens of Osuna  
RUBICUNDUS

POLUPRAGMATICUS, Jesuit, magician, &c.  
EQUIVOCUS, Servant of the Jesuit  
LODOVICUS PANTOMETER, Mathematician  
PANTOMAGUS, Physician & Alchemist  
SIMON ACUTUS, A sophist  
THEANUS, A theologaster  
PEDANUS, A teacher of grammar  
AMPHIMACER, A poetaster  
ANTONIUS, A Fresh-man, the son of Stephanio

} *Philosophasters*

STEPHANIO  
POLUPISTOS } Country noblemen

DROMO, A servant of Polupistos  
STAPHYLA, An old woman, & bawd

CAMÆNA  
TARENTILLA } "Daughters" of Staphyla, posing as seamstresses

A SERGEANT  
A DRAWER    FLUTE-PLAYERS  
SLAVE       SERVING MAID  
PATIENTS    BOY, &c.

| | |
|---|---|
| *Desiderius Dux,* | Sr. KINGE, the Bishop of London's sonne |
| *Eubulus,* | Mr. GORGES, Sir Arther Gorges' sonne |
| *Cratinus,* | Mr. BARTLIT, a Gentleman Commoner |
| *Polumathes,* | Sr. BENNET, Sir John Bennett's sonne |
| *Philobiblos,* | Sr. HAYWOOD, Student, Bac. |
| *Polupragmaticus,* | Mr. GOFFE, Master of Artes, Student |
| *Æquivocus,* | Mr. JONSON, Master of Artes, Student, Bac. |
| *Simon Acutus,* | Sr. FORTYE, Student, Bac. |
| *Lod. Pantometer,* | Sr. WESTLYE, Student, Bac. Art. |
| *Pantomagus,* | Sr. OSBOSTON, Student, Bac. of Arts |
| *Amphimacer,* | LIMITER, Scholler of the House, Stud. |
| *Theanus,* | Sr. VAUGHAN, Student, Bac. |
| *Pedanus,* | MORLY, Scholler, Student |
| *Stephanio,* | Sr. ARUNDALL, Student, Bac. |
| *Polupistos,* | Sr. PRICE, Bac. Art. Student |
| *Dromo,* | HILSINGE, Scholler of the House |
| *Sordidus, Cornutus,* ⎱ 3 Towns- ⎰ Sr. INGOLSBY, HARRIS, | |
| *Rubicundus* ⎰ men, ⎱ PARSONS | |
| *Staphyla,* | BENEFEILDE, Scholler of the House |
| *Camæna,* | PRISE, Scholler of the House |
| *Tarentilla,* | STROUDE, Scholler of the House |
| *Lictor, Promus,* | COTTON, Scholler of the House |
| *Patientes,* | PORTRY, BLUNT, SERLE |
| *Fidicen,* | HERSEN, a Quirister |

ACTED ON SHROVE-MONDAY NIGHT, 1617, FEB. 16,
DIE LUNAE.
IT BEGAN ABOUT FIVE AT NIGHT AND ENDED AT EIGHT.
AUCTORE ROBERTO BURTON,
LINLIACO LECESTRENSE

ACTED ON SHROVE-MONDAY NIGHT, 1617, FEBRUARY 16.
IT BEGAN ABOUT FIVE AT NIGHT AND ENDED AT
EIGHT.
WRITTEN BY ROBERT BURTON,
OF LINDLEY IN LEICESTERSHIRE.　17

QUOD EST poetis nunc, quod antiquis fuit
Solenne, et usu semper in ludis erit,
Orare, adesse ut mente benignâ velint,
Pro more solenni nos petituri sumus.
Si quid pervulgatum hâc fabulâ fuerit
Absoletum, si quid quod minus arriserit,
Emendicatum e nuperâ scenâ aut quis putet,
Sciat quod undecim abhinc annis scripta fuit,
Inter blattas et tineas in hunc diem delituit,
Ab authore in æternas damnata tenebras,
Aliorum importunitate nunc in scenam venit.
Et hoc inpræsentiarum scire vos æquum fuit.
Comœdiæ summam eloqui non eſt opus,
Nomen vel ipsum quæ sit abunde docet.
Scenaque prima ne quis ignoret tamen,
Hæc terra quæ vos tenet eſt Andalusia:
Hoc oppidum Osuna, a duce hujusce loci
Jam de nupero erecta Academia.
Viros undequaque accersivit doctissimos,
Mox aderunt, unà omnes admittendi illicò.
Hic non agetur de bonis, pseudophilosophi
Quid perpetrârint fabulæ finis docet.
Nec plura dicam, cuncta se sponte explicant.
Vos unum hoc obiter admonitos volo,
Philosophaſtros, si qui tales saltem sient,
Quam primum ut eant, pleni rimarum sumus.

As was the custom in the Ancient days,
And now with Poets who have fashioned Plays,
It is the wont to shew themselves, to say in sooth
A word to gain good will of age & youth,
So even we now call on Custom's name.
If aught here told be obsolete and lame,
If aught be disapproved, or give annoy,
Should any man suspect somewhat 's alloy,
Ta'en from another's work of late,—
Know then this Play eleven years agone was writ,
And since then hid, with moth & bookworms bit,
Condemned by its Author to dark night,
And only now, by others urged, is brought to light.
'T is only fit that ye should know the right.
The Comedy's pith to tell there is no need,
The name itself is there for all to read.
Howbeit, lest ye should fail this scene to place,
Andalusia 's the land to which ye 've come apace;
This town Osuna is, and here a Duke, of late,
An University hath built, led on by Fate.
He summoned learned men from ev'ry side,
Anon they 'll come, and welcomed be, full tide.
With honest men this fable will not deal;
What pseudo-sages dare at length we shall reveal.
I 'll say no more; they 'll all themselves explain.
Of one thing, by the by, I wish to warn ye well,
Philosophasters, if any such there be to tell,
That quickly ye get hence; we blab too much, I swear.

Sed salva res eŝt, nullus exsurgit loco,
Nemo reus, digni omnes Academici;
Opere magno rogatos vos omnes volo,
Attentionem noŝtro ut præŝtetis gregi,
Saltem Theatro quanta vulgari datur.

But all is well; not one hath left his chair,
None guilty is, good scholars all & fair;
I wish ye all most earnestly besought
For our Company, that ye give at least the heed,
That unto vulgar stage ye deem the meed.

# PHILOSOPHASTER

## ACTUS PRIMUS
### SCENA PRIMA

POLUPRAGMATICUS.       LOD. PANTOMETER.

PANTOMAGUS.    SIMON ACUTUS.    ÆQUIVOCUS.

*(Cum togis et reliquo apparatu.)*

*[Dum alii loquuntur,*
*Polupragmaticus.*                    *reliqui se parant.*

OMPONITE, componite, componite in-
quam ocyus
Tunicas, togas, barbas, vestes, habitus.
*Lod. Pant.* Sed eſtne certus hic admis-
sionis dies?
*Polupr.* Certo certius, hodie ad horam
decimam
Dux aderit, unaque admittendi Academici.
Tu libros hos, tuque inſtrumenta hæc cape,
Tu præ te feres Mathesin, tu Philosophiam,
Tu Medicinam, ego qualemcunque Scientiam.

22

# PHILOSOPHASTER

## ACT I

### SCENE I

POLUPRAGMATICUS. LOD. PANTOMETER. PANTOMAGUS.
SIMON ACUTUS. EQUIVOCUS.

*(With togas and the rest of the equipment.)*

*Polupragmaticus.*       [*Whilst some are talking, others dress themselves.*

GET ye ready, get ye ready, get ye ready! Tunics, togas, false-beards, cloaks, & gowns. Quick, I say!

*Lod. Pant.*  But is it certain that this is the day of admission, Sir?

*Polupr.*  Sure and more than sure; this day at the tenth hour the Duke will arrive and all shall be admitted to the University. Take thou these books, thou these instruments; thou shalt represent Mathematics, thou Philosophy, thou Medicine, and I Knowledge of any sort whatsoever.

23

*Lod. Pant.*   Sed unde Scientiam?

*Polupr.*                              Stipes; librum hunc cape,
   Edisce hinc verba quædam sesquipedalia.

*Lod. Pant.*   Sed qui verbis aut arte hâc uti potero?


*Polupr.*   Qui? sic: si fueris ad mensam, vel in colloquio,
   Cape quadram aut librum, si sit altera parte longior,
   Dic esse Parallelogrammum rectangulum,
   Dic Rhombum, vel Rhomboidem; si multilaterum
   Ac regulare, Polygonum; secus, Trapezium.


*Lod. Pant.*   Egone hæc?

*Polupr.*                              Panem scinde in formam Icosaedron,
   Dic conum, cylindrum, prisma, parallelopipedum;
   Habensque semper in promptu hunc circinum,
   Describes figuras quasdam geometricas.
   Docebis in dato cubo pyramidem efficere,
   Ex datâ pyramide octaedron, ex octaedro
   Dodecaedron, tetraedron, aut exaedron.

*Lod. Pant.*   Ego nunquam recordabor horum nominum.

*Polupr.*   Loqueris inde de Algorismo et Algebra,
   De numeris contractis, surdis, sursolidis,
   De radice, zanzenique, zinzizanzizenique.

                         (*et hujus modi.*)

*Lod. Pant.*   Zinzizan: quid hoc?

*Polupr.*                              Vel de Musica,
   Vocali, Harmonica, Rhythmica, Organica;
   Ut chromatium juvetur Hemitonio.
   De B *fa* B *mi,* elamire et elami,
   Inducendis apte in cheli et in organo,
   De diapente, diapason, et diatessaron,

*Lod. Pant.*   But whence get we the Knowledge, Sir?

*Polupr.*   Blockhead! take this book and learn by rote some
long words.

*Lod. Pant.*   But how shall I be able to make use of the words,
or of this art?

*Polupr.*   How?   Like this: Should'st thou hap to be nigh a
table, or in conference with any man, take up a trencher
or a book, if 't is longer on the one side declare that 't is
a rectangular parallelogram, or call it a rhombus, or a
rhomboid figure; if 't is many-sided and regular, declare
it a polygon; otherwise declare 't is a trapezoid.

*Lod. Pant.*   Am I to say this?

*Polupr.*   Cut some bread and fashion an icosahedron, shew a
cone, a cylinder, a prism, a parallellopiped; and having
ever at hand this pair of compasses, describe thou certain
geometrick figures.   Shew how to fashion a pyramid out
of a cube, an octahedron out of a pyramid, a dodecahedron
from an octahedron, a tetrahedron, or an exehedron.

*Lod. Pant.*   I 'll never be able to remember these words!

*Polupr.*   Thou mayeſt then discourse of Algorism[3] & Algebra, of the limited numbers, of surds, subsolids, roots, and
of the Zanze,[4] and the Zinzizanzizenique (*and others of
like sort*).

*Lod. Pant.*   Zinzizan!   What in God's name is this?

*Polupr.*   Or speak of Musick, singing, harmony, rhythm, of
inſtruments; whether chromatic semitones are of any use.
Of B *fa* B *mi, ela* & *elami*,[5] about the proper manner of
performing on lyre & lute, of octaves, fifths, double octaves, how they may sound the midmoſt A, the loweſt
ſtring, B *mi*, E *la mi*, B *mi*, the higheſt note on the tetra-

Ut sonent meson proslambanomenos,

Hypate hypaton, parhypate meson, hypaton

Lichanos, nete, trite, paranete, et nete diazeugmenon.

*Lod. Pant.*   Ludis operam, nunquam hæc imitari potero.


*Polupr.*   Nihil est.

*Lod. Pant.*        At hæc si quis demonstrari velit?

*Polupr.*   Tum dic ab *a* et *c,* et ab *a* ad *d,* et *l* per *e* alterum,

Duc rectam per *n* et *o,* et ipsum *d* diagonaliter,

Et per sextum primi scindet medium *f* æquale *c* alteri.


*Lod. Pant.*   Hoc tam obscurum ut nemo possit intelligere.

*Polupr.*   Eo melius. Sic demonstratur quod demonstrandum
erat.

Tuum est disputare de Infinito, Ente, Vacuo,

Natura naturante, et hæcceitate Scoti,

De causalitate causæ, et quidditativa Materia,

De Gabrielitate Gabrielis, et spiritali animâ.

*Simon.*   Vellem quod jubes si possem.

*Polupr.*                              Potes fingere,

Jactare, et mentiri, et hoc satis.

*Simon.*                        Dabo operam.

*Polupr.*   Ne dubites: unica virtus erit impudentia.

Heus, Medice, tu præ te feres Spagiricum,

Disputabis de paramyro, bili, Tartaro, mummia,

Elixir extrahendo, cæmentis, gradationibus;

Quo pacto sublimandus sit Mercurius,

Saturnus calcinandus, florificanda Venus,

Ferrum crocificandum, reverberandus Juppiter.

Audin' quæ dico?

chord, the third ſtring, next to the higheſt, & the higheſt split-note.

*Lod. Pant.* Alack, Sir, thou doſt labor in vain: I shall ne'er be able to repeat these things!

*Polupr.* Pish! 't is nought.

*Lod. Pant.* But happen some man desire the proof, what then?

*Polupr.* Ah, then thou wilt reply thus: Draw a line from *a* to *c*, from *a* once more to *d* & *l*, and back once more through *e*, lead ſtraightway through *n* & *o* and back to *d* diagonally, and divide by one-sixth of the firſt, the median *f*, equal to the other *c*.

*Lod. Pant.* 'T will be so obscure that none may comprehend it.

*Polupr.* So much the better, my good man. 'T is thus we prove what 's to be proven. Thy business is to speak of the Infinite, of Entities, Voids, formative Nature, of the hæcceity of Scotus,[6] of the causality of causes, of the quiddity, of Gabriel's Gabrielites,[7] and the life of the Spirit.

*Simon.* I am willing to obey, if only I 'm able.

*Polupr.* Thou 'rt able to deceive, boaſt, & pretend, and that 's quite sufficient.

*Simon.* I 'll undertake the task.

*Polupr.* Be not afraid: the only virtue required of ye will be impudence. Harkee, Doctor, thou 'lt profess the Spagyric art, treating of paramirum,[8] choler, Tartarism, mumia, the concoction of elixir, of cementation, gradation; how Mercury ought to be sublimed, Saturn calcined, Venus flour'd, iron saffronated, and how Jupiter is to be reverberated.[9] Heed ye what I say?

*Lod. Pant.*                    Dictum sapienti satis.

*Polupr.*    Aut si te mavis Iatromathematicum,
    Tum sit sermo de crisi, et morbis chronicis,
    De Jove directo aut stationario, Marte retrogrado,
    De tetragono, radio partili et platico.
    Tenesne?

*Lod. Pant.*    Teneo.

*Polupr.*                    Suum quisque curet officium.
    Ego meum, bilinguis, ambidexter, omniscius,
    Jactabo quidvis, prout dabitur occasio,
    Callere me omnes linguas, artes, scientias,
    Nescire, aut hæsitare, stolidum existimo.
    Sed verbo dicam Jesuitam præ me feram.

*Simon.*    Cur Jesuitam?

*Polupr.*                    Quid non audet hoc genus hominum,
    In regum aulas, gynæcia, quo non ruit?
    Quod intentatum reliquit scelus?
    Hos agam Ruffinos, et ad unguem exprimam.
    Sed heus Æquivoce, nostin' officium tuum?

*Æquiv.*    Here, ne dubites de sedulitate mea.
    Lacti lac, ovum ovo non magis est simile,
    Quam ego tibi; quod dico, dissimulo;
    Æquivocare jamdudum ab utroque parente didici,
    Amphibologia enim mater meretrix et lena fuit,
    Pater Agyrta, magus et impostor unicus;
    Ego vero qualis quantusque sum, totus sum tuus.

*Polupr.*    Bene se res habet, suas quisque partes agat.

*Lod. Pant.*   A hint 's enough for a wise man.

*Polupr.*   Or should'ſt thou prefer to represent an Iatromath-
ematical Doćtor, then muſt thou discourse of crises,
chronic disease, whether Jupiter moveth aright or is fixed,
Mars retrograde, of quadrangles, of the semidiameter, in
general and in particular. Doſt thou comprehend?

*Lod. Pant.*   I comprehend, Sir.

*Polupr.*   Each man to his duty. I to mine, speaking double-
tongued, an ambidexter, omniscient, I shall speak whatever
I please, as the occasion requireth; I 'm skilled in all
languages, arts, sciences; in my belief to be ignorant or
to hesitate is the height of folly. But *Jesuit* is the word
that describeth me beſt.

*Simon.*   Why Jesuit?

*Polupr.*   What will a man of this class not dare? Into what
King's palace, or woman's chamber will he not rush?
What daſtard deed doth he leave untried? I shall repre-
sent them as Rufflers,[10] and shall imitate 'em to a hair.
But hark 'ee, Equivocus, doſt know thy part?

*Equiv.*   Doubt not my zeal, O Maſter. We are as like as two
drops of milk, or the yolks of eggs; what I intend, I hide;
I learned to equivocate from both parents long ago;
mother had the double meaning, whore and bawd; father,
Agyrta,[11] a wizard and a passing good impoſter; in sooth
I am so much in that sort that I am wholly thine.

*Polupr.*   Our business now is well in hand; let each man aćt
his part.

## SCENA SECUNDA

Desiderius.    Eubulus.    Cratinus.    Lictor.
Philosophastri, etc.

*Des.*  Eubule, quis novæ jam status Academiæ?

*Eu.*  Bellus et magnificus; parata sunt omnia,
   Bibliothecæ, scholæ, reditus, salaria.

*Des.*  Sed ubi sunt interim Scholares, ubi Academici?

*Eu.*  Præsto sunt.

*Crat.*          Ingredi jube.

*Des.*                  Paretur convivium.

           [*Intrant Philosophastri.*

   Aspectus haud ingratus, ita me Deus amet.
   Salvete ad unum omnes florentes Academici,
   Grati venistis Osunam, sed cujus magisterii,
   Quales, unde, quas artes profitemini?

*Crat.*  Dicat pro se quisque, seorsim singuli.

*Eu.*  Tu qui primus es quam profiteris scientiam?
   Vel unde venis, e Peripato an a Stoâ?
   Cujus sectator, Platonis an Aristotelis?
   Scotista, Thomista, realis, nominalis, an quis alius?

*Polupr.*  Nullius et omnium.

*Crat.*                  Opinor Elius Hippias.

*Polupr.*  Non sed illius e sorore nepos octuagesimus.

*Des.*  Quâ polles arte potissimum?

## SCENE II

DUKE DESIDERIUS.  EUBULUS.  CRATINUS.  A SERGEANT.
PHILOSOPHASTERS, &c.

*Duke Des.*   Tell me, Eubulus, juſt what is the ſtate of the
new University?

*Eu.*   'T is fair and doeth handsomely, my Lord; all things
are ready, libraries, colleges, revenues, stipends.

*Duke Des.*   But where, betimes, are the Scholars, where the
learned men?

*Eu.*   All are here, my Lord.

*Crat.*   Bid them enter.

*Duke.*   Let the banquet be made ready.

[*The Philosophaſters enter.*

As God loveth, they look by no means unpleasing.  Greetings to ye, one and all, ornaments of the University; right
pleased am I that ye 've come to Osuna; but may not the
Maſters tell us of their rank, their native countries and
their arts?

*Crat.*   Each man may speak for himself, one at a time.

*Eu.*   Thou, then, Sir, who art foremoſt, wilt thou not tell us
thy special branch of learning? or whether thou deriveſt
from Peripatetic or Stoic? whether thou 'rt a disciple of
Plato or Ariſtotle? whether thou doſt call thyself Scotiſt,
Thomiſt, realiſt, nominaliſt, or what not?

*Polupr.*   I 'm all of these, yet none.

*Crat.*   Methinks he is Hippias[12] of Elis.

*Polupr.*   Nay, not so, but I am the eightieth descendant from
that man's siſter.

*Duke.*   In which of the Arts haſt thou the moſt skill?

*Polupr.*                              Men' rogas?
   Grammaticus, Rhetor, geometres, pictor, aliptes,
   Augur, schoenobates, medicus, magus, omnia novi.
   Vel si mavis Jesuita, ut dicam semel.
*Eu.*   Mirus hic artifex.
*Polupr.*                          Fac periculum in Theologiâ,
   Philosophiâ, Medicinâ, Staticâ, Stenographiâ,
   Politiâ, Thaumaturgiâ, fac in Uranoscopiâ,
   Chirosophiâ, Magiâ, Bial, Hartumim, Jedoni,
   Notis, ignotis, licitis aut illicitis scientiis,
   Solertem me dabo, senties qui vir siem.
*Cr.*   Quod nomen?
*Polupr.*                 Polupragmaticus.
*Des.*                              Erit forsan a consiliis
      mihi.
   Inscribe nomen ejus.  Tu quis?
*Pant.*                           Medicus ego.
*Eu.*   Rationalis, Dogmaticus, Methodicus, Empiricus?


*Pant.*   Nullus horum, sed novæ medicinæ assecla,
   Quam nuper docuit D^{us}. Philippus Aureolus
   Theophrastus Paracelsus ab Hohenheim Bumbast medicus.


*Des.*   Hic est futurus reipublicæ necessarius.
*Eu.*   Quod nomen?
*Pant.*                 Pantomagus.
*Eu.*                              Quis tibi proximus?
*Lod.*   Lodovicus Pantometer, Professor Matheseos.
*Eu.*   Quid potes?
*Lod.*                 Cœlorum motus exactè calleo,
   Et totius orbis terræ quemvis ferè angulum.

*Polupr.*  Dost thou question me?  I excel as grammarian,[13] rhetorician, geometer, painter, wrestler, soothsayer, ropedancer, physician, wizard; all trades are mine.  Or, if ye will, call me, in a word, a Jesuit.

*Eu.*  Wondrous clever, this man.

*Polupr.*  Try me in Theology, Philosophy, Medicine, statics, stenography,[14] politics, thaumaturgy; try me in piss-prophecy, palmistry, magick—through Bial, Hartumim, Jedoni; in the know & the unknown, the lawful & unlawful arts. I 'll shew thee my wisdom, and ye shall learn what a man I am.

*Cr.*  What is thy name?

*Polupr.*  Polupragmaticus.

*Duke.*  He will, peradventure, serve in my Council.  Write down his name.  And who, now, art thou?

*Pant.*  Sir, I am a physician.

*Eu.*  What school—Rationalist, Dogmatic, Methodistic, Empiric?

*Pant.*  None of these, Sir; I am a follower of a new school of Medicine lately instructed by Doctor Philippus Aureolus Theophrastus Bombastus Paracelsus von Hohenheim, a physician.

*Duke.*  This man will be helpful to the country.

*Eu.*  What is thy name?

*Pant.*  Pantomagus.

*Eu.*  Next, who art thou?

*Lod.*  Lodovicus Pantometer, Professor of Mathematics.

*Eu.*  And what, pray, canst thou do?

*Lod.*  I know to a hair the motion of the heavens, and wellnigh every corner of the earth's globe.

*Des.*   Novi hoc hominum genus: admittatur illico.

*Cr.*   Instrumentorum illorum quem usum habes?

*Lod.*   Utor in Architecturâ, Gnomonice, Geodæsiâ.
*Eu.*   Quis ille alter?
*Simon.*                    Sophista Peripateticus.
    Mihi proprium est syllogismis concludere,
    Retia sermonum doceo, qui contra me disputant
    Tacere cogo: nomen Simon Acutus, homo Italus.
*Cr.*   Tu quis?
*Theanus.*      Rhetor si placet (auditores humanissimi)
    Non ita pridem fui, jam vero Theologus.
*Cr.*   Quid cum staterâ tibi?
*Th.*                         Pondus verborum trutino,
    Affectus moveo, Suadæ medullam exerceo.
*Des.*   Concionator opinor egregius, a sacris sis mihi.
    Finitimus oratori poeta: sed quis es?

*Amph.*   Sum—quicquid conor dicere carmen erit—
    Scribo quosvis versus, carmen Elboicum.
    Ad omnes numeros Tricolos, Tetrastrophos,
    Dicolos, distrophos, pedesque Choriambos catalecticos.

*Des.*   Ede nomen.
*Amph.*                 Amphimacer enutritus in Alcala de las
        Heneras.
    Literasque exhibeo serenitati tuæ a dominâ
    Illustrissimâ Ducissâ de Medinâ Sydoniâ.
*Des.*   Non curo literas: specimen artis exhibe.

*Duke.* I 'm familiar with men of this class; he is admitted
directly.

*Cr.* Prithee, Sir, to what use doſt thou put those inſtruments?

*Lod.* I use them in Architecture, dialing & surveying.

*Eu.* And now who is this other man?

*Simon.* A Peripatetic Sophiſt. 'T is my business to demon-
ſtrate the Syllogism. I teach the tricks of speech; I silence
them that argue againſt me. My name is Simon Acutus,
an Italian.

*Cr.* And thou, Sir?

*Theanus.* But a little while ago I was a rhetorician, an ye
please, moſt kind Sirs, but now, in sooth, I 'm a theologian.

*Cr.* Of what use to thee those balances?

*Th.* I weigh heavy words, ſtir the passions, I can thrill the
very goddess of Persuasion to the marrow.

*Duke.* A passing good preacher, methinks thou shalt be my
Chaplain. A poet 's next-door to an orator;[15] but who art
thou?

*Amph.* I am (whatso I 'tempt to say will be a poem neat)[16]—
I write the verse of every kind, a Sibyl's song.
In all three measures classic, not one wrong—
A Tetraſtrophe, a Dicolon, a Diaſtrophe sweet,
Choriambic-catalectic—all in measured feet.

*Duke.* Tell us thy name.

*Amph.* Amphimacer, reared in Alcala de las Henares,[17] I
bear letters to your Grace from my Lady, the moſt illuſtrious Duchess of Medina-Sydonia.

*Duke.* I care not a fig for thy letters. Shew us a sample of
thine art.

*Amph.*    *O Desiderî Dux, vultus tuus emicat ut lux,*
    *Et vos, O proceres, quorum sapientia, mores,*
    *Splendent ut flores, quorum admiramur honores.*
    *Vos Mæcenates date, nos erimusque Marones.*
    Per Jovem ex tempore.


*Des.*                              Ita videtur, ut ut
    Admittatur.  Sed gesticularius ille quis?
*Ped.*    Dicor, vocor, salutor, appellor, habeor, existi-
    mor,
    Pædagogus, puerorum præfectus ab officio,
    Pedanus apud vulgus, præceptor apud pueros.
    Per Antiphrasin Ludimagister, per Periphrasin
    Major juvenum castigatorque minorum,
    Quod est tanquam, quasi, perinde ac si diceres
    Gymnasiarcha, Pædotriba, vel Hypodidascalus,
    Magister, Magistellus, sive Magisterculus.
    Sed utrum horum mavis accipe.
*Des.*    Scribe Grammaticum.  Sed qui reliqui?
*Eu.*    Nostrates, Angli, Galli, Germani, Itali.


*Des.*    Unà inscribantur omnes et gratuito.
    Quod bonum, felix, faustumque sit reipublicæ,
    Ego Desiderius, Osunæ Dux, authoritate meâ
    Admitto vos omnes, universos et singulos.
    Dono vos immunitatibus et privilegiis,
    Do vobis potestatem legendi, practicandi sedulò
    Suam facultatem, suum cuique Magisterium.


*Omnes.*    Gratias habemus Serenitati tuæ.

*Amph.*  *O Desiderius, Duke of Grace,*
    *The light now shines about thy face;*
    *And ye, O courtly Nobles wise,*
    *Like fairest flow'rs, your honors prize.*
    *Grant ye Mæcenases to be,*
    *And we will let ye Virgils see.*
    'T was done off-hand, by Jove.

*Duke.*  So 't would seem—however, he is admitted.
    But who is that pantomiming person?

*Ped.*  Sir, I'm reported to be, called, greeted, named, held, &
    esteemed a pedagogue, by profession a teacher of boys;
    Pedanus to the common lot, Master amongst the lads.
    Antiphrastically, a schoolmaster; periphrastically, the elder
    and corrector of the young, which is the same as if, for-
    sooth, ye call the Master of the Gymnasium an instruc-
    tor; or an usher, the Master, a little master, or a sorry
    little master. But choose what ye will.


*Duke.*  Write him down grammarian. But who are left?

*Eu.*  Englishmen, French, Germans, Italians, & natives from
    round about.

*Duke.*  Enroll them every one, and that freely. And now
    may what follows make for the well-being, happiness, &
    good fortune of the State. I Desiderius, Duke of Osuna,
    by virtue of the authority vested in me, admit ye all, indi-
    vidually & collectively. I hereby present unto ye its rights
    & privileges & grant ye opportunity for study, for the dili-
    gent exercise each man of his own powers, and for each
    the subject of which he is master.

*All.*  We give thanks, Your Grace.

*Des.*   Conviventur, inde suum quisque cedat ad locum.


                                        [*Exit Dux, et consiliarii.*
*Servus.*   Sedeatis si placet, paratum eſt convivium.


*Polupr.*   Et quidni sedemus? primus locus erit meus.


*Th.*   Atqui per Jovem meus.
*Pant.*                    Et quidni meus?
*Amph.*   μὰ Δία καὶ τοὺς ἄλλους Θεούς, primus ego.


*Pol.*                                    Scurra ineptissime!
          [*Concertant de loco. Polupr. dat alapam Pedano.*


                                              [*Intrat.*
*Eu.*   Quis hic tumultus?  Lapitharumne convivium?
*Pol.*   Nil mali, sed orta quædam eſt contentio
     Inter Peripateticum et Medicum de vitæ principio,
     Nos de Ideis, illi contendebant de atomis.
*Amph.* (*Potat.*)   Quicunque vult meus esse frater bibat semel,
          bis, ter, quater.


*Eu.*   Hiccine ebrius.
*Pol.*                    Non, sed enthusiasmo quodam percitus.
*Eu.*   Hoccine philosophari? non tam verum quam dictum
          vetus,
     Tam convenire Philosophis quam Horologiis.
     Veſtrum eſt inter vox rem totam componere.
     (*Servo loq.*)   Heus tolle cyathos, suum quisque cedat in
          locum.

*Duke.*   Let them feaſt together, and then each may hie him
to his own place.

> [*Exit the Duke & his advisers.*

*Servant.*   Be seated, an ye please, good gentlemen, the banquet
is ready prepared.

*Polupr.*   And in what order sit we?  The head seat shall be
mine!

*Th.*   But it shall be mine, by Jove!

*Pant.*   And where, pray, is mine?

*Amph.*   By Jupiter and all the other gods, the head place
shall be mine!

*Pol.*   Impertinent parasite!

> [*They quarrel amongſt themselves concerning their
> places.  Polupragmaticus giveth Pedanus a box on
> the ear.*

> [*Enter Eubulus.*

*Eu.*   What's all this hurly-burly?  A Lapithian feaſt?

*Pol.*   Naught that's serious;  it arose out of a contention
'twixt a peripatetic and a physician concerning the origin
of life: we hold for the Idea, they for the Atom.

*Amph.*   (*Drinking*) Whosoever wisheth to be my brother,
let him drink once, twice, thrice, or two times two with
me.

*Eu.*   Is this man drunk?

*Pol.*   Nay, only moved by a kind of inspiration.

*Eu.*   Calleſt thou *this* philosophizing?  There's naught so
true as the old saw, "As well expeᴄt agreement amongſt
Philosophers as amongſt clocks." [18]  'T is yours to settle
the whole matter amongſt ye.  (*To a servant*) Ho, there,
take away the cups; and let each man to his own place.

## SCENA TERTIA

CORNUTUS.     SORDIDUS.     RUBICUNDUS.

*Cor.*   Amice Sordide, scio te virum politicum,
   Prudentem, ditem, si quem alium in hoc oppido.
*Sord.*   Verum dicis.
*Cor.*                 Et bis prætorem.
*Sord.*                          Immo ter prætor fui.
*Rub.*   Et senex es sexagenarius.
*Sord.*                 Diis gratia.
*Rub.*   Et loquutus es non semel coram ipso duce.


*Sord.*   Ita sane.
*Cor.*            Dic mihi tandem pro tuâ prudentiâ
   Num credas hanc nuper erectam Academiam
   Cessuram in rem nostram an in incommodum?
*Sord.*   Spinosam, Cornute, quæstionem proponis mihi,
   Sed dicam quod sæpe patrem audivi dicere,
   Conimbræ civem et tonsorem Academicum,
   Se plus lucratum fuisse illic, idque anno unico,
   Quam decem Osunæ; credo cessuram in commodum.


*Rub.*   Idem et ego.
*Sord.*                 Proferre possum rationes meas.
*Rub.*   Et ego meas.
*Cor.*                 Sed date mihi veniam
   Vobis dicendi quæ sequentur incommoda;
   Primum ubi vili nunc vænit lignum, cerevisia,
   Mox caræ fruges, annona, cara omnia,
   Nam sunt gulones et potatores strenui.
*Sord.*   Id nihil est, abundè lucrabimur alias.

## SCENE III

### CORNUTUS.     SORDIDUS.     RUBICUNDUS.

*Cor.*  Friend Sordidus, I know full well thou 'rt a politick, prudent, & wealthy man if any such there be in this town.

*Sord.*  Aye, thou speakeſt truly.

*Cor.*  And twice a Prætor.

*Sord.*  Nay, but I was thrice a Prætor.

*Rub.*  And thou 'rt an old fellow of three-score years.

*Sord.*  The gods be praised.

*Rub.*  And more than once haſt thou spoken in the presence of the Duke himself.

*Sord.*  Aye, true.

*Cor.*  Then tell me, prithee, out of thy wisdom, whether this new-built University be more apt to work us good or ill?

*Sord.*  A knotty queſtion, Cornuto, but I 'll say what oft I 've heard my father tell—and he was a citizen of Coimbra & barber by appointment to the University there—that he had more profit there in the space of a single year than in ten at Osuna: 't is my belief, therefore, that 't will work to our advantage.

*Rub.*  Yea, I agree.

*Sord.*  I 'm able to shew my reasons.

*Rub.*  And I mine.

*Cor.*  But, Good Sirs, give me leave I pray ye, to point out the disadvantages: In the first place, where now wood & beer are sold cheap, soon we shall have them dear; fruits, corn, all expensive; for these men are mighty guzzlers & gluttons.

*Sord.*  That is nothing; in the end we shall be rich.

*Cor.*   Sed qui demum? œnopoli, pandochei—

*Rub.*   Immo etiam omnes oppidani reliqui,
Sartores, piſtores, sutores, crepidarii,
Pharmacopolæ, tonsores, coci, lanii,
Bibliopolæ, Architecti, et hoc genus hominum,
Ubi nunc fere omnes aridâ reptant fame,
Mox crescent in infinitum opulentiâ.

*Cor.*   Sed non solvent Scholares, non habent pecuniam.

*Sord.*   Habent, sed nugis impendunt ut plurimum.
Si non solvunt, quorsum lex, in idem recidit,
Diem des, duplum solvant, fœnus optimum.

*Cor.*   Sed cives verberant.

*Rub.*                      Raro, nugas agis.

*Cor.*   Fures autem sunt, auferent ligna, poma, anates.


*Sord.*   Tirones, pueri.

*Cor.*                      Sed audi gravissimum,
Periclitabitur, opinor, uxorum pudicitia.

*Sord.*   Leve vulnus, et contemnendum, quod non nocet.
Quid si voceris corniger? quæſtus uberrimus.
Sed habesne formosam aut nubilem filiam?
Ducent indotatam.


*Rub.*                      Vultis dicam quod sentio,
Et vobis clam? credo nos omnes fuisse corni-
geros,
Antequam scholares adirent hoc oppidum.

*Cor.*   Verum perpetuas alent nobiscum inimicitias,
Contemnent, irridebunt.      •

*Rub.*                      Oderint, irrideant,

*Cor.*   But juſt which one precisely? taverns, inn-keepers——

*Rub.*   Furthermore, the remaining townsfolk, butchers, bak-
ers, shoemakers, slipper-makers, drug-venders, barbers,
cooks, weeders, booksellers, surveyors, and all of this class,
where now they crawl around with lean bellies, soon shall
they ſtrut about with infinite wealth.

*Cor.*   But scholars pay no bills; they have no moneys.

*Sord.*   They have it, but they waſte it, moſt part, on trifles.
Should they pay not, ye should set a day, according to law,
on which they should pay twofold, the very beſt intereſt.

*Cor.*   But they flog the citizens.

*Rub.*   Seldom! thou dealeſt in trifles.

*Cor.*   But they are indeed thieves; they run off with wood,
apples, ducks.

*Sord.*   Mere boys, tyros.

*Cor.*   But harkee to somewhat more serious: methinks the
chaſtity of our wives is jeopardized.

*Sord.*   Pish! 't is but a slight wound, and to be despised, for
that it giveth no pain. What if thou haſt been called a
cuckold? 'T is a most fruitful trade. But haſt thou not a
comely, or at leaſt marriageable, daughter? They 'll wed
without a dot.

*Rub.*   Will ye that I speak my mind and tell ye mine inmoſt
thought? 'T is my belief that every man of us was a
cuckold ere ever the scholars came to town.

*Cor.*   Nathless they will ever be at odds with us; they 'll
ridicule us & hold us in contempt.

*Rub.*   Let them hate, ridicule, despise, and hornify: we are

Contemnant, cornutos vocent, deteriores non sumus.
Me vocant nasutum, Rubicundum, sordidum,
Et vocent usque, dum me vocent divitem.

*Sord.*　Mecaſtor, non dubito, quin intra annos decem
Videre hanc noſtram perpusillam urbeculam
Sivillæ, Salamancæ, aut Cordubæ similem,
Si me de rebus hisce consulentem velitis sequi—
Solvant, inquam, solvant: quod reliquum eſt, eat.

*Cor.*　Quando vos vultis, idem et mihi placet.


### SCENA QUARTA

### STAPHYLA.　TARENTILLA.　CAMÆNA.

*Sta.*　Mecaſtor, lege durâ vivunt mulieres,
Et misera eſt imprimis vetularum conditio,
Quibus eſt nix in capite, et sulcus in genâ.
Mihi quidem tres sunt dentes, capilli totidem,
Nec magis video quam sereno die noctua,
Sed quod dolet magis suspecta sum veneficii.
Olim cum fueram virgo ambiri a multis me memini,
Sed jam a nullis rogor; oblinam et pingam licet,
Cachinnantes rejiciunt; nardoque perfundam caput,
Ubicunque nauseant. Proh dii quid agerem?
Dicuntque halitum quendam poſticum exire a me clanculum,
Nam et quod res eſt dicam, ano meo non possum fidere,
Quin ad singulos quosque gressus ferè sibilet,
Et a poſterioribus exhalet quendam spiritum.
Sed quid? alia mihi ineunda eſt via,
Quam ut mendicem quidvis tentandum prius;
Lena futura sum, faveat Venus precor.
Ædes conduxi in suburbanis hortulis,

none the worse for 't. They may call me big-nosed, dirty
Rubicundus even now, as long as they call me rich.

*Sord.*  By Caſtor, I doubt not that ere a decade hath passed
we 'll see this our little town like unto Seville, Salamanca,
or Cordova; if ye wish to follow my advice in these matters, they should pay, say I, they should pay: what 's left
over, let it go.

*Cor.*  Be it as ye will; the idea pleaseth me, likewise.

### SCENE IV

STAPHYLA.     TARENTILLA.     CAMENA.

*Sta.*  By Caſtor, women live under a rule that 's hard to bear,
and moſt wretched is the ſtate of aged dames, for whom 's
gray hair & furrowed cheeks. To me, in sooth, but three
teeth are left intaċt, and on mine ancient pate three locks
to match; I see no better than an owl at clear noontide.
'T is hinted that I 'm a witch: that grieves me most of all.
Time paſt I was a maid besought of many, but now de-
sired by none. I paint & primp: they laugh & spurn. I
'noint my head with nard, and lo, they 're all disguſt. Ye
gods, what have I done? They tell in private of my
nether breath; for—and now I 'll tell the truth concerning
this—to truſt mine arse I 'm quite unable; nay, as I go
along it hisseth at every step I take, and at those who follow nigh it puffeth reeking fumes. How now? Another
way muſt be devised for mine affairs, attempting any means
before I 'm forc'd to beg. I 'll be a bawd—pray Venus may
be kind! Within a garden nigh unto the town, I 've hired
a house, and now behold I 've got two juicy, snout-fair

Nactaque sum duas succi plenas adolescentulas,
Alteram Polupisti nobilis e rure filiam,
Civis alteram, cedent spero in lucrum mihi.
Nam cùm catervatim huc accedent Academici,
Lotrix insidiabor cum meis mercibus,
Scholares sunt apti ad practicandum scio,
Det Plutus ut sit illis pecuniarum satis.
Experiemur utrumque, nam Romæ fuimus,
Lisbonæ, Sivillæ, Cordubæ, Valentiæ,
Sed ibi tot sunt numero meretrices, tam vili pretio
Scortum vænit, ut omnino lucrandum sit nihil.
Unaquæque fere domus lupanar Venetiis,
Dedi operam incassum illic, sed eccas filiolas.     [*Intrant.*

*Tar.*   Non est cerussa, neque gypsum in hoc oppido,
Nulli colores.

*Staph.*          Non refert: non est eadem ratio
Osunæ ac alibi, variantur pro loco et homines,
Non hic opus unguentis, pigmentis, cæterisque,
Quibus fucum faciunt aulicæ mulieres;
Sunt hic tirones rudes qui capiuntur illico.
Simul ac puellam prætereuntem vident,
Jurant Brisein esse, Atalantam, aut Deam Gnidiam,
Aut qualem olim Euphranor depinxit Venerem.
Nam quod ad artem attinet meretriciam,
Ne norunt quidem recentes Academici,
Nisi sit in tenebris puellam non audent aspicere,
Secus rubent, pallent, præ timore dentes quatiunt.

*Cam.*   Abjiciemus ergo versicolores caligas,
Auratam bombicinamque supellectilem?

*Staph.*   Nihil nimis.

*Cam.*          Ego non abjiciam.

maids; one sired by Polupistos, a rustic noble; t' other is a
citizen's wench. I hope to profit by 'em both. A laundress
am I, waiting with my wares. These scholars are apt in
practice, that I know full well—Plutus grant 'em all
sufficient funds! I 'll try both ways; we have dwelt at
Rome, aye and Lisbon, Seville, Cordova, & Valentia, too:
but there whores are too abundant, and the price for what
an harlot sells so low that naught is gain'd. In Venice
well-nigh every house is a brothel, the struggle 's all in
vain. But lo, here come the daughters twain.

[*They enter.*

*Tar.*  There 's no ceruse, nor gypsum, nor dye-stuffs in all
this town.

*Staph.*  It mattereth not: the fashions of Osuna are unlike
the rest, and tastes of men do vary with the place. Here
there 's no need of perfumes, dyes, & all that stuff where-
by the women folk at court do make their ointments: here
are but rude tyros who fall at the wink of an eye. An they
but see a girl pass by they swear 't is Briseis, Atalanta, the
Cnidian goddess, or such as Euphranor of old hath painted
Venus. For so she 's clever in the strumpet's art, these raw
Collegians notice not—they look upon no wench, save in
the dark; nigh to, they first blush, and then turn pale; out
of very fear their teeth do chatter in their jaws.

*Cam.*  Shall we then cast away our varicolored hosen,
our skirts and petticoats of silk & cloth of gold?

*Staph.*  Do nothing in excess.

*Cam.*  I shall cast off nothing.

*Staph.*    Cum fuerint comitia vel concursus nobilium,
Tum sint in usu crines hyacinthini,
Armillæ, inaures, tiaræ, plumæque tremulæ;
Tunc incedetis auratis sandaliis,
Unguentis, oleis, emplastris utemini,
Hic non opus.
*Tar.*                Quid ergo faciendum velis?
*Staph.*    Indutæ hic tanquam civis honesti filiæ
Incedetis per omnes plateas die quolibet
Ad macellum, ad forum; si scholaris exeat,
Aliud agentes ite; si rimetur accuratius,
Subridebis aliquando; si propius accesserit,
Erubesces; si quid obscænum urget, indignabere.
O si ego jam, qualis tu nunc es, forem.
*Cam.*    Benè mones.
*Staph.*                Vos horum recordemini,
Quod reliquum est detur fortunæ et mihi.

### SCENA QUINTA

#### POLUMATHES.    PHILOBIBLOS.

*Phil.*    Polumathes Osunam venisti gratissimus,
Tu qui spectatas ubique terrarum Academias
Vidisti, quid de Osunâ censes, quid de Andalusiâ?
*Pol.*    Ducatus hic sanè longè florentissimus,
Ubique vitalis, et perennis salubritas,
Et quod advertendum Cato jubet, nitent accolæ.
*Phil.*    Pulchra sanè laus, sed hæccine ea regio,
In quâ tot olim floruerunt Arabes?
*Pol.*    Ipsa: nam cum per Europam sæviret barbaries,
In hunc se locum contraxit philosophia.

*Staph.* Whenas there shall be elections, or assemblies of nobles, then ye may display the hyacinthine locks, bracelets, ear-rings, tiaras, & fine feathers; there ye 'll mince along in gilded slippers, making proper shew of perfumes, oils, & unguents; at this time there 's no need for 't.

*Tar.* How, therefore, dost thou wish us to act?

*Staph.* Array yourselves as daughters of respectable citizens here, and move about the streets any day ye like, to the market, or the forum; if a student venture forth, go thy way, and pay no heed; should he seem interested, bestow a smile now and again; should he draw nigh, blush; should he attempt some act of wantonness, seem highly offended—oh, if I could only be what ye are now!

*Cam.* Thou 'rt a good teacher.

*Staph.* Heed well these things; leave the rest to me—and Chance.

### SCENE V

### POLUMATHES.    PHILOBIBLOS.

*Phil.* I 'm delighted, Polumathes, to see thee in Osuna: thou who hast seen every university of repute throughout the world, what thinkest thou of Osuna? what of Andalusia?

*Pol.* This Duchy is by far the most flourishing: life aboundeth, & the best of health the year around; and, as Cato tells us we should note, "the dwellers round about wax prosperous."

*Phil.* 'T is high praise assuredly, but is not this the region in which the Arabs once flourished?

*Pol.* Yea, the very same: for when Barbarism raged throughout Europe, Philosophy took refuge here.

*Phil.*   At quæ causa tam longæ peregrinationis tuæ?

*Pol.*   Ut cum Pontani Suppatio sapientem consulerem.

*Phil.*   Quasi per tot urbes erranti non occurrat sapiens.

*Pol.*   Ne unus quidem.

*Phil.*                              Incredibile.

*Pol.*                                           Ita est.

*Phil.*                                                        Quid ita?

*Pol.*   Ob inopiam.

*Phil.*                        Mira narras: Romæ fuisti, an apud
          Italos?

*Pol.*   Vagatus per compita, plateas, diversa urbis loca;
          Obviam fiunt peregrinantium greges incompositi,
          Fœneratores, causidici, lenones, lucro dediti,
          Rhetores passim, poetæ, et id genus hominum,
          Sapientes vero nulli; quod ad reliqua,
          Cardinalium ferè mulabus subtritus fueram,
          Et meretricum manus vix salvus evaseram.

*Phil.*   Abires itaque; brevis inde trajectus in Greciam.

*Pol.*   Non audebam.

*Phil.*                    Quî sit?

*Pol.*                                      Ne, si in Turcas inciderem,
          Damnarer ad remos.

*Phil.*                              Cur non in Germaniam?

*Pol.*   Vixi illic per menses aliquot, sed illorum ibi
          Frequenti compotatione obruitur ingenium.

*Phil.*   An apud Batavos fuisti?

*Pol.*                                        Non, ob tumultus bellicos.

*Phil.*   An apud Gallos?

*Phil.*   But to what end haſt thou made so long a journey?

*Pol.*   So that, like unto Suppatius of Pontanus, I might counsel with wise men.

*Phil.*   As if, wandering about so many cities, he might not
meet the wise!

*Pol.*   Nay, not even one.

*Phil.*   'T is paſt all belief!

*Pol.*   Nathless 't is true.

*Phil.*   How can that be?

*Pol.*   By reason of their scarcity.

*Phil.*   'T is a marvellous thing thou telleſt: haſt thou been at
Rome, or amongſt the Italians?

*Pol.*   I 've wandered through the by-ways, ſtreets, & all parts
of the city; one may easily meet with disorderly rowtes
of ſtrangers, advocates, usurers, pimps, money-grubbers,
orators, poets, & men of that ilk, all abroad—none truly
wise; as for the reſt, I was well-nigh trampled under foot
by the Cardinal's *mules*,[19] & I scarce managed to escape a
band of ſtrumpets.

*Phil.*   So thou didſt take thy departure: 't is but a short passage from there into Greece.

*Pol.*   I dared not venture it.

*Phil.*   Wherefore?

*Pol.*   Leſt I should fall amongſt the Turks & be condemned
to the galleys.

*Phil.*   Why not then into Germany?

*Pol.*   I dwelt there for a little time, but there they 've drowned
their wits in drink.

*Phil.*   Haſt thou dwelt amongſt the Hollanders?

*Pol.*   Nay, for reason of the hurly-burly of war that 's there.

*Phil.*   Nor amongſt the Gauls?

*Pol.*                    Utique leves inveni et subdolos,
  Magisque curantes corpus quam animum.
*Phil.*   An apud Anglos?
*Pol.*                      Dii boni! belluam vidi multorum
      capitum,
  Annus ipse non est adeo varius, adeoque mutabilis,
  Ac eorum ingenia.
*Phil.*              Vidistine veterem Oxoniam?
*Pol.*   Et instructam illorum bibliothecam, tum in eâ
  Mortuos multos inveni, sed catenis malè habitos,
  At vivum illic sapientem vidi neminem.
*Phil.*   Doctos ubicunque viros vidisti sat scio?
*Pol.*   Profecto paucos: exulant artes, exulat philosophia;
  Jurisperiti imprimis quæstum uberem faciunt,
  Reliqui sordent.
*Phil.*          De Osunensibus hisce quid statuis?
*Pol.*   Nondum contraxi familiaritatem cum Academicis,
  Verum, si vis, post mensium unum aut alterum
  Quod petis dicam, at hâc lege interim,
  Ut, si tu quid observes, communices mihi.
*Phil.* (*Susurrat.*)   Volo: sed aurem admove.
*Pol.*                                Cautum benè.


### SCENA SEXTA

POLUPRAGMATICUS.     STEPHANIO, *cum Servo.*
ÆQUIVOCUS.           ANTONIUS.

*Pol.*   Laudo consilium paternumque animum,
  Qui filium cupis erudiendum bonis artibus,
  Ut sis voti compos, dabo operam sedulò.

*Pol.*  Only the light & crafty are there to be found, more giv'n to belly than brains.

*Phil.*  Nor amongſt the English?

*Pol.*  May the gods forbid!  I have seen the many-headed monſter—the weather itself is not so mutable, so unconſtant, as their minds.

*Phil.*  Haſt thou beheld old Oxford?

*Pol.*  Aye, and their well-appointed library, wherein many dead are found, unhappily held by chains,[20] but I can not recall having seen any wise men living there.

*Phil.*  I am sure thou haſt seen learned men everywhere?

*Pol.*  But few, forsooth; the Arts are banished, Philosophy in exile; in the main, 't is the law-cats that thrive—the remainder are to be contemned.

*Phil.*  What thinkeſt thou of these Osunites?

*Pol.*  I am not yet acquainted with the University men, but i' faith, after a month or two, I 'll answer thee; but this condition betimes, that, whatsoever thou noteſt, report it unto me.

*Phil.* (*Whispering*)  That I will: but keep thine ear open.

*Pol.*  Be very careful.

SCENE VI

POLUPRAGMATICUS.     STEPHANIO WITH SERVANT.
      EQUIVOCUS.     ANTONIUS.

*Pol.*  I commend the judgment & the fatherly spirit of a man who wisheth his son well trained in the Arts, and I shall mind well that thy wishes are fulfilled in good measure.

*St.*   Ago grates: habebis me nec ingratum, nec immemorem.
At si paternitati tuæ placeat, quæram hoc obiter.

*Pol.*   Quid vis?
*St.*                  Quo sumptu sit opus, quo temporis spatio,
Priusquam ad culmen conscendat artium?
*Pol.*   De sumptu dicam alibi; jam si velis omniscium,
Sicut ego, viginti annis opus existimo;
Nam ego septem annos dabam Grammaticæ,
Totidem Rhetoricæ, totidemque Dialecticæ,
Sex Musicæ, sex Metaphysicæ, decem Morum studio,
Novem Politiæ: at in Mathesi annos quatuordecim.

*St.*   Numeravit octuaginta! Quot annos natus es?

*Pol.*   Captus per Deos!
*Æq.*                  Implicitè, non explicitè.
*St.*   Capio: sed quot annis informabis filium?

*Pol.*   Bono sis animo.  Quot vis? video quosdam igniculos,
Nam multum pollicetur mihi bona indoles,
Quæ elucet in hoc adolescente secundum physiognomonas,
Frontem habet elatam, Mercurialem lineam
Habet conspicuam, quæ juxta Metoposcopos—
Pilorumque color, et, et ipse oculus,
Magnum ostentant ingenium, bonamque memoriam.
*St.*   Benè dicis.
*Pol.*                  Audin'? docebo filium tuum
Artem dicendi et disputandi tribus hebdomadis,
Uno mense totius systema Philosophiæ,
Ad meam methodum.

*St.* I thank thee, Sir: thou 'lt find me neither ungrateful nor unmindful. But if 't is agreeable to thee, Father, I 'd like to ask this question.

*Pol.* What wilt thou, good Sir?

*St.* What then should be the cost & what time must elapse before the lad can climb to the very summit of the Arts?

*Pol.* Concerning the cost I 'll have my say at another time; but should'st thou desire thy son to be as all-knowing as I, why 't would require a full score years, I trow; for I gave to Grammar seven years, full as many to Rhetoric, the same to Logic, six to Music, six to Metaphysick, ten to Morals, nine to Statecraft; but to Mathematicks, twice seven years I devoted full.

*St.* That addeth up to four-score years in all! Good Sir, what is thine age?

*Pol.* (*Aside*) Caught, by Jove!

*Eq.* Ah, mark thou well, implicitly, not explicitly.

*St.* I see, I see: but in how many years wilt thou educate my son?

*Pol.* Be of good courage. How many dost thou wish? I behold some indications that augur a sound native ability; following his physiognomy, 't is clear in this youth that he hath an high forehead, a strong Mercurial line, which, taken together with the Metoposcopy, the color of the hair, & the eye itself, indicate a good mind & an excellent memory.

*St.* Thou speakest sooth.

*Pol.* Payest thou good heed? I 'll teach thy son the art of speaking & disputation in three weeks; in a month, by my method, the entire body of Philosophy.

*St.*                    Itane?

*Pol.*                        Factum puta.

    Possem docere pro sex coronatis, pro decem,

    Pro quingentis, sed si vis filium tuum

    Instituendum brevi, majori opus industriâ,

    Et magnus labor magnam mercedem petit.

*St.*    Mercedem quamvis; impende quidvis, dabitur,

    Modò sit ad usus honestos et necessarios.

*Pol.*    Modò sit, inquis, quid interponis modò?

    Quasi nescirem quid esset necessarium,

    Tot Comitum, Baronum, præceptorque nobilium.

*St.*    Ne succenseat paternitas, viginti en minas;

    Vis aliud quid?

*Pol.*                    Tu numerabis pecuniam.

    Quod reliquum est fidei committes meæ,

    Brevique faciam ut cum Philippo lætabere

    Genuisse te filium quem fidei committas meæ.

*St.*    Benè dicis: commendo natum meum tibi

    Erudiendum tam moribus, quam scientiâ.

[*Æq.* (secum.)   *Commisit ovem lupo!*]

    Jubeo te valere.

*Pol.*                Nos te.

*St.*                        Fili vale.

                       [*Dat Æquivoco pecuniam.*

    Heus serve?

*Pol.*                Tu sequere me intus puer.

*St.*   Is it possible?

*Pol.*   Consider it already done. 'T is possible to teach for six
crowns, for ten, or for five hundred; but an thou desireſt
thy son to be taught in a short time, why then the effort is
greater, & great enterprise requireth a generous wage.


*St.*   Whatever wage thou desireſt; expend what thou wilt,
't will be provided, so be 't is for honorable & necessary uses.

*Pol.*   "So be," thou sayeſt, why doſt thou put in "so be"? As
though I did not *know* what 's necessary—and I the teacher
of so many Earls, Barons, & Noblemen!

*St.*   Be not angry, good Father; there are twenty pounds; doſt
thou wish for anything more?

*Pol.*   Thou shalt caſt an account of the money. The reſt
thou 'lt leave to my good faith; and I will shortly give thee
cause to rejoice, like Philip,[21] that thou haſt begotten a son
to entruſt to my charge.

*St.*   Thou speakeſt sooth: I entruſt my son to thy keeping:
inſtruct him as well in morals as in knowledge. . . . .

*Eq.* (*Aside*)   Entruſt the sheep to the wolf![22]

*St.* (*Continuing*) . . . . I bid thee farewell.

*Pol.*   We bid thee the same.

*St.*   Farewell, my son.

                                   [*Gives money to Equivocus.*

   Ho! Varlet!

*Pol.*   Follow thou me within, my lad.

SCENA PRIMA

POLUPISTOS.    DROMO.    SIMON ACUTUS.
AMPHIMACER.    ÆQUIVOCUS.

*Polupistos.*

ROMO, quod erat nomen iſtius hominis,
Cujus tam celebris fama eſt apud Aca-
demicos?

*Dr.*   Sesquipedale nomen habet, sed omnino
excidit.

*Pol.*   Poteſtne rem furto sublatam repe-
tere?

*Dr.*   Ita ferunt, et locum indicare, et numerum furum.

*Pol.*   Dii boni servetis hunc hominem in salutem meam!
Sed ubi habitat?

*Dr.*                Viden' deambulantem Academicum?
Roges eum.

*Pol.*            Tace.

> [*Intrat Simon Acutus cum duobus
> tironibus, legens ad eos.*

*Sim.*            "*Quoniam necessaria eſt, Chrysiorare ad
Categoriarum rationem quæ ab Ariſtotele tradita eſt, etc.*"
Notate bene, "*quoniam necessaria eſt.*" 1. quia necessitas
cogit me, pauper fortasse fuit. "*Chrysiorare,*" 1. aurum
rogare, vel mendicare, verbum infinitivi modi, a Græco
verbo *Cecarrasoraomi;* "*ad Categoriarum rationem,*" vel

58

SCENE I

POLUPISTOS.    DROMO.    SIMON ACUTUS.
AMPHIMACER.    EQUIVOCUS.

*Polupistos*

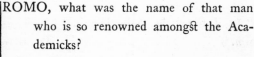ROMO, what was the name of that man who is so renowned amongſt the Academicks?

*Dr.*  He hath a name three-span long, but I've clean forgotten it.

*Pol.*  Would not he be able to recover the stol'n property?

*Dr.*  So they report, and furthermore to reveal both the place and the number of thieves.

*Pol.*  May the good gods preserve this man for my salvation! But where doth he dwell?

*Dr.*  Seeſt thou not that perambulating Academick? Queſtion him.

*Pol.*  Hold thy peace.

> [*Enter Simon Acutus, with two freshmen, to whom he reads.*

*Sim.*  "*Quoniam necessaria eſt, Chrysiorare ad Categoriarum, rationem quæ ab Ariſtotele traditia eſt,*[23] &c." Now mark well,—"*quoniam necessaria eſt.*" 1. Since necessity compelleth me,—doubtless he was a poor man. "*Chrysiorare,*" 1. "to ask gold" or "to beg," a verb of the infinitive mood, from the Greek word, *Cecarrasoraomi;* "*ad Categoriarum*

59

ad rationem Categoriarum, non refert. Categoriæ sunt
aves quædam Macedonicæ, rationales, ut canes, et equi;
notate et hoc per viam: et eſt Græcum, licet scribatur
Latinis literis: notetur et illud valdè, *"quæ ab Ariſtotele
tradita, etc."* Sic arbitrabar, hic Ariſtoteles fuit valdè pau-
peribus munificus: novi fontem ejus nominis. Tu nihil
notas?

*Pol.*   Interpellabo. Salve Domine!

*Sim.*                                 Tu salve, quicunque sis,
        quoque!

*Pol.*   Noſtin' magiſtrum quendam Polupragmaticum,
        Ubi habitet?

*Sim.*          Video quo tendis, sed majorem nego.

*Pol.*   Quo tendam ego?

*Dr.*                      Contendit forsan de viâ.

*Sim.*   Quæſtio tua sumi poteſt dupliciter—
        Primum ubi quæritur ad hoc, *num magiſtrum sciam,*
        Dico quod sic—sed an *hunc,* dico quod non sciam.

*Pol.*   Pace tuâ dicam, hoc ego non intelligo.

*Dr.*                                      Pol! nec ego.

*Sim.*   Sic explico. *Duplex* eſt *scientia: Intuitiva,* quæ hic non
        intelligitur; vel *Discussiva,* quæ pendet a sensu; et sic,
        *"scire"* eſt *"per causas scire";* vel sic, scio *formaliter,* qua-
        tenus *Ens,* in quantum *Ens* habet in mente nostrâ unum
        conceptum omnibus communem, sicut habet Scotus in
        Metaphysicis: sed non *quidditativè,* quatenus Individuationis
        principium propriam habet entitatem, vel singularizetur per

*rationem,*" for categorical reasons, or in accordance with
the reckoning of the Categories, it mattereth not. Cat-
gories are certain Macedonian fowls, having a sense of
reason, like unto that of dogs & horses; note this, by the
by: 't is all Greek, e'en though 't was written in Roman
letters; and note this especially—"*quæ ab Aristoteles traditia, &c.*" . . . . which hath been handed down from
Aristotle. Just as I 've ever held, this Aristotle was exceeding liberal to the poor: I know the source of his name.
Hast thou made a note of this?

*Pol.*   I shall interrupt. God save thee, Master!

*Sim.*   God save thee likewise, whoever thou art!

*Pol.*   Knowest thou a certain Master Polupragmaticus, and
where he dwelleth?

*Sim.*   I see thy drift, but I deny thy major.[24]

*Pol.*   See my drift?

*Dr.*   Mayhap he disputeth concerning the way.

*Sim.*   Thy question may be taken in a double sense; first, when
't is asked thus: Whether I know *a* Master; I reply yes.
But whether I know *this* Master: I reply that I do not know
him.

*Pol.*   By thy leave I 'll say that I comprehend nothing of this.

*Dr.*   Nor I, by Pollux!

*Sim.*   I 'll explain it in this manner. Knowledge is twofold:
Intuitive, which is not here considered; or Discursive,
which dependeth upon reason; and so, *to know* is *to know
through discussion;* or thus, I know *formally,* as far as the
*Ens,* inasmuch as the *Ens* hath in our mind one common
concept, such as Scotus hath it in his Metaphysick: but not
*quidditatively,* since the principle of Individuation is held

accidentia, secundum D. Thomam, aliquid addens posi-
tivum suum subjectum Individuans, non secundum *esse*
cognitum, sed reale repræsentativum; et sic, non scio
magistralitatem suam.

*Pol.*   Tu me homo adiges ad insaniam.

*Sim.*                              Concludam syllogisticè;
Omnis scientia Dianoetica fit a præcedente cognitione,
Sed non habeo præcedentem cognitionem. *Ergo*—

*Pol.*   Quorsum hæc? quid mihi cum scientiis?


*Sim.*   Per Jovem! est Aristotelis posteriorum lib. i., cap. i.


*Pol.*   Nugas agis.

*Sim.*                    Quia tu non intelligis.

*Pol.*   Proh Deum!

*Sim.*                    Quid quæris?

*Pol.*                              Num scias hunc hominem.
Responde ad rem quæso, vel prorsus tace.

*Sim.*   Si non loquaris *ad idem, secundum idem,* et *eodem
        tempore,*
Meum respondere non est necessarium.
Respondebo tamen, et ad utramque quæstionem, breviter—
Scio per Intellectum, *Speculativum,* non *Practicum;*
Vel sic, scio quatenus est in prædicamento *Substantiæ,*
Sed non quatenus est in prædicamento *Ubi.*


*Pol.*   Quid hoc ad rem? non respondes mihi.


*Sim.*                              Possem aliter,
Sed nolo, nam quod 8° Topicorum dicit Aristoteles,
Respondere vanæ interrogationi non est necessarium.

to be an entity, or is singularized by accidence, according to Doctor Aquinas, the Individual adding somewhat to his positive Subject, not according to the known *esse*, but representing Reality; and so I know not his Master.

*Pol.*   Man, thou 'lt drive me mad![25]

*Sim.*   I infer syllogistically; all reasoned knowledge deriveth from precedent thought, but I have not the precedent thought. *Therefore*——

*Pol.*   What, pray, is the end of all this? What have I to do with this knowledge?

*Sim.*   By Jove! 't is after Aristotle's [*Analytica*] *Posteriora*, *Book I, chapter i.*

*Pol.*   Thou dost jest with me.

*Sim.*   Because thou dost not understand.

*Pol.*   Ye gods!

*Sim.*   What dost thou wish to know?

*Pol.*   Whether thou knowest this man. Either answer to the point, else hold thy peace.

*Sim.*   If thou dost not speak to the same point, in accord with the same & suitably as well, 't is not necessary for me to make reply. Nathless reply I shall, and that to each question briefly:

I understand through the intellect, *Speculatively*, not *Practically;* or, let me explain it thus—I understand as far as the predicament of *Substance,* but not as far as the predicament of *Place.*

*Pol.*   What hath all this to do with the matter? Thou hast not answered my question.

*Sim.*   I am quite able to answer, but I 'm loath nathless, for Aristotle saith, in the eighth chapter of the *Topics,* that to answer vain questions is not necessary.

*Pol.* Ilicet.

*Sim.* Eo. [*Exit.*

*Pol.* Proh dii! qualis hic est homo?

*Dr.* Opinor vel Melancholicum, vel morionem Academicum.


*Pol.* Ita videtur; sed eccum appropinquantem alium.

*Am.* *"Conticuere omnes, intentique ora tenebant."*

*"Ora tenebant"*: os pro vultu: elegans, per Jovem!

*"Inde toro pater Æneas," "pater"* ob Ascanium filium.


*Pol.* Alloquamur. Nostin' magistrum Polupragmaticum?


*Am.* Nescio per Charitas!

*Pol.* Nec ædes suas?

*Am.* Per mare, per terras, et per pia numina juro!

*Pol.* Ne jures.

*Am.* Testor humum, tum testor aquas, tum testor Olympum!

*Pol.* Dromo quid ait?

*Dr.* De Olympo loquitur.

*Am.* At vos qui tandem, quibus aut venistis ab oris?


*Pol.* Populares tui.

*Am.* At quæ tanta fuit Osunam tibi causa videndi?

*Pol.* Ut convenirem hunc hominem, nostin' hospitium?


*Am.* Novi: subjungamque descriptionem Topographicam.


*Pol.* *Topograph*—quid hoc?

*Am.* Poeticam, exemplo capies?

*Pol.*   Begone!

*Sim.*   I 'm off.   [*Exit.*

*Pol.*   Ye gods! What manner of man is this fellow?

*Dr.*   Methinks he is either melancholick, or one of these academick asses.

*Pol.*   So 't would seem; but lo, another draweth nigh.

*Am.*   "*Keep silent all, with closed mouths take heed.*" "*With closed mouths*": the *mouth's* used here to mean the face: 't is an elegant line, by Jove! "*Thence from the bed of Father Æneas,*" "father" to Ascanius, the son.

*Pol.*   Now we may say somewhat. Knoweſt thou Maſter Polupragmaticus?

*Am.*   By the Three Graces, I know him not!

*Pol.*   Not e'en his dwelling place?

*Am.*   By the sea, by the lands, & by the blessed gods, I swear!

*Pol.*   Swear not, I pray.

*Am.*   I call the earth to witness, then upon water, & finally upon Olympus!

*Pol.*   Prithee, Dromo, what doth the man say?

*Dr.*   He speaketh of Olympus.

*Am.*   But how now, Gentles, who are ye, and from what shores have ye come?

*Pol.*   We are fellow-countrymen of thine.

*Am.*   But for what high cause do ye look in Osuna?

*Pol.*   That I might meet with this man: knoweſt thou a lodging-place?

*Am.*   Aye, that I do: and I can furnish a topographical description.

*Pol.*   Topograph—what manner of thing is this?

*Am.*   'T is a poetical expression: wilt thou take an illuſtration?

*"Regia Solis erat sublimibus alta columnis,*
*"Clara micante auro, flammasque imitante pyropo;*
*"Cujus ebur nitidum fastigia summa tegebat;*
*"Argenti bifores radiabant lumine valvæ."*
Hæc est Topographica Solis descriptio.
Sed si vacet—

*Pol.*                    O, non vacat, non vacat.

*Am.*    Si non forte vacet, tum generose vale.

                                                              *[Exit.*

*Pol.*    Dromo quid suades?

                                         *[Intrat Æquivocus.*

*Æq.*                    Quis quærit Polupragmaticum
Tam diluculo?

*Pol.*                    Is sum: estne herus tuus domi?

*Æq.*    Domi non est, tuæ scilicet, at est suæ.
Nam reverà nondum surrexit Juppiter meus,
Alcumenam suam Tarentillam nunc complexu fovet.

*Pol.*    Quando aderit?

*Æq.*                    Ad pomeridianam tertiam.

*Pol.*                    Interim vale.


SCENA SECUNDA

THEANUS.          PEDANUS.

*The.*    Quid vis Pedane?

*Ped.*                    Ut chartæ huic nomen apponas, si
placet.

*The.*    Quid sibi vult?

*Ped.*                    Testimoniales literæ.

*The.*    Fiet, sed quam nunc vitæ rationem inis?

*"The Court o' the Sun was aloft with columns tall,*
*"With shining gold resplendent as burning flame;*
*"Against the roof gleams iv'ry, bright over all;*
*"The double doors of silver make all who see acclaim."* [26]
. . . . Now that's a description of the Court of the Sun;
but if thou hast the leisure. . . . .

*Pol.*   O, but I have no leisure, no time at all.

*Am.*   If then thou hast no spare time, I bid thee a most
gracious farewell.                                    [*Exit.*

*Pol.*   Dromo, what dost thou advise me to do?

                                    [*Enter Equivocus.*

*Eq.*   Who is 't that seeketh Polupragmaticus so very early in
the morning?

*Pol.*   I am the man; is thy Master at home?

*Eq.*   He's not at home, that is, not to thee, but he is to himself. For, truth to say, my Jupiter hath not yet arisen, at this
moment in his arms he clippeth Tarentilla, his Alcmene.

*Pol.*   At what time will he be at home?

*Eq.*   This afternoon, at the third hour.

*Pol.*   Until then, farewell.


### SCENE II

#### THEANUS.     PEDANUS.

*The.*   What wilt thou, Pedanus?

*Ped.*   An 't is pleasing to thee, that thou 'lt sign thy name to
this paper.

*The.*   What's the meaning of it?

*Ped.*   Testimonial letters.

*The.*   It shall be done; but what manner of life art thou
entering?

*Ped.*    Rus eo, docturus nobilis cujusdam filios.

*The.*    Tege caput.
*Ped.*                    Benè est.
*The.*                                Ita volo, tege caput.
    Pedane, et ubi primum rus adieris cave
    Ut sit gestus gravis, et quam primum poteris
    Ut sint vestes nitidæ: cavendum id unicè:
    Sit vultus comis plerumque, et blandus, nisi sit in scholâ,
    Tum vero nasum corruga, et frontem capera.

*Ped.*    Fiet.
*The.*        Sed si vis insignis haberi grammaticus,
    Comparandi sunt libri plurimi in *folio*.
*Ped.*    Habeo *Calepinum*, et cum commento *Virgilium*.
*The.*    Sic oportet; sed si fueris ad mensam adhibitus,
    Sit sermo plerumque de rebus philosophicis,
    Quam diu vivant culex, et apis, vel de meteoris;
    Sed in quibusvis sis supra modum criticus.

*Ped.*    Attendo.
*The.*                    Inter confabulandum debes historiolam
    Inserere aliquando, vel e Græcis sententiam.
    "δὶς καὶ τρὶς τὸ καλόν."    καὶ, "ἢ πῖθι ἢ ἄπιθι."

*Ped.*    Enitar: sed in scholâ quid agendum mones?
    Virgamne suades an ferulam?

*The.*                                Non refert, quam velis;
    Nunc hanc, nunc illam.
*Ped.*                                Sed quot plagas oportebat dare?

*Ped.*   I hie me to the countryside for to teach the sons of a certain nobleman.

*The.*   Cover thy head.

*Ped.*   'T is well.

*The.*   So I advise thee, cover thy head. As soon as ever thou 'rt in the country, Pedanus, see to 't that thou movest with dignity, and as soon as 't is possible fit thyself out in fitting garments: this in especial thou must heed: keep a cheerful countenance & a smooth tongue, unless peradventure 't is in the schoolroom; then, by all means, wrinkle up thy nose & frown heavily.

*Ped.*   'T will be as thou sayest.

*The.*   But should'st thou wish Grammar thought important, thou must needs display many folio volumes.

*Ped.*   I have already a *Calepino*[27] & an annotated *Virgil*.

*The.*   So thou should'st: but should'st thou, perchance, be holding counsel at the table, the discussion may turn more to philosophick matters, such as how long doth a bee or a gnat live, or about meteors; but whatever 't is, thou 'rt to be critical beyond measure.

*Ped.*   I give heed.

*The.*   In the midst of discussion thou must needs now and then introduce somewhat from history, or an aphorism from the Greeks, such as: "Good things are worth thrice repeating," and "Either drink or begone."

*Ped.*   I shall endeavor to do well: but in the school what dost thou think should be done? Which dost thou command the more, rod or ferrule?

*The.*   'T mattereth not, whichever thou wilt; sometimes this, sometimes that.

*Ped.*   But how many strokes had one ought to give?

*The.*    Erras, non est dicendum *oportebat* sed *oportuit.*
 Plebeio sex, tres tantum generosi filio,
 Nisi sis bene potus, iratus, vel melancholicus.


*Ped.*    Quot inquis dare debueram?
*The.*                                        Erras iterum.
 Dicendum est *debui*, non autem *debueram.*
 Sed audi, cave ut flagelles nobilis filium,
 Nisi prius impetratâ a matre veniâ.
*Ped.*    Quid ita?
*The.*                            Cave etiam: sed alibi instituam,
 Profecturum te nunc video, benè vale.


### SCENA TERTIA

#### PANTOMAGUS *solus.*

Tanti eris aliis quanti tibi fueris,

Et qui se vilipendit vilipendetur ab aliis.

Ego, ne quid ignoretis, sum doctor medicus.
Sed cur medicus? quia nobis ex furto vivere,
Solisque licet impunè hominem occidere.
Doctor Osunensis divortor his ædibus,
Et apud Idiotas audio vir doctissimus;
Quod ad artes quibus utor, incedo gravis,

Decenter amictus, sicut videtis, annulis
Ornatus, et quoad barbam summè conspicuus.

*The.*  Thou art in error; thou should'st not say "had ought,"
   but "should." For the common lads six, three only for a
   gentleman's son; that is, unless thou 'rt very drunk, angry,
   or o'ercast with melancholy.

*Ped.*  How many didst thou say I had ought to give?

*The.*  Once more thou dost blunder. Thou should'st say "I
   ought," not "I had ought." But hearken to me, take care
   how thou goest about to thrash the son of a nobleman
   save first thou hast obtained permission from his mother.[28]

*Ped.*  Why so?

*The.*  Again I say, take care: but I shall instruct thee other-
   where, for I perceive that thou 'rt now about to depart, so
   I 'll bid thee a fond farewell.


### SCENE III

### PANTOMAGUS *alone.*

Thou 'lt be of as much worth to others as thou 'rt unto
   thyself,

And whoso contemneth himself is contemned by all mankind.

I, though ye may not know it, am a Doctor of Medicine.

But why a Doctor be? For that we may live by trickery,

We alone may slay a fellow man without punishment.[29]

The Doctor of Osuna is lodged in this house,

And I, the most learned of men, give ear to fools;

According to the wont of the profession, I move with
   dignity,

In fitting raiment, as ye see, deck't out with rings,

And with a beard most venerable, of great esteem.

Si quis me quærat, duco in Musæum ſtatim
Ornatum vitreolis, chartis, libris omnium generum,

Quos ego tamen omnini non intelligo,
Ornamenti causâ ſtant secundum classes suas.
Huc ubi ventum de naturâ morbi rogo,
Discurro de Essatis, Essentificatis, localiter, emunctoraliter,

De Anatron Embrionato, et minerali Sulphure,
Subjungens diversas opiniones diversorum hominum,
Quid Avenzoar, quid Rhases, et quid Mesue,
Quid Paracelsus; miratur ille singularem peritiam,
Infinitamque lectionem; quando reverâ mihi
Sunt tantum pervulgati Receptus duo,
Quorum sacerdos alterum, anus alterum edocuit,
Compôſti de Scammoneo vel Helleboro.

Hos alternatim plerumque miniſtrare soleo;
De Enematis, Emplaſtris, Apophlegmatismis tamen
Loquor, de Julapiis, Syropiis, Electuariis,
De Dropace, Sinapismo, Opiatis, Topicis,
Suffitu, et Suffumigatione, ac si Galenus forem.
Quibuscunque commendo victum salubrem,
Quando ego delectum ciborum non scio,
Nisi quod flatulenta cogant crepitum;
Porgo plerumque singulos nulla ratione habitâ

Ætatis, morbive, nec prosim, nec obsim; sed fores crepant.

When one seeks me out, I lead him straight into my study,
Trick't out with glasses, parchments, & books of every
    sort,
Although of these all told I comprehend no word.
They stand, arranged by class, to ornament th' room.
When folk here enter, the nature of their ills I ask,
Discourse of diet, essentification,[30] local symptoms, emunc-
    tions
Of embryonated soda, & the mineral sulphur,
Summing up the several opinions of divers men;
Thus Avenzoar, thus Rhases, and so Mesue & Paracelsus:
He marveleth at my exceeding skill & vast reading; whenas,
    in sooth,
I know no more than two common concoctions, made of
    scammony &
Hellebore, one of which a priest taught me, t' other an
    old dame.
These, one after t' other, full oft was I wont to 'minister;
I make talk of clysters, emplasters, apophlegmatisms,
Likewise of juleps, syrops, & electuaries,
Of dropax, sinapisms, opiates, and topick medicines,
Of suffites and suffumigations, as if I were Galen's self.
I commend to every man an healthy diet,
Although I never know the foods to choose,
Save that flatulent food-stuffs force a fart;
I purge oft, with no reckoning of condition, age, or ail-
    ment:
I neither hurt nor help: but the doors are opening.

## SCENA QUARTA

### ANTONIUS.    ÆQUIVOCUS.

*Æq.*   Optatus mihi advenis Antoni; quo tam diluculo?

*Ant.*   Ad publicas lectiones.

*Æq.*                           Ad lectiones?   Quid ita?

*Ant.*   Ut ediscam.

*Æq.*                 Et quid edisces, si Diis placet?
   Quot sunt prædicabilia?   nugas hasce apagesis.

*Ant.*   Has nugas vocas?

*Æq.*                       Nugas omnium nugacissimas.

*Ant.*   Itane?

*Æq.*           Ita.   Quid tibi cum genere et specie?
   An tu filius et hæres, isque patris unicus?

*Ant.*   Quid inde?

*Æq.*                   Quid ergo tibi cum scientiis?
   Viderint has tricas fratres natu minimi,
   Quos ad servitutem novercans natura peperit,
   Vile vulgus, inopes, et id genus hominum,
   Quos ad laborem damnavit tristis Horoscopus.

*Ant.*   At quid vis interim faciam?

*Æq.*                           Quid faciam, rogas?
   En tibi pictas chartas, et omne genus aleæ,
   Hæ Musæ sunt studiis aptiores tuis.
   Da te mihi per dies aliquot discipulum modò,
   Dedocebo te mores istos, effingam de novo,
   Et efficiam te peritissimum omnium artificem.

*Ant.*   Artificem cujus artis?

*Æq.*                         Artis potatoriæ,
   Veneris, aleæ, ut potare possis strenuè,

### SCENE IV

#### ANTONIUS.    EQUIVOCUS.

*Eq.*   I 'm well pleased that thou haſt come unto me, Antonius; but why at the dawn of day?

*Ant.*   For the public readings.

*Eq.*   For the readings?  Why so, I prithee?

*Ant.*   So I may learn the better.

*Eq.*   And what, please God, doſt thou wish to learn?  How many predicables there are?  Away with such nonsense!

*Ant.*   Calleſt thou these things nonsense?

*Eq.*   The sillieſt nonsense in the world.

*Ant.*   Can it be possible?

*Eq.*   It really is.  What haſt thou to do with genus & species? Art thou not the son & heir, thy father's only son?

*Ant.*   What of that?

*Eq.*   What therefore haſt thou to do with knowledge? Younger brothers know well enough the vexations that, springing from an unfortunate birth, have dragged into servitude the vulgar, the poor, and all that sort of men whom an evil Horoscope hath condemned to weary drudgery.

*Ant.*   But what wilt thou have me do betimes?

*Eq.*   Thou askeſt what to do?  Lo, 't is cards for thee & all games of chance: these ſtudies are more suited to thy desires.  Entruſt thyself to me as a ſtudent for yet a little while, and I 'll teach thee better manners; I 'll make a new man of thee, and the moſt skillful Maſter of Arts.

*Ant.*   Maſter of which art?

*Eq.*   The art of toping, of wenching, of gaming, so thou 'lt

Et cum decore fumum e naribus evomere,

Obvios salutare, et ambire dominam.

*Ant.*   At compotationes hasce interdixit serio pater.

*Æq.*   Interdixit pater—quid? eris etiamnum puer?

*Ant.*   Jussitque ut darem operam studiis noctes et dies.

*Æq.*   Non refert quid jussit, satis superque doctus es.

*Ant.*   Egone doctus satis?

*Æq.*                             Potes chartæ nomen apponere?

*Ant.*   Possum.

*Æq.*           Iterum dico, satis superque doctus es.

*Ant.*   Sed Latinum vult pater.

*Æq.*                             Bene se res habet.

Audi, hoc ubi memoriter edidiceris,

*Qui nescit dissimulare nescit vivere,*

Ne quid ultra de Latinitate cogitaveris.

*Ant.*   Quî demum tempus impendam?

*Æq.*                                     Etiamne rogitas?

Tu sis solicitus de cane venatico,

De cantu, et choreâ, venatione, et aucupio,

De lanistâ, et dominâ; hæc studia te magis decent.

Sed heus tu, invitor ego ad proximum œnopolium

Hâc nocte ad cœnam, eris hospes meus.

Aderunt puellæ illic, combibones optimi, tibicines;

Pergræcabimur unâ, genio noctem addiximus;

Ne quid hæsites, mecum ibis, eris acceptissimus.

*Ant.*   Quando ita suades, Æquivoce, duc quovis, sequar.

be able to drink bravely & to puff smoke through the nose handsomely, to salute familiars, & to woo a mistress.

*Ant.*   But my father most particularly forbade drinking bouts.

*Eq.*   Thy father forbade—what's this? Wilt forever be a mere boy?

*Ant.*   And he commanded that I give good heed to study, both day & night.

*Eq.*   What he commandeth is no concern of thine; thou knowest more than enough.

*Ant.*   I know enough, I?

*Eq.*   Canst thou not sign thy name unto a paper?

*Ant.*   I can.

*Eq.*   Then I say again that thou dost know enough.

*Ant.*   But my father wisheth Latin.

*Eq.*   Well enough. Now harkee, when thou hast learnt this without book, *"Qui nescit dissimulare nescit vivere"*— "whoso knoweth not how to dissemble, knoweth not how to live," why no better Latin can be conceived.[31]

*Ant.*   How, then, shall I occupy my time?

*Eq.*   Gad! art yet enquiring that? Thou should'st be concerned about hunting-dogs, a song, a dance, the chase, hawking, fencing, & a mistress: these be the studies that would fit thee better. But stay, I'm bid to a nearby tavern this night to sup, thou 'rt my guest. There'll be wenches, the heartiest toss-pots & pipers; we'll carouse together, & give the night to joy: fear not, thou 'lt fare thither with me, and be well received.

*Ant.*   For that thou art so persuasive, Equivocus, lead me whithersoever thou wilt, & I'll follow.

## SCENA QUINTA

POLUMATHES.          THEANUS.          PHILOBIBLOS.

*Th.*    Ambo peregrinantes studiosi?
*Pol.*                              Ambo sumus.
*Th.*    Sed quæ causa apud nos moræ tam diutinæ?

*Phil.*    Discendi.
*Th.*    Quid est quod scire desideras?
*Pol.*    Multa sunt in quibuscunque ferè scientiis
         In quibus hæreo, quæ solvi quam primum cupio.

*Th.*    Roga quid vis, modo sit in artibus,
         Nam per annos triginta nunc magister fui,
         Octies bursarius, bis subpræfectus collegii mei.

*Phil.*    Vir doctus proculdubio.
*Pol.*                              Solvesne quod rogo?
*Th.*    Solvam si potero.
*Pol.*                      Tentabo prius in grammaticâ.
*Th.*    Quid a me scire cupis quæ spectant ad pueros?

*Phil.*    Aquila non capit muscas, roga quid serio.

*Pol.*    Quod est summum bonum?
*Th.*                              Bonum sacerdotium.
*Phil.*    Lepidè per Jovem!
*Pol.*                        Dubitatur de generatione meteorôn,
         Incremento Nili, et origine fontium,
         An mare per polos sit navigabile?

### SCENE V

POLUMATHES.     THEANUS.     PHILOBIBLOS.

*Th.*   Are ye both foreign students?

*Pol.*   Aye, both of us.

*Th.*   But for what reason have ye tarried amongst us so long?

*Phil.*   We seek knowledge.

*Th.*   What do ye wish to learn?

*Pol.*   There be many matters in well-nigh all ranges of knowledge concerning which I 'm in doubt, and which I hope to have settled as soon as may be.

*Th.*   Ask what thou wilt, provided only 't is within the realm of the Arts, for I 've now been a Master for thirty years, eight times a Bursar, and twice a Sub-prefect of my College.

*Phil.*   Without doubt a most learned man.

*Pol.*   Wilt thou answer whatso I ask of thee?

*Th.*   I 'll answer an I 'm able.

*Pol.*   I 'll try thee first about the rules of Grammar.

*Th.*   Why dost thou require of me what is but the concern of mere lads?

*Phil.*   The eagle stoopeth not to catch flies; ask rather of weighty matters.

*Pol.*   What is the greatest good?

*Th.*   A good Benefice.

*Phil.*   A witty reply, by Jove!

*Pol.*   Is there any doubt concerning the cause of meteors, the rising of the Nile & the fountains thereof, or whether the Sea about the Pole be navigable?

*Phil.*   De sympathiâ ammonii et hydrargyri,
   Sulphuris, chrysocollæ, et plumbi cinerei,
   Infinitisque aliis; ſtatue quid, supersedebimus tibi.

*Th.*   Credendum eſt in his cum Catholicâ Ecclesiâ.
*Phil.*   Dissimulat, opinor, roga quid in artibus.
*Pol.*   Quid censes de quadraturâ circuli?
*Phil.*                                   De volutâ Deinoſtrati?
*Pol.*   Quid de contaĉtûs angulo? dividatur?

*Phil.*                                      Daturne minimis?
*Th.*   Legebam in Euclide ad pontem asininum semel.
*Pol.*   Qualis Arithmeticus?
*Th.*                           Scio numerare pecuniam.
*Pol.*   De triplici terræ motu quid exiſtimas?
   De ſtellâ novâ, sublunaris an ætherea?

*Phil.*   Novam Raimarus induxit hypothesin,
   Novam Tycho Brahe, novam Fracaſtorius,
   Novam Helisæus Roeslin, novam Patritius,
   Novam Thaddeus Hagesius ab Hagecke medicus.
*Th.*   Domine salvum fac! quænam hæc incantatio?
*Pol.*   Hi omnes excludunt elementum igneum.
*Th.*                                      Iterum!
*Pol.*   Hos omnes Maginus perſtringit, qui de nupero
   Sphæram novam effinxit undecimam;
   Hic peccat contra mathematica principia,
   Ille optica, at ille philosophica;
   Cui credendum? quid ſtatuis? obnixè a te rogo.

*Th.*   Quod supra nos nihil ad nos.

*Phil.*  Or concerning the sympathy betwixt ammoniack salt
& quicksilver, sulfur, borax, & pewter, and of countless
others? whatsoever thou judgeſt, that we will yield unto
thee.

*Th.*  In this matter ye should hold with the Catholic Church.

*Phil.*  Methinks he dissembleth; ask him concerning the Arts.

*Pol.*  What 's thy opinion about squaring the circle?

*Phil.*  Or concerning the scroll of Dinoſtratus?

*Pol.*  Or what concerning the angle of contingence?  How is
it divided?

*Phil.*  Is that at all permissible?

*Th.*  I once read in *Euclid,* as far as the *Pons asinorum.*[32]

*Pol.*  What sort of an Arithmetician art thou?

*Th.*  I know how to count money.

*Pol.*  What thinkeſt thou of the threefold movement of the
earth?  What doſt thou think of the new ſtar—is it sub-
lunary, or of the Heavens?

*Phil.*  Raimerus hath fetch'd forth a new hypothesis, Tycho
Brahe a new one, Fracaſtorius[33] a new one, Helisæus
Roeslin a new one, Patricius a new one, Thaddeus Hag-
gesius, the Hegeck Doɛtor, a new one.

*Th.*  Lord save us! what kind of incantation is this?

*Pol.*  All these rejeɛt the element of fire.

*Th.*  Harping on that again!

*Pol.*  Maginus inveigheth againſt all these, and hath lately
made out eleven Heavens; herein, belike, he offendeth
againſt the firſt principles of mathematicks: opticks on
the one hand, philosophy on t' other.  Whom, then, shall
we believe?  To what conclusion haſt thou come?  I en-
treat thee earneſtly.

*Th.*  What 's above is naught to us.

*Pol.*                                   Neque curas Aſtronomiam?

*Th.*   Non omnino; caput mihi calendarium,

Nasus index, venter horologium;

Diis gratia, scio prandendi cubandique tempora,

Dies feſtos; et quid opus Aſtronomiâ?

*Pol.*   Quid profiteris?

*Th.*                       Quidquid animo collibuit meo.

*Phil.*   Dic mihi, medice, quod eſt morborum initium?

*Th.*   Non sum medicus.

*Phil.*                       Dic mihi, juridice,

Quid arbitreris de Papiniani lege Arithmeticâ,

Expone nobis legem Falcidiam si poteris.

*Th.*   Non sum juriſta.

*Phil.*                       Sacerdos procul dubio.

*Th.*   Quidni sacerdos?

*Pol.*                       Habes itaque linguarum peritiam.

Præfert Hebreæ Belgicam Goropius, Punicam

Alter, Græcam Apollinaris; interpone judicium.


*Th.*   Nil mihi cum linguis, quid opus tantâ scientiâ?

Scio Missam celebrare, legere, et scribere,

Et concionari possum cum ad vicem meam venit.


*Pol.*   O virum indignum, miserum, et ſtolidum!


*Th.*   Cur sic exclamas?

*Pol.*                       Miseresco tui.

*Th.*   Ego tui.

*Pol.*           Sapientum octavus!

*Phil.*                       Merum pecus!

*Pol.*  Carest thou nothing for Aſtronomy?

*Th.*  Not a fig: head is mine almanack, nose my compass, & belly my clock: thanks be to the gods, I know the times to eat & sleep—I know the feſtal days. What 's the need for Aſtronomy?

*Pol.*  What doſt thou profess to teach?

*Th.*  Whatsoever tickleth my fancy.

*Phil.*  Pray tell me, Doctor, what is the cause of disease?

*Th.*  I am not a Doctor.

*Phil.*  Tell me, Judge, thy opinion of Papinianus, his Arithmetical law? or explain, an thou 'rt able, the Falcidian Law.[34]

*Th.*  Marry, I 'm not a Judge.

*Phil.*  Beyond a doubt thou 'rt a Prieſt.

*Th.*  Why not a Prieſt?

*Pol.*  And so thou haſt knowledge of the languages. Goropius preferreth the Dutch to the Hebrew, another the Carthagenian; Apollinaris preferreth the Greek; tell us thy judgment in this matter.

*Th.*  I have naught to do with languages; what profit is there in such knowledge? I know enough to celebrate the Mass, to read & to write, and whenas it falleth to my lot I 'm able to preach.

*Pol.*  O wretched mannikin, miserable wretch, and what a fool!

*Th.*  Why such exclamations?

*Pol.*  I pity thee.

*Th.*  And I thee.

*Pol.*  The Eighth Wise Man!

*Phil.*  An unadulterated beaſt!

SCENA SEXTA

TARENTILLA. AMPHIMACER.

*Tar.*   Inter omnes eos, qui me simul ambiunt,
Scholares, oppidanos, rusticos, aulicos,
Unus est qui se poetam nominat,
Homo rudis, et qui ridetur ab omnibus.
Hunc ego quum non curem (nam quid mihi cum eo
Qui non habet argentum?) vanâ spe lacto tamen,
Eo quod omnem nostram exhilaret familiam,
Cantilenis, rhythmis, et fabulis suis.
Sed eccum, venit: præ me feram melancholiam.

*Amph.*   Hæccine Tarentilla? sic est, compellabo magnificè;
Salve pulchricoma nympha, et roseum fulguris jubar,

Virginum decus, honor ætatis tuæ,
Formâ, proceritate, et candore animi—

[*Hæret.*

*Tar.*   Hæres ne? Juno Lucina fer opem.
*Amph.*   Quæ mulierum genus superas fæminarum,

Cujus a vertice et nigricantibus oculis,
Tale quiddam spirat ac ab aureâ Venere——

*Tar.*   Quorsum hæc? quasi me ne nôris quidem.

*Amph.*   Ne nôrim, meæ delitiæ, mea rosa, meum suavium!
Quid agis? quid reluctaris? da mihi basium.
Tantisper da suaviolum, dum basia restant,
Ex animâque tuâ dum spiritus in mea labra
Influit, inque jecur mulgenti dulcia philtra.

## SCENE VI

TARENTILLA.    AMPHIMACER.

*Tar.*  'Mongſt all them that hither come, incontinent, to pay
me court—scholars, townsmen, ruſticks, courtiers—one
there is who calleth himself a Poet, a loutish fellow & the
butt of every man's laughter.  Though I care no whit for 's
company (what have I to do with a man who hath no
moneys?), yet I lure him on by vain hopes, for that he
maketh all the household merry by his songs, rhymes, &
facete fables.  But look! he cometh; I 'll feign an air of
melancholy.

*Amph.*  Is this then Tarentilla?  Ah ha, so 't is then; I shall
speak out bravely: All hail, fair nymph, roseate morning-
ſtar,

> *Moſt beauteous of virgins, ornament of thy age,*
> *In form, in ſtature, and in sincere affection——*

> > [*He ſtammers & breaks off.*

*Tar.*  Do thy words stick faſt?  Juno-Lucina grant him aid!

*Amph.*  *Thou'rt above all female womankind, of a race*
> *apart;*

> *From thy head's crown and eyes of jet,*
> *Thou'rt such an one as was never yet;*
> *Thou mov'st me so, by Venus' crown, my heart——*

*Tar.*  To what end all this talk? as if thou didſt not even
know me!

*Amph.*  Not know thee, my darling, rosebud, my sweetheart!
> What doeſt thou?  Why doſt thou struggle so?
> Give me a kiss, then seal thy lips, but oh!
> Grant one brief kiss, that whilſt thy breath I drink,
> And quaff thy soul, from lips that ever shrink,

Quod apud Theocritum Venus Adonidi,
Serenissima Tarentilla id ego tibi.

*Tar.*    Ne sis molestus.
*Amph.*                    Quæso ne frontem capera.
*Tar.*    Non vacat nugis tuis nunc operam dare.
*Amph.*    Nugis! attamen hæ nugæ pondera vocis habent.
  Liceat deosculari manum aut calceamentum tuum.
  Quid? an gravaris dolore dentium?
  An forte furtivum vereris osculum,
  Ut semper ferè ori admoveas manum?
*Tar.*    Osculum et basium, et nil præter osculum.
*Amph.*    Viri amantis osculum apud volentem puellam
  Tacitæ petitionis obtinet locum, apud nolentem
  Precationis. *Achilles Tatius lib.* 1 *mo.*
*Tar.*    Quorsum venis? quid ergo vis? quid petis?

*Amph.*    Non ego divitias Arabum, rubrive lapillos
  Æquoris insignes cupio, nec quicquid Iberus
  Amne Tagus rutilante vehit, populosque superbos
  Sceptrigerâ domitare manu etc. sed unum basiolum.

*Tar.*    Si te donarem basio, quid subires causâ meâ?

*Amph.*    Tuus, o regina, quid optes
  Explorare labor; mihi jussa capessere fas est.
  Quidvis impera.
*Tar.*                    Impero silentium.
*Amph.*                                    Audi poema prius,
  Quod hesternâ nocte de te composui.
*Tar.*                                    Recita.

My heart with love's sweet potions may be fill'd.

With old Theocritus, his *Venus to Adonis* rare,

I sing to thee, my sweet, my Tarentilla fair.

*Tar.*  Nay, leave me alone.

*Amph.*  Prithee, wrinkle not thy brow.

*Tar.*  Marry, I have not the time to pay heed unto thy nothings.

*Amph.*  Nothings! Nathless these same nothings have the weight of words.[35] Pray give me leave to kiss thy hand, or e'en thy shoe. What! art thou suffering of a toothache? Or mayhap thou 'rt in fear of a stol'n kiss, seeing that thy hand moveth ever round thy mouth?

*Tar.*  Kissing, bussing, kissing, and naught else beside!

*Amph.*  The kiss of a lover to a willing wench is a silent wooing, to an unwilling one is but an humble petition. (*Achilles Tatius*, Book I.)[36]

*Tar.*  What are thy intentions? What dost thou wish? What art thou asking?

*Amph.*  "I yearn not for the whole wealth of Arabia, nor the rare jewels from the Red Sea, nor aught of the yellow gold Iberiam Tagus beareth in its stream, nor with sceptered hand to conquer a proud people," &c.[37] .... but just one little kiss.

*Tar.*  Happen I should give thee a kiss, what then wouldst thou undertake in my behalf?

*Amph.*  Thine, O queen, is the task to search out thy desire; to do thy bidding is my duty.[38] Command whatsoever thou wouldst have.

*Tar.*  I command silence.

*Amph.*  Prithee hear first a poem which I composed yester-night in thy honor.

*Tar.*  Read it then.

*Amph.*   "Da mihi te facilem, dederisque in carmina vires,
    "Ingenium vultu ſtatque caditque tuo."
*Tar.*   Hoccine poema?
*Amph.*                    Prologus: attendas: incipio.
    "Te Tarentillâ non eſt formosior illa—"
*Tar.*   Quænam illa? si diis placet.
*Amph.*                              Taceas obsecro.
    "In totâ Osunâ non eſt te pulchrior una;
    "Si digitos speƈtes, digiti sunt consule digni,
    "Sive oculos, oculi sunt tanquam sidera cæli."
*Tar.*   Tam bonus in versu quam Mulciber eſt in *a horse shoe.*
*Amph.*   "Frons sursum a dorso, dorsum ſtat fronte deorsum.
    "Crus quasi thus, et pes velut æs, mamma eſt quasi flamma."


*Tar.*   Poetarum facile princeps! at cur mamma quasi flamma?


*Amph.*   "Ut ſtipulam flamma exurit, sic me tua mamma."


*Tar.*   Perge.
*Amph.*          "Eſt umbilicus medio velut æquore ficus,
    "Inter se partes septem neƈtuntur ut artes."
*Tar.*   Si vis, vel non vis, debes comedere *Stock fishe.*
*Amph.*   "Laudaremne genas, currentes corpore venas,
    "Candida colla nitentia coƈtum lac velut ollâ.
    "Quod reliquum eſt versu non possum dicere, cum tu
    "Tantum præcellas quantum inter Cynthia ſtellas."
*Tar.*   Cum faciam vitulâ pro frugibus, ipse venito.
    Interim ad Anticyras, nisi me modo spreveris, ito.

                                                  [*Exit.*

*Amph.*   "Be kind to me, and thou 'lt give power to song,
By thy glance I stand or fall ere long." [39]

*Tar.*   Is this a poem?

*Amph.*   'T is but the Prologue: hearken to me, I begin:
"Than Thee, O Tarentilla, not fairer is she . . . ."

*Tar.*   Who, pray, is this "she"?

*Amph.*   I beg thee be quiet.
"In all Osuna there is not one more fair;
See those fingers, they worthy of a Consul are;
Behold the eyes, eyes like the stars of Heaven."

*Tar.*   Thou 'rt as good at poetry as Vulcan is at—a horse shoe.

*Amph.*   "Thy lofty brow from ev'ry point stands true.
Thy legs shed frankincense upon the dew,
Thy tiny feet as though they were of brass,
Thy paps are as a burning flame, my lass."

*Tar.*   Easily the Prince of poets! But why paps like a *burning flame?*

*Amph.*   E'en as a flame consumeth stubble, so am I consumed
by thy paps.

*Tar.*   Go on, go on!

*Amph.*   "The navel in thy belly's midst is like a fig, full sweet,
E'en as the Arts, these seven parts are knit in one complete."

*Tar.*   Willy-nilly, thou should'st be made to eat *Stock-fish.*

*Amph.*   "I praised not thy cheeks, the coursing veins,
Thy fair & milk-white neck complains.
At all the rest I'm stricken dumb; the word but mars:
Thou dost excell 'em all, a moon amongst the stars."

*Tar.*   Whenas I sacrifice the heifer for the harvest, come
thyself. Meantime, get thee to Anticyra,[40] unless thou
dost despise me, begone.

*[Exit.*

*Amph.   Ipse venito cum faciam etc.*, i.e. quando eo cubitum.
    Capio, mi Tarentilla! at cur interim ad Anticyras?
    Ut sis facetus, et ingeniosus, sicut semper es.
    Benè monet, et hoc sedulò præstitero.


### SCENA SEPTIMA

POLUPRAGMATICUS.              POLUPISTOS.
    ÆQUIVOCUS.          DROMO.

*Polupr.*   Torquem, inquis, aureum die Veneris ad primum
    gallicinium.
    Hoccine totum?
*Polupiſt.*        Me miserum, vix totius dimidium.
    Amisi gemmas inæſtimabiles utique et innumerabiles.
*Polupr.*   Quæ summa totius?
*Polupiſt.*          Decem opinor myriades.
*Æq.*   Cognatus meus eſt, mentitur tam egregie.
*Polupiſt.*   Præter paternum annulum, et torquem illum
    aureum,
    Qui fuit avi, abavi, atavi, abatavi nonagesimi,
    Pondo talentis ter centum, catenis octodecim.


*Dr.*   Præter hæc suffurati sunt duos equos Frisios,
    Comederunt capones tres, gallum gallinaceum,
    Ova centum, duo farta, tres ingentes artocreas.
*Polupr.*   Mira narrat: os huic sublinam probè.


*Dr.*   Par caligarum ab Hedione noſtro et ligulas novas,
    Vas lactis demoliti.
*Polupiſt.*        Tacen' verbero?

*Amph.* So, *come thyself whenas I sacrifice* &c. . . . . that is to say when it's bed time. I'm delighted, my Tarentilla! But why, meantime, muſt I to Anticyra go? "So that thou mayeſt be as facete & witty as ever." She adviseth well, and I'll set about this thing in good earneſt.

### SCENE VII

POLUPRAGMATICUS.          POLUPISTOS.
          EQUIVOCUS.     DROMO.

*Polupr.* A golden necklace, sayeſt thou, on Friday at cock-crow. Is this all?

*Polupiſt.* Ah, wretched man that I am, 't was barely half the whole. In faſt I loſt countless jewels of priceless value.

*Polupr.* What is the total value?

*Polupiſt.* Ten times ten thousand, methinks.

*Eq.* He muſt be blood-kin of mine, he lieth in such good part.

*Polupiſt.* Above all my father's ring, and that golden necklace, which was my grandsire's, my great-grandsire's father's, my great-grandsire's grandsire's grandsire's, back unto the ninetieth generation; eighteen links the length, in weight three hundred talents.

*Dr.* Moreover they've stol'n two Frisian horses, eaten three capons, a dunghill-cock, an hundred eggs, two puddings, & three huge meat-pies. . . . .

*Polupr.* He spinneth a marvellous tale: I'll cozen him right well.

*Dr.* . . . . and a pair of my Hedio's buskins[41] & new buckles; moreover they waſted a bowl of chitterlings.

*Polupiſt.* Wilt thou be silent, knave?

*Polupr.*   Ludos huic miros faciam.

*Æq.*                         Patellâ dignum operculum.

*Polupr.*   Quid petis?

*Polupiſt.*                 Peto fures capi si posses efficere.


*Polupr.*   Si posses! Si vis, terram suo movebo de loco,
    Lunam e cælo, ciebo grandinem, et tonitrua,
    Arte meâ faciam ut mus loco dimoveat
    Quod quadringenta boum juga non trahant.


*Polupiſt.*   O illuſtrem artificem!

*Dr.*                         O execrandum carnificem!

*Æq.*   Boves pictos aut mortuos herus intelligit.

*Polupr.*.   Possum, si libet, unius ope herbeculæ
    Fugare totum exercitum, seras quaslibet
    Aperire, ope hujusce quem vides annuli
    Prandere apud Batavos, cœnare in Italiâ.

*Æq.*   Non eodem die, et sic verum eſt totum quod ait.


*Polupiſt.*   O admirandam peritiam!

*Dr.*                         O execrandam inscitiam!

*Polupr.*   Si vis huc in medium proferam, idque ſtatim,
    Umbram Agamemnonis, aut Achillis animam.


*Polupiſt.*   Virum procul dubio doctissimum!

*Dr.*                         Sapientum octavum!

*Polupr.*   Nil me latet, non quid agatur apud Inferos,
    Colocynthropiratas, aut Madagascar accolas ——


*Æq.*   Scilicet in genere sed non in specie.

*Polupiſt.*   Jupiter ipse nihil poteſt majus.

*Polupr.*  I 'll make rare sport of this.

*Eq.*  The lid 's worthy of the pot.

*Polupr.*  What doſt thou require of me?

*Polupiſt.*  I ask that these robbers be taken, an thou 'rt able to do it.

*Polupr.*  If I am *able!*  Sirrah, should'ſt thou desire 't, I 'll swing the very earth from its orbit, the moon from the heavens, bring down hail, & summon thunder.  By mine art, I 'll cause a mouse to drag from its place a weight that four hundred yoke of oxen could not budge.

*Polupiſt.*  Oh, illuſtrious artificer!

*Dr.*  Oh, what a cursed hangman!

*Eq.*  The Maſter meaneth painted oxen, or dead ones.

*Polupr.*  I 'm able, an it liketh thee well, by aid of one little herb, to put an entire army to flight, to open any lock, or, by means of this ring which thou canſt see, to breakfaſt in Holland & dine in Italy.

*Eq.*  Not on the same day, however: thus what he saith is altogether true.

*Polupiſt.*  Oh, what marvellous skill!

*Dr.*  Oh, what damned folly!

*Polupr.*  An thou wilt, I 'll fetch forth, here in your very midſt, and that at once, the shade of Agamemnon or the soul of Achilles.

*Polupiſt.*  Beyond doubt a moſt learned man!

*Dr.*  The Eighth Wise Man!

*Polupr.*  Naught is hid from me, no not even what is done 'mongſt the inhabitants of Hell, the Pumpkin-pirates, or the Madagascar borderers——

*Eq.*  In general, no doubt, not in particular.

*Polupiſt.*  Jove himself can do nothing more wonderful.

*Dr.*                                Hic impostor nihil minus.

*Polupr.*   Quid Juno in aurem insusurret Jovi.

Musicam accire, flammamque e pugnis excutere——

*Polupist.*   Deus bone, homo homini quid interest!

*Dr.*                                Stulto intelligens.

*Polupr.*   Possum, in medio ære arcem extruere,

Quod fuit et quod futurum ad unguem prædicere.

*Æq.*   Testis ego sum prædixisse quidem, sed falso omnia.

*Dr.*   Pol, hoc periclitabor: quo fui natus in loco?

*Polupr.*   Tuguriolo fortasse.

*Dr.*                                Mentiris per Jovem.

Quoties enim matrem meam audivi dicere

Me natum fuisse, simul et genitum in scrobe.

Sed quod fatum me manet?

*Polupr.*                          Volam manus et frontem in-
spiciam.

In fronte distorta Martialis lineola,

Divulsa, crassa, cruciformis, Solarem intersecans,

Biothanandum ostendit; sed cedo manum?

Hic a Rascettâ descendens Saturnina pallida—

Quid? semicirculus in Mensali, signum homicidii.

*Polupist.*   Rem tenes.

*Polupr.*                Divulsum Thenar salacem et furem.

Cave ut dolatas posthac conscendas arbores,

Ne demissum lapsus per funem repentè concidas,

Cadendo collum frangas. Noli altum sapere.

*Polupist.*   Rubet, pallet, scrupulum injecisti homini.

*Dr.*   This man is nothing short of an impostor.

*Polupr.*   .... Whatever Juno whispereth into Jove's ear is revealed to me.[42] I can call forth music & dispel the heat of battle.

*Polupist.*   Good God! what a difference there is 'twixt one man & another!

*Dr.*   What a difference 'twixt a fool & a man of brains!

*Polupr.*   I'm able to build a tower in midair, to predict perfectly what hath been, and what will be.

*Eq.*   In sooth, I am a witness to what he hath predicted, but they're all lies.

*Dr.*   By Pollux, I'll put this to a test! In what place was I born?

*Polupr.*   In a cottage, peradventure.

*Dr.*   Thou'rt a liar, by Jove! For full oft have I heard my mother tell how that I was both born & begot in a ditch. But what fate lieth in store for me?

*Polupr.*   I'll read the palm of the hand & the brow. On the brow is a little writhen line—the line of Mars—divided, thick, cruciform, intersecting the Sun; it sheweth that thou'lt die by violence; but wilt thou shew me thy palm? This pale line of Saturn descending from the Rascetta— What's this? a semi-circle on the Mensal line's a sign of murder.

*Polupist.*   Thou understandest thy business.

*Polupr.*   The divided Thenar denoteth the letcher & thief. Beware henceforth of climbing upon hewn timbers lest, sliding down the rope, thou'rt suddenly slain; the fall may break thy neck. Aspire not to high things.[43]

*Polupist.*   He blusheth, he turneth pale; he hath given him a bone to gnaw.[44]

*Dr.* Ego te per deos ——

*Æq.* Vin' sceleste? quid agis?

*Polupist.* Liceat hoc unum interrogare si vacet.

Ubi nunc isti fures sunt aut quid agant?

*Polupr.* Sunt, sunt, sunt, in hoc ipso temporis articulo

(*oculo famulum admonet*)

In campo Calatravæ, prope de la Ponte pagum,

Toleti cras pernoctabunt, ad signum solis, foro veteri.

*Polupist.* Beasti: sed quâ demum potes arte reducere?

*Polupr.* Confide, reducam vel e faucibus Erebi,

Faciamque, si vis, ut seorsim singuli

Cum capistris in manu domum tuam adeant.

*Polupist.* Siccine ais?

*Polupr.* Factum puta. Sed quid interim dabis?

*Polupist.* Cape has viginti minas.

*Dr.* Dabitur per Jovem.

Os tibi longè non abest ab infortunio.

*Æq.* Quid tu facies?

*Dr.* Faciam ——

*Polupist.* Etiamne furcifer?

*Polupr.* Bellè. Cape hoc unguentum, et hunc pulverem,

Inunge postes omnes circa ædes tuas,

Sepelito scriptum hoc ad ingressum vestibuli,

Tum circumcirca sternes hunc pulverem.

*Polupist.* Sed quando faciam?

*Polupr.* Die et horâ Mercurii,

Proximè sequenti: fures ultro domum venient.

*Dr.*   I 'll give thee one, by the gods——!

*Eq.*   Doſt thou purpose some wickedness? What sayeſt thou?

*Polupiſt.*   If thou haſt the time, I should like to ask this one question. Where now are these robbers, and what are they doing?

*Polupr.*   They are . . . . ah, um, they are . . . . they are at this inſtant (*with a warning glance at his servant*) on the plains of Calatrava, near by the village of Pons; they will abide tomorrow night at Toledo, at the Sign of the Sun, in the old market.

*Polupiſt.*   I am rejoiced: but through what contrivance art thou able to fetch them back again?

*Polupr.*   Be assured; I can, in fact, fetch them from the very jaws of hell, & I can contrive, shouldſt thou so wish, that each one will betake him to thy house, halter in hand.

*Polupiſt.*   Is it really so?

*Polupr.*   Count it already done. But meantime what wilt thou pay me?

*Polupiſt.*   Here take these eighty pounds.

*Dr.*   'T will be given away, by Jove! Thy face is not far from misfortune.[45]

*Eq.*   What wilt thou do?

*Dr.*   I 'll——

*Polupiſt.*   What! again, thou gallowclapper?

*Polupr.*   Well said. Take this ointment & this powder: anoint all the door-poſts about thy dwelling; bury this writing near the courtyard entrance, then scatter this powder round about the place.

*Polupiſt.*   But when shall I do this?

*Polupr.*   This time Wednesday following: the thieves will then return to thy house of their own accord.

*Polupist.*    Cum bonis?

*Polupr.*            Cum bonis—at hoc obiter cave.

     Ne tu, vel servulorum tuorum quispiam,

     Per tres ante horas et novem scrupulos,

     Mingat, cacet, vel e postico sibilet,

     Nullus sit fœtor; si sit, labor erit irritus,

     Ludetisque operam.

*Polupist.*        Curabo diligenter omnia.

*Polupiſt.*  With the goods?

*Polupr.*  Aye, with the goods—betimes heed this warning: neither thou nor any of thy young servants, for the space of three hours and nine minutes before the time, shall piss, dung, nor break wind from 's backside; none must let a stink: if this be done the enterprise will come to naught & thou 'lt waſte thine efforts.

*Polupiſt.*  I'll take good pains in everything.

## SCENA PRIMA

Æquivocus.          Antonius.

*Antonius.*

EUM immortalem! quantus ignis in me
                   æstuat,
              Venas totumque cor incendens flammis
                   furentibus,
              Ut videar mihi pro verbis flammam
                   emittere.
              Non apud Ætnam ita furit Enceladus gigas,
Adeo Camæna mea coquit et formæ decus.
Cujus tantus eſt splendor et lepos, ut vix putem
Esse aut fuisse aliquam cum quâ conferri queat.
Quæ de Helenâ et Cytereâ poetæ ferunt
Vana sunt, præ hâc sordent, una omnibus
Præcellit, aureum pomum quæ ferret dignissima.

*Æq.*   Auscultabo hìc quid secum mussitet Antonius.


*Ant.*   Quid hìc referam nigricantes oculos,
Laſteam cervicem, aut auream cæsariem,
Turgentes mammas, deos deasque omnes reor


Naturamque posuisse in hâc quod pulchrum fuit.
Nam non ut reliquæ videntur mulieres aulicæ,
Quæ fucatæ cerussâ, purpurisso, aut ſtibio,
Se cingunt, poliunt, curaturâ reddunt amabiles,

EQUIVOCUS.            ANTONIUS.

*Antonius*

REAT God! how furious a fire rageth
  within me,
  Kindling my veins & my whole heart
   with fierce flames!
  Methinks I utter flames inſtead of words.
  The giant Enceladus doth not so rage
   'neath Etna;
So my Camena & her body's grace do torture me.
I scarce can credit, such is her wit & glory,
That any, paſt or present, can compare with her.
What of Helen & Venus the poets have sung
Are empty nothings, compar'd to her they 're sluts;
Excelling all, the golden apple she should win.

*Eq.* I 'll ſtand here & liſten, to catch what Antonius mut-
tereth unto himself.

*Ant.* How shall I speak of her dark brown eyes,
Her milk-white neck, her golden hair,
Her swelling paps? All gods & goddesses, and Nature's
 self,
Methinks, have her endowed with beauty.
Not so the women of the court, those other dames,
Who, painted with ceruse, ſtibium, & carmine dye,
Gird & primp themselves; by tricks they make their beauty;

Soli uſtæ debentes aut arti quod pulchrum habent.

At in hâc genuinæ formæ gratia, et verus color,
Simplex, sincera, clara, divina, elegans,
Tam suaviter arridet, bellè canit, concinnè tripudiat,

Ut spectatores ferè omnes adigat ad insaniam.
Me quod attinet, ita mulieres omnes delevit ex animo,

Ut quo me vertam nesciam, ita jactor, crucior miser.

*Æq.*   Quo me vertam? quid faciam? caudex, stipes, asinus —
Et dignus qui jactere, et cruciere, et sis miser.

*Ant.*   Quid interim suades?
*Æq.*                     Quid vis?
*Ant.*                                Ut amicâ fruar.
Hoc precor effice, et emancipatum do me tibi.
*Æq.*   Mitte suspiria, et ſtolidas hasce querimonias.
Ad cuſtodem vetulam rectâ te proripias,
Huic aurum des, muneribus agendum non suspiriis.
Hanc si feceris tuam, facilem invenies aditum.
*Ant.*   Benè mones. Sed quî cum puellâ me geram?

*Æq.*   Mitte pathicas querelas, *meum cor, meæ delitiæ.*
Jacta te filium et hæredem patris unicum,
Juratoque te ducturum, si secus frui non poteris.

*Ant.*   Quid? egone jurem hoc?
*Æq.*                            Securè et liberè.
Sed heus! linguâ jures oportet, non autem animo,

To gowns alone they owe it all; such loveliness hath come
    from art.

But her's the grace of natural form & color real,

Without deceit, pure, lovely, divine, & rare,

Her laugh so sweet, so wonderful her song,

So trippingly doth she dance along,

That nigh all who see she driveth unto madness.

As for me, from out my mind she hath driv'n all other
    womankind,

So that I know not where to turn me,

So am I rack't, miserable, and tortured beyond endurance.

*Eq.*   "Whither shall I turn me? What shall I do?" Thou 'rt
a blockhead, a fool, an ass—well deserving to be rack't,
miserable, & tortured.

*Ant.*   Aye, but what wouldst thou have me do?

*Eq.*   What dost thou wish to do?

*Ant.*   Marry, I would enjoy my mistress. Bring this to pass
I beg of thee, and I 'll be thy slave.

*Eq.*   Then leave off these moans & doltish complaints. Hasten
straightway to the old hag that guards her; give her a bit
o' gold: 't may be done with gifts but not with groans. An
thou 'lt do it thus, thou 'lt find an access easy.

*Ant.*   Wise counsel, forsooth; but how now shall I demean
myself with the damsel?

*Eq.*   Cease these snivelling moans—"My heart! My darling!" Set thyself forth as son & sole heir of thy father;
be sure to swear thou 'lt wed the wench, otherwise thou 'lt
not enjoy her.

*Ant.*   How now? Am I to swear this thing?

*Eq.*   Freely & withouten a single care. But harkee! let the
oath be from the lips, not from thy heart: "I swear I 'll

Juro te ducturum me—in altero sæculo—
Nunquamne audivisti me sic jurantem aut tutorem tuum?
Fac imitere, simulatque armillas dabis,
Aut monile, aut quod fatuæ virgines volunt.

*Ant.* Armillas, inquis, et monile—sed unde pecunias?
Illud est quod me nunc torquet maximè.
Quid comminiscar? aut quam tendam fabricam
Ut pecunias emungam? hoc doce.

*Æq.* Opportunè memoras.
Scribe literas ad matrem tuam quam ocyssimè,
Dic te ægrotum febricitasse per menses aliquot,
Febremque tuto jures, sed amoris reserves tibi,
Apud pharmacopolas et medicos insumpsisse pecuniam;
Hæc cito fieri cures, aliò me avocant negotia.

[*Exit.*

*Ant.* Ago tibi gratias, scribamque ad matrem illicò,
Quæ credula quum sit, et supra modum misericors,
Plorabit statim, et *O mi Antoni puer,*
*Mi fili Antoni, suavis puer,* neque dormiet scio
Ingemiscens ad hæc, dum miserit pecuniam.


SCENA SECUNDA

PANTOMAGUS ET PATIENTES.

*Rusticus.* Hæc est ni fallor Pantomagi domus.
*Hospes.* Et hæc hora pomeridiana tertia.
*Rust.* Paulisper expectabimus.
*Hosp.* Eccum venit.

wed thee, lass"—in an hundred years or so—Haſt thou
ne'er heard me swearing thus? or else thy tutor? Do thou
likewise, so soon as thou haſt giv'n her the bracelets, necklace, or whatever toys & baubles silly wenches want.

*Ant.*  With bracelets & a necklace sayeſt thou—but where's
the money? That now's what vexeth me above all else.
How shall I contrive this affair? Or shall I fabricate some
tale to cozen forth the moneys? What sayeſt thou to that?

*Eq.*  A seasonable reminder, that. Address a letter to thy
mother without delay, saying that thou haſt been ill of an
ague for some months—thou mayeſt in safety swear to th'
fever, but that it's a fever of love, keep that to thyself—
'twixt apothecaries & doctors thy money's quite spent.
Take care that this be done with all haſte. But now mine
own affairs call me elsewhere.

[Exit Equivocus.

*Ant.*  I thank 'ee, Sir, and I shall write to my mother at once.
Sithen she is credulous & tender beyond moſt, she'll forthwith begin to weep, crying: "O my Son Antonius, my Son
Antonius, my sweet boy!" and I trow she'll not sleep a
wink for bewailing this matter; meanwhiles she'll despatch the moneys without delay.


### SCENE II

#### PANTOMAGUS & HIS PATIENTS

*Ruſt.*  An I miſtake not, this be the house of Pantomagus.
*Stranger.*  Aye, and this the third hour of the afternoon.
*Ruſt.*  We shall see him in a little while now.
*Stranger.*  Lo, he cometh now.

*Pant.*  Qui primus venit sit prior; cujus hoc lotium?

*Ruſt.*  Ægroti.

*Pant.*                 Sed cujus ætatis? sexus? quod nomen habet?

*Ruſt.*  Annon patet ex urinâ?

*Pant.*                         Nihil minus.

*Ruſt.*  Uxoris eſt.

*Pant.*                 Ubi dolet?

*Ruſt.*                         Lecto.

*Pant.*                                 Non intelligis?

In mesaraicis hic dolor, sævit calor hypocondriis,

Et in regione convulsio epigaſtricâ.

*Ruſt.*  Non capio.

*Pant.*                 Per partes umbilicales tumor,

Ingens etiam diaphoresis apud hæmorrhoides.

*Ruſt.*  Committo rem totam, et salutem suam fidei tuæ.

Ego planè rudis, quod videtur consules.


*Pant. (scribit.)*  Hunc habe receptum, adi Pharmacopœum
     meum,

Habitat in viâ Jacobeâ ad signum bovis.

                                [*succedit alius.*

Oſtendit hæc urina cruciatum arthriticum,

Affectu quodam ischiadico, sed ubi dolet?


*Hosp.*  Afficior aliquando mirâ quâdam vertigine,

Pedes labuntur, impingo in parietes caput.

*Pant.*  Tu plus æquo potas, et ille eſt morbus tuus.

Jejunandum eſt tibi per tres dies continuos.

*Hosp.*  Illud non placet.

*Pant.*                 Nec potandum.

*Hosp.*                                 Illud minus.

*Pant.*  Firſt come, firſt serv'd; whose urine 's this?

*Ruſt.*  It come of a sick person, Sir.

*Pant.*  Aye, but of what age? sex? What 's his name?

*Ruſt.*  'T is evident from the piss,[46] is 't not, Sir?

*Pant.*  In no wise, Sirrah.

*Ruſt.*  Then 't is wife's, Sir.

*Pant.*  Where doth she suffer?

*Ruſt.*  In the bed, Sir.

*Pant.*  Haſt thou no wit at all? This pain resideth in the mesentaries, heat rageth in the hypochondries, & there are cramps in the belly.

*Ruſt.*  I comprehend it not, Sir.

*Pant.*  There 's a tumor about the navel, & there 's already a great sweating 'round the emerods.

*Ruſt.*  I entruſt the whole matter to thee; her health 's in thy hands. I 'm but an ignorant fellow: do what seemeth beſt.

*Pant.*  (*Writing*) Take this prescription, and get thee to mine apothecary who dwelleth at the Sign of the Ox, in Jacobean Road.

> [*Exit. Stranger comes forward.*

(*Examining urine*) The urine we have here revealeth a moſt painful gout, affected in a measure by sciatica, but where doth it give unease?

*Stran.*  I 'm troubled sore, betimes, by a monſtrous giddiness, my feet ſtumble, I crack mine head 'gainſt the walls.

*Pant.*  Thou drinkeſt all out of reason, that 's thy disease: I 'll have thee faſt for three successive days.

*Stran.*  I like not that.

*Pant.*  Drink not a drop.

*Stran.*  I like that e'en less.

*Pant.*  Dic decem Credos, quinque Paternosters, tres Avema-
          rias,

Quolibet die ter: dein hoc suspende ad collum tuum.

*Hosp.*  Fiet.

*Pant.*          Cujus hoc lotium?

                              [*succedit alter oppidanus.*

*Opp.*                    Meum.

*Pant.*                              Quid cruciat?

*Opp.*  Uxor, uxor. Annon potes mederi uxori malæ?


*Pant.*  Non insanit?

*Opp.*                  Et me ferè adigit ad insaniam,

Ut neque dies neque noctes pacatus agere valeam;

Sed et totam strepitu suo impedit viciniam,

Clamores ejus sunt supra galli cantum, aut horolo-
          gium.

*Pant.*  Quomodo afficitur?

*Opp.*                        Rixatur, clamat, dentitonat,

Hinnifremit, titionatur, jaculatur pelves et patinas,

Candelabratur, me et ancillas delumbat fustibus.


*Pant.*  Mira narras.

*Opp.*                Si quid potes quæso fer opem.

*Pant.*  Illine lumbos suos bis vel ter quercino baculo.

Remedium ad hoc non habetur excellentius.


Cujus hæc?

                              [*succedit quartus generosus.*

*Gen.*          Mea.

*Pant.*                    Quomodo tecum se res habet?

*Pant.*    Say ten *Credos,* five *Paternosters,* three *Ave Marias,*
say anything whatever thrice a day; furthermore hang this
about thy neck.

*Stran.*    'T will be done, Sir.

*Pant.*    Whose urine's this?

                    [*Townsman comes forward.*

*Town.*    Mine, Sir.

*Pant.*    How art thou afflicted?

*Town.*    'T is my wife, my wife, Sir.  Art able to effect a
cure for 'n evil wife?

*Pant.*    Is she not mad?

*Town.*    Aye, marry, and nigh driveth me unto madness, for
that I get me no peace, neither by day or night; moreover
she setteth the whole neighborhood agog with her clatter:
her cries are louder than cock's crow or the clock's gong.

*Pant.*    In what manner is she affected?

*Town.*    She scoldeth, bawleth, gnasheth her teeth, brayeth like
a mule, hurleth firebrands, flingeth down pans, plates, &
candlesticks: with cudgels she hath so laid about the loins
of the maidservants, and mine own, that we are by now
quite feeble.

*Pant.*    A marvellous tale, this.

*Town.*    If thou 'rt able to do aught, I beseech thine aid.

*Pant.*    Lay about her loins twice or even thrice with a stout
oaken cudgel.  For this ailment 't is held to be a sovereign
remedy.

*Pant.*    Whose water 's this?

                    [*Exit Townsman: succeeded by Gentleman.*

*Gent.*    'T is mine.

*Pant.*    In what way doth thy trouble shew itself?

*Gen.*   Oculi, aures, ſtomachus, male se habent,
Si placet, et sum supra modum melancholicus.

*Pant.*   Si consultum vis oculis, advocatum poſthac ne videris,
Auribus autem si vis, domi mulierem non habueris.
Ad ſtomachum, cave ne devores ferrum, aut chalybem,
Fragmenta ollarum, lapides, aut paleas,
Nam præterquam quod duræ concoctionis sunt, ſtomacho nocent
Ad melancholiam: si ad diem vis esse hilaris, vinum bibe,
Si ad mensem, porcum occide; si ad annum, uxore ducito.

Cujus hoc lotium?

[*succedit ancilla.*

*Anc.*          Heræ.
*Pant.*              Ubi, aut quid dolet?
*Anc.*   Cruciatur prolis procreandæ desiderio.
*Pant.*   Cruciaturne prolis procreandæ desiderio?
In hoc morbo vulgaris medicina praum valet.
Sunt hic multi ſtudentes, multi Academici,
Inter quod procul dubio reperiatur aliquis
Ejus naturæ concors, a quo forsan concipiat.
*Anc.*   Hos dudum fratres, monachosque expertæ fuimus.
*Pant.*   At hoc variis modis et sæpe tentandum fuit.

*Anc.*   Veremur ne sola multitudo nobis nocuerit.

*Pant.*   Itane? Salutem dices heræ tuæ meo nomine,
Eamque me visurum fortasse die craſtino,
Laturumque Diasatyrion quod sit in rem suam.

*Gent.*   Mine eyes, ears, & belly behave ill amongst themselves, an you please, and, above all, I am most grievously melancholy.

*Pant.*   If thou desirest consultation concerning thine eyes, then henceforth thou shouldst not visit an advocate; but if concerning thine ears, thou shouldst not keep a woman in thy house. As to thy belly, have a care lest thou swallow iron or steel, bits of pottery, stones, or the beard of a cock, for besides being of stiff concoction, they do the belly ill. As to thy melancholy: if thou wouldst be merry for a day, drink wine, if for a month, butcher an hog; but if for an whole year, take a wife.

Whose urine 's this?

> [*A Maidservant approaches.*

*Maid.*   'T is that of my mistress, Sir.

*Pant.*   What 's the location of pain & how doth she suffer?

*Maid.*   She 's vexed by want of begetting a child, Sir.

*Pant.*   Vexed by want of begetting a child, thou sayest? For this common ailment, there 's little need of medicine. There are many students, many Academicks hereabouts, 'mongst whom some agreeable fellow should be discover'd by whom, forsooth, she could conceive.

*Maid.*   But lately we 've been trying those friars, those monks.

*Pant.*   But ye should have tried this in many ways and at many times.

*Maid.*   We fear lest the multitude of itself may have been harmful to us.

*Pant.*   Is that so? Salute thy mistress in my name, say that I 'll see to the matter, peradventure on the morrow, & fetch along some compound of Satyrion which may be useful in her affairs.

*Anc.*   Gratus aderis.
*Pant.*                  Herusne domi?
*Anc.*                                   Non.
*Pant.*                                              Benè eſt.
                                                    [*exit ancilla.*

Vos autem curate vos, et si quid male fuerit
Hic me consulite, aut veſtram accersite me domum.
Valete. Sic damnum aliorum eſt lucrum mihi,
                                                    [*Exeunt.*

Et fama mea ex idiotarum infortuniis.
Sic efflorescam faxit Æsculapius.


### SCENA TERTIA

#### ANTONIUS.      STAPHYLA.

*Ant.*   Nisi me fallit animus bonum refert nuncium,
         Nam ædepol venit hilarior, movet ocyus,
         Et me quam primum vidit exiluit animo.
         Quæ nova?

*Staph.*              Ita me deus amet, optima.
*Ant.*   Non sum apud me; cedo, quî succedit negotium?

*Staph.*   Quin tu cessas veſtem meam trahere,
           Trita eſt, et lacerabitur cito.
*Ant.*                          Dic sedulò,
         Ut se res habet, cave ne fingas aliquid.
*Staph.*   Non per Jovem, sed tu ſtes tamen propius,
           Ne quis auscultans nos interim audiat.

*Maid.*  Thy visit will be most welcome.

*Pant.*  Is not the master at home?

*Maid.*  Nay, Sir.

*Pant.*  'T is well.

*[Exit Maid.*

*Pant.*  (*To all*)  All of ye take heed to care well for yourselves, & if aught goeth amiss, consult me here, or else
summon me unto your homes.  Be of good health!

*[Exit Patients.*

*Pant.*  (*Alone*)  Thus the loss of others is gain for me, and
my renown groweth out of the folly of the fools.  Thus
may Esculapius grant that I may ever flourish.


### SCENE III

ANTONIUS.          STAPHYLA.

*Ant.*  If my wits deceive me not, she beareth back good tid-
ings, for, by the temple of Pollux, she cometh with more
jocundity, moveth more swiftly, & whenas she saw me she
sprang forward with confidence.  What new news is there,
my dame?

*Staph.*  As I hope to be saved, it 's very good indeed.

*Ant.*  I 'm beside myself; tell me, how doth the business
prosper?

*Staph.*  Nay but let go my gown, 't is already worn &
presently 't will be torn.

*Ant.*  Tell me quickly how matters stand, and take care not
to counterfeit.

*Staph.*  Nay, by the gods, but draw nigh unto me, lest an
eavesdropper overhear.

*Ant.*   Narra jam: proh! quam fœtantem habet hæc anus ha-
*Staph.*   Quo abis?                                    [litum!
*Ant.*                Ausculto.
*Staph.*                        Dico te perditè amare eam,
    Et alloqui velle.
*Ant.*                Quid illa?
*Staph.*                        Rubet faciem,
    Subrisitque sibi ad nomen tuum.
*Ant.*                        Conjectura optima,
    Non recusavit munus.
*Staph.*                Non.
*Ant.*                        Et id non malum.
*Staph.*   Dico te tandem emoriturum idque subito,
    Nisi potiaris saltem pretio vel precario.


*Ant.*   Hem, quid tum ipsa?
*Staph.*                Erubuit iterum,
    Sed ne time, totus sermo placuit.
*Ant.*   Uno verbo expedi.
*Staph.*                Attende, decrevimus
    Iturum te cras ad ædes.
*Ant.*                Subaudi tuas.
*Staph.*                        Ita.
*Ant.*   Illudis.
*Staph.*        Crede si lubet.
*Ant.*                        Ad horam quotam?
*Staph.*   Ad horam antemeridianam undecimam.
    Sed quod signum amoris remittes, quod symbolum?
*Ant.*   Post salutem dabis hanc catenulam,
    Et sudarium hoc auro intertextum meo nomine.

*Ant.*    Tell me at once: Good God! what a ſtinking breath!

*Staph.*    Why doſt thou draw back?

*Ant.*    I 'm liſtening closely enough.

*Staph.*    I report that thou 'rt head over ears in love with her, and burn for an interview.

*Ant.*    What did she?

*Staph.*    'T red'neth her cheeks & she smiled at mention of thy name.

*Ant.*    'T is a good omen; she refuseth not the gift.


*Staph.*    Nay.

*Ant.*    That, too, is not bad.

*Staph.*    At the laſt I tell her thou 'lt die outright & that at once, save that thou doſt enjoy her, if through none other way, by reason of money or entreaty.

*Ant.*    Ah ha! what then did she?

*Staph.*    Once more she blushed: but have no fear, she was pleased with all I said.

*Ant.*    In one word, woman, tell me everything.

*Staph.*    Mark well, then; we have appointed that on the morrow thou 'lt betake thyself to the house.

*Ant.*    I know, thy house.

*Staph.*    So.

*Ant.*    Thou doſt make mock of me.

*Staph.*    Believe it or no, an it liketh thee.

*Ant.*    At what hour?

*Staph.*    At the eleventh hour, before noon. But what token of love wilt thou send, what sign?

*Ant.*    After that thou haſt delivered my greetings, present her with this little chain & this handkerchief, whereon my name hath been embroider'd in gold.

*Staph.*    Nimis exile munus, mittes crumenam tuam.

　　Volenti nolenti extorquebo hunc annulum.

*Ant.*    Matris donum.  Sed habe.

*Staph.*                        At quid das mihi?

*Ant.*    Iterumne tibi? habe.

*Staph.*                    Do tibi gratias.

　　Sed Antonî, virum te præbe, bellum erit arduum.

*Ant.*    Missa iſtæc fac: ad horam præscriptam adero.


### SCENA QUARTA

### POLUPISTOS.    DROMO.

*Polupiſt.*    Ut dii illum perduint sceleratum hominem,

　　Qui primum nobis hanc cudit Magiam,

　　Zoroaſtrem, Artefium, aut quemlibet alium!

　　Unquamne quisquam ita ludificatus fuit,

　　"Cape hoc unguentum," "fures ultro domum venient?"

*Dr.*    Here, prædixin' ego hoc antea?

*Pol.*    O credulam ſtultitiam, seramque pœnitentiam!

*Dr.*    Et modo nil præter admirandam peritiam.


*Pol.*    Herumne illudis, scelus? abi in malem crucem.

　　　　　　　　　　　　　　　*[Exit Dromo.*

　　Quasi solſtitialis herba paulisper fui,

　　Repente exortus sum, repente occidi.

　　Sed quid agam, quam rationem, quam inibo viam?

　　Nobilis a naturâ laborare nequeo.

　　Aut suffurandum, aut emendicandum eſt mihi.

　　Furem certa manet crux, mendicum infamia.

　　Quibus querar? amicis? habebunt ludibrio.

*Staph.*   A moſt trifling gift! thou 'lt send thy purse.
But will or nil, I 'll take this ring.

*Ant.*   'T was my mother's gift, but take it.

*Staph.*   But what doſt thou give to me?

*Ant.*   More, for thee? Well, take this.

*Staph.*   I thankee kindly, sir. But O Antonius, prove well thy
manhood; 't will be a ſtiff battle.

*Ant.*   Never mind about that: I 'll come at the appointed
hour.


### SCENE IV

#### POLUPISTOS.   DROMO.

*Polupiſt.*   May the gods deſtroy that wicked wretch, Zoro-
aſter, Artesius, or whoever 't was invented this magick
for us! Hath any man ever been so vilely mocked! "Take
this ointment"—"The thieves will return to the house
of their own accord!"

*Dr.*   Did I not warn thee of this before, O Maſter?

*Pol.*   O credulous folly! O late repentance!

*Dr.*   And yet, but a moment ago, thou couldſt speak of
nought save his wondrous skill.

*Pol.*   Art making sport of thy Maſter, knave? Go hang thyself !                                              [*Exit Dromo.*
Like unto the flow'r of but a single day,—lo I am arisen,
& lo, I have perished. But what shall I do? What business shall I undertake? Which way shall I turn? A nobleman by birth, I 'm unequal to toil. I muſt either beg or
ſteal. Sure for thief 's the gallows; for beggar 's sure dis-
grace. To whom shall I make lament? To my friends?
they 'll laugh. To the people? they 'll make sport of me.

Popularibus? illudent. Ignotis? nihil dabunt.
Dicamne me miserum? dedignor, abominor.
Mille supersunt modi, et mille sequar.
Restat adhuc domi supellex, prædiolum,
Hoc ego vendam. Est Osunæ medicus,
Qui pro certo lapidem habet philosophicum.
Hunc conducam, et hujus unius operâ
Quicquid habeo domi, tripodas, trigas,
Æs, cuprum, stannum, ferrum, plumbum, chalybem,
Et supellectilem omnigenam circa ædes meas,
Transmutabo in aurum; boves etiam, et oves,
Vehiculares equos, pullos, et asinos,
Una cum ephippiis, plaustris, curribus,
Vertam in aurum; et sic favente Mercurio
Fortunam et opes recuperabo pristinas.


SCENA QUINTA

PEDANUS.    PHILOBIBLOS.    THEANUS.

*Ped.*   Salve, vir Academice!
*Ph.*                         Salve, vir humanissime!
*Ped.*   Salutis tuæ causâ ambulare te puto.


*Ph.*   Rem tenes.
*Ped.*            Et tu beatus qui tali frueris otio,
   Et tam felici Academicorum consortio;
   Ad institutionem docta familiaritas multum valet.
*Phil.*   Sed unde tu?
*Ped.*                  Pueris edocendis ruri operam eloco,
   Ubi non urbanam, sed villaticam Palladem colunt;

To ſtrangers? they 'll give me naught. Shall I cry "O wretch that I am, I 'm undone?" Nay! I loathe & abominate such behavior. A thousand devices yet remain; a thousand shall I attempt. The household-ſtuff 'till now remaineth at my home, the little farm I 'll sell. There 's a physician at Osuna who, 't is believed, hath the Philosopher's Stone. This man I shall hire, and by his power whatsoever I have at home, trivets, carts, brass, copper, pewter, iron, lead, ſteel, & ſtuff of ev'ry kind about mine house, I 'll transmute into gold: e'en the oxen & the sheep, coach-horses, colts, & asses, together with harness, waynes, chariots, I 'll turn 'em all to gold: and thus, Mercury favoring, I 'll regain my former riches & eſtate.

## SCENE V

PEDANUS.     PHILOBIBLOS.     THEANUS.

*Ped.*   Hail, Academician!

*Phil.*   God save thee, moſt courteous gentleman!

*Ped.*   I presume thou doſt walk abroad for the sake of thy health.

*Phil.*   Thou underſtandeſt the matter.

*Ped.*   And thou 'rt bleſt to have such leisure & so pleasant a fellowship as that of the University men; to mingle with the learned is of great benefit in one's education.

*Phil.*   Whence haſt thou come?

*Ped.*   I 'm hired out in the country, at the business of teaching boys, where they serve, not the Minerva of the town,

Nactus sum otium visendi Matrem Academiam.
Ut latinè loquamur me tibi occurisse gaudeo,
Nobis enim doctis utilis ac jucunda est exercitatio.

*Phil.*    Nobis doctis! profecto tu es asinus! sed bone vir
     Multum te laudo quod nec in viâ vis otio marcescere.

*Ped.*    Honestè quidem, domine, loqueris, sed incongruè,
     Et quam primum corrigas moneo.

*Phil.*                      Satis pro imperio!
*Ped.*    Nam vide, *splendesco, liquesco, tabesco,* et verba hu-
     jusmodi
Respuunt casum illum.
*Phil.*             Ciceronem auctorem habeo.
*Ped.*    Mentiris, garris, cæcutis, non intelligis.

*Phil.*    Oportet peregrinum injuriam pati, secus ——

*Ped.*    Quid malum? Nonne te pudet tam barbarè loqui?
     Ubi tu gentium legisti *injuriam pati,* quo libro?

*Phil.*    Non contendo, nec enim ultra vacat ob negotium.

*Ped.*    Quo vadis?
*Phil.*          Ad consulendum medicum.
*Ped.*                        Comes ero.
     Sed quâ de re?
*Phil.*          An ad distillationem frictio sit utilis.
*Ped.*    Absurdè et stolidè, non est dicendum *frictio* sed *frica-*
     *tio;*

but of the field; having got a bit of leisure, I 'm visiting
the Mother University. I rejoice to 've met with thee,
inasmuch as we may converse in Latin, for 't is a profitable
& most delectable practice amongst us learned men.

*Phil.* "Us learned men!" Verily thou 'rt an ass! But, my
good fellow, I commend thee heartily for being unminded,
e'en when taking a stroll, to get slack through idleness.

*Ped.* Verily thou hast spoken honestly, Master, but incor-
rectly, and I advise that thou shouldst mend thy speech as
soon as ever 't is possible.

*Phil.* 'T was spoken in accord with good authority.

*Ped.* But note that *splendesco, liquesco, tabesco,* & verbs of
that sort, do not take that case.[47]

*Phil.* I consider Cicero an authority.

*Ped.* Thou 'rt a counterfeit-scholar, a chattering-magpie, all
but blind & without understanding.

*Phil.* It behooveth an alien to endure an insult, otherwise
———

*Ped.* What insult? Shouldst thou not be ashamed to speak
so barbarously? Where in the world hast thou read
*injuriam pati*—"to endure an insult?" in what book?

*Phil.* I 'll not dispute with thee, nor does my business permit longer delay.

*Ped.* Whither goest thou?

*Phil.* To consult a physician.

*Ped.* I 'll go with thee. But for what reason dost thou go?

*Phil.* To learn whether frication 's good for a rheum.

*Ped.* Absurdly & stupidly said; the word is not *frictio* but
*fricatio;* for that a noun of the first conjugation which

Quia nomen primæ conjugationis quod *tum* vel *itum* habet
In supino, præter cæterorum legem et ordinem,
Desinit in *atio* (attendis?) non *itio* vel *iɛtio*.

*Phil.*   Mirus hic homo.

                                        [*Intrat Theanus.*

*Th.*                         Quid? an Pedanum meum video?
Is ipsus eſt. Pedane auspicato advenis, ut vales?


*Phil.*   Sic me servavit Apollo.

                                                  [*Exit.*

*Th.*                         Unde venis, quid agis?
Novus mihi quispiam videris tam veſte nitidus.


*Ped.*   Pancraticè, athleticè, basilicè, commodè,
Glisco, glisco, glisco.

*Th.*                         Lætor, ita me Dii ament!
Sed quid tibi nobiscum nunc negotii?

*Ped.*   Ad visitandos amicos, et coemendos libros,
Doɛtosque consulendos.

*Th.*                         Sed quem nunc locum geris?

*Ped.*   Eundem quem ante, nisi quod sit paulo auɛtior,
Nam et ego pædagogus jam, et capellanus simul,
Quovis Sabbato bis concionem habeo.

*Th.*                                     Mira loqueris.

*Ped.*   Et præleɛtor præterea sum proximo in oppidulo.

*Th.*   Ditesces illicò; sed jam non ultra curas grammaticam?


*Ped.*   Vel maximè, et opportunè nunc in mentem venit.
Sunt ibi quædam quæ me valde sollicitum tenent.

*Th.*   Quænam ea?

*Ped.*                   Opinor esse Magicen in **Grammaticâ**.

hath *tum* or *itum* in the Supine (contrary to the law & order of the others) endeth in *-atio* (art attending?), not *-itio* or *-iĉtio*.

*Phil.*   This is a marvellous fellow.

[*Enter Theanus.*

*Th.*   What's this? Is't not Pedanus that I see? Aye, marry, 't is the fellow himself. Pedanus thou'ſt arrived at a timely hour; art well?

*Phil.*   So hath Apollo delivered me![48]

[*Exit Philobiblos.*

*Th.*   Whence comeſt thou, and how's thy health? In all ways thou seemeſt unto me quite youthful in thy neat apparel.

*Ped.*   I'm like unto a wreſtler, a ſtout champion; royally, profitably, I'm waxing fat, swelling, & yearning for more.

*Th.*   As God loveth, I rejoice! But what's thy business with us now?

*Ped.*   To visit my friends, purchase books, & consult with learned men.

*Th.*   But unto what position haſt thou now attained?

*Ped.*   The same as aforetime, save that 't is a little more important, for I am now both a teacher & a chaplain; well-nigh every Sabbath I'm twice in the pulpit.

*Th.*   Thou telleſt wonders!

*Ped.*   And moreover I'm a leĉturer in the adjacent town.

*Th.*   Come presently thou'lt be rich; but doſt thou any longer eſteem thy grammar?

*Ped.*   Moſt of all, and seasonably enough it cometh to mind. There be certain matters that keep me much diſturbed.

*Th.*   What are these?

*Ped.*   Methinks there's magick in the grammar.

*Th.*   Dii melius!

*Ped.*          Ita dico. Hæc sibi quid volunt?
   *Arx, stridens, rostris, sphinx, prester, torrida, seps, strix,*
   Et alibi, *vim, ravim, tussim, sitim, maguderim, amussim.*
   Inspexi Catholicon, Mammotrectum, et vocabularios,
   Et non invenio, opinor esse exorcismum aliquem.

*Th.*   Longè erras, et ostendam tibi errorem tuum alibi.

*Ped.*   Pace tuâ liceat interrogare hoc unicum?
   Quo pede prius Helena Trojanum littus appulerit?
   Et quot vini cados Æneæ Acestes dederit?

*Th.*   Ne quid ultra jam quæras, tu mihi cœnam dabis,
   Quod reliquum est inter cœnandum disceptabimus.

### SCENA SEXTA

#### ANTONIUS.          CAMÆNA.

*Ant.*   Hæc est hora quam statuit anus, sed Camænam video,
   Auscultabo hic quales sermones secum habeat.

*Cam.*   O quam ego misera, insana, et stulta olim fui,
   Quæ sic amorem, et tam sæpè execrata indignissimè,
   Omnesque puellas tanquam non sanæ mentis habui,
   Quæ saltem amarent, Medeam, Scyllam, aut Minois
      filiam!
   Agnosco errorem, et jam cano palinodiam;
   Major vis est fateor aligeri Dei,
   Quam ut resisti possit ab imbelli mulierculâ;
   Experior jam serò misera, Antonii siquidem mei

*Th.*  God save us then!

*Ped.*  So say I. What do these words mean? *Arx, ſtridens, roſtris, sphinx, preſter, torrida, seps, ſtrix,* &, of another sort: *vim, ravim, tussim, sitim, maguderim, amussim?* I 've sought throughout the *Catholicon,* the *Mammotreĉtus,*[49] & other Glossaries, and I find naught; methinks 't is conjuring of some sort.

*Th.*  Thou 'rt greatly deceived, and muſt be shewn thine error elsewhere.

*Ped.*  Saving thy displeasure, may I ask this one queſtion? On which foot did Helen land on the shores of Troy? And how many jars of wine did Aceſtes give unto Æneas?

*Th.*  Nay, no more queſtions now; later thou 'lt sup with me: we 'll discourse of these matters whilſt we are eating.


SCENE VI

ANTONIUS.    CAMENA.

*Ant.*  'T is the hour that the old dame set; but lo, I see Camena: here I 'll hearken to what kind of communion she holdeth with herself.

*Cam.*  Out on 't! what a wretched, mad, and foolish creature I have been till now, thus cursing love full many a time moſt shamefully, and holding all girls diſtraught, e'en those that loved—Medea, Scylla, or the daughter of Minos! I own the fault, and now I recant all I 've ever said: I own that the Winged God hath greater power than a poor, helpless woman is able to withſtand; I 'm taught this now at laſt, poor thing that I am. Yea, by reason of mine Antonius, whose shapely form & lovely

Ita coquit venusta forma, et vultus elegans,
Adeoque urit, ut si non ipsius complexu fruar,
Statutum sit vitam finire ferro aut laqueo.
Quare te Junonem, Venerem, et Cupidinem precor,
Ut vel nos Hymenæis jungatis optatissimis,
Aut me morti dedatis; non possum hanc flammam pati.

*Ant.* Non possum me continere quin salutem et alloquar.
Salve mea Charis, mea Venus, meæ delitiæ,
Immortalem vitam agere inter mortales me facis.

*Cam.* Euge, Antoni, salve ab imo calce ad summum ver-
ticem!
Cur tam tristis? quid palles? doletne quicquam? dic sodes.
*Ant.* Hei mihi!
*Cam.* Per Deos te oro, animule mi,
Ne quid me celes obsecro.
*Ant.* Jura silentium,
Daque fidem te nulli commissuram usquam gentium.
*Cam.* Habe fidem: Angeronam me dices aut Harpocratem.

*Ant.* Paucis dicam. Perditè te amo. Semper mihi formo-
sissima,
At nunc supra modum visa es pulcherrima,
Et tua forma ita semper obversatur mihi,
Ut si non expleam amorem derepentè peream.
Jube quidvis, posce quidvis, nummos, gemmas, opes,
Denegare nec possum nec volo. Hoc unum supplex peto,
Ut mihi vitam dones, cum sit in manu tuâ.
Aut mihi nunc acquiesce, aut hâc sicâ me interfice.
*Cam.* O indignum facinus, et singularem impudentiam!
Tu me audes sollicitare de stupro?

face so fret me that I burn with passion, insomuch that if
I may not enjoy his embrace, 't is fixed that my life end
by knife or noose. Wherefore I pray ye Juno, Venus,
Cupid, that ye either make us one in happy wedlock, else
give me up to Death; this burning flame I cannot bear.

*Ant.*   Nor can I longer bear to ſtay my greetings, I 'll speak
to her. God save thee, my darling, my Venus, my sweetheart; 'mongſt mortal men thou haſt given me immortal
life!

*Cam.*   Well done, Antonius, God save thee, e'en from heel
to head! But why so sad? Why so pale? Doth aught
trouble thee? Prithee, speak to me!

*Ant.*   Ah, deary me!

*Cam.*   In God's name I pray thee, sweetheart, hide naught
from me.

*Ant.*   Swear silence then, and pledge thy faith thou 'lt not
breathe a word of it anywhere in the world.

*Cam.*   Thou haſt my pledge: thou 'lt say that I am Angerona
Dea or Harpocrates.

*Ant.*   I 'll speak but briefly. I love thee desperately. Ever to
me thou 'rt the faireſt of women, but this inſtant thou 'rt
beyond all compare; always thy beauty seemeth thus to me,
so that if I appease not my passion, even now I shall wither
away. Command what thou wilt, ask for whatsoever thou
doſt desire, money, precious ſtones, great riches; I could
nor would deny thee aught. This one boon I humbly pray:
Give me life, sithen 't is in thine own hand. Either satisfy
my longing now, or slay me with this dagger.

*Cam.*   Oh, what a base exploit, what brazen impudence! Doſt
thou dare to ask my maidenhead? Or doſt thou think me

An me venalem putes meretriculam,
Aut cum scorto publico te verba facere,
Nec mei rationem habes, canis impudens?
Ni fidem dedissem, proh, quantas turbas darem.

*Ant.*   Quæso ne me malè capias serenissima,
Voveo, do fidem, juro, sanctèque polliceor,
Per Premam, Premundam, Hymenæum, et reliquos
Conjugales Deos, me ducturum te in uxorem statim,
Hæres sum, et patris idem filius unicus.
Ne repelle, Camæna. Regiam vitam ages.

*Cam.*   Dii te perduint cum hâc procacitate tuâ.

[*Exit.*

*Ant.*   Quo fugis? audi verbum unicum.


*Cam.*                               Non audio.

*Ant.*   Non possum non admirari mulierum versutiam,
Quæ cum viris tam bellè dissimulare didicerint,
Ac si omnes eâdem edoctæ essent in scholâ.
Scio Camænam me perditè amare, sed quam bellè tegit.
Sic est ingenium muliebre, et his plerumque moribus,
Ut quanto plus petant tanto opponant se fortius,
Quo magis exoptent, eo reluctentur plus et negent,
Nam cogi volunt nolentes, reluctantes petunt.
Sed ad eam me conferam intus, ut reconciliem mihi.

a little strumpet, all out for sale? Or that thou talkest to a public whore? Hast no respect for me, thou shameless cur? Had I not given thee my pledge, out on 't! What a stir I 'd make.

*Ant.*  I beg thee judge me not amiss, sweet lady: I take the vow, I give thee my pledge, I swear by all that 's holy, I promise in the name of Prema, Premunda, Hymen, & all th' rest o' the connubial gods & goddesses, I 'll make thee my wife at once. I 'm the heir, my father's only son. Reject me not, Camena. Right royally thou shalt live.

*Cam.*  For this thy malapert lechery, may the gods destroy thee!                                        [*Exit Camena.*

*Ant.*  Why art thou running away? I prithee hear one word more!

*Cam.*  I 'll not listen to another word.

*Ant.*  I cannot but admire the guile of women, whose wont it is to dissemble so skillfully with mankind, as though all of 'em were trained in the same school. I 'm sure Camena loveth me exceedingly well, but 't is neat how she contriveth to hide it from me. Such is the genius of woman, and, most part, these whims are such that what they earnestly seek after, that they boldly decry: the more they desire, the more they hold back and deny 't. For unwilling maids wish to be forc'd, and those who draw away are asking for 't. But I 'll betake me unto her within, that I may be restor'd to favor.

## SCENA SEPTIMA

POLUMATHES.                SIMON ACUTUS.

*Sim.*   Quid est quod scire desideras?

*Pol.*                          Scire volo

Quid arbitreris de concentu Pythagorico.

*Sim.*   Scire te vellem imprimis concentum esse duplicem,
activum et passivum, vocalem et Rhythmicum; vocalis qui
procedit ab arteriis et diaphragmate, Rhythmicus qui fit ab
æquilaterâ vocum collisione, juxta proportionem choriam-
bicam, continuam, superpartientem, submultiplicem.

*Pol.*   Quorsum hæc?

*Sim.*                          Elucescet illicò.

Hæc autem proportio fit vel secundum quantitatem, vel
qualitatem: quantitativè, idque ad mensurantis benè placi-
tum, ut enim numerus numerans a numerante fluit in
numeratum, sic mensura a mensurante in rem mensuratam,
per quandam sympathiam et Apotomen Harmonicam.  Tu
non olfacis responsionem meam?

*Pol.*   O cælum, O terras, O maria Neptuni, sapit hic?

*Sim.*   Vel secundum qualitatem: et sic quoad Euphoniam, vel
gratiam: rursus in Euphonia sex occurrunt consideranda,
longitudo, brevitas, pondus, et levitas, filorum tenuitas,
et oris ingenuitas.

*Pol.*   Fleat Heraclitus, an rideat Democritus?

*Sim.*   Concludam determinando metaphysicaliter, et ad mentem philosophi.

*Pol.*   Facesse in malam rem, asine!

*Sim.*   Non intelligis fortasse?

## SCENE VII

### POLUMATHES.    SIMON ACUTUS.

*Sim.*  What, pray, dost thou desire to know?

*Pol.*  I wish to know what thou thinkest concerning the Pythagorean Harmonies.

*Sim.*  Know then, first of all, that Harmony is two-fold— Active & Passive, Vocal & Rythmick. Vocal is that which issueth from the arteries & the Midriff; Rythmick is occasioned by the equilateral concussion of tones, equally proportioned, choriambic, continuous, superpartient, submultiplicate.

*Pol.*  What 's the purpose of all this?

*Sim.*  'T is quickly shown. This proportion is either according to quantity or quality: Quantitatively—according to the fancy of the measurer—for, as the number numbered, by the numbering, mergeth into the numbered, so a measure, by the measuring, mergeth into the thing measured, by means of a certain agreement in nature & the Harmonic Apotome.[50] Dost thou not understand mine answer?

*Pol.*  O Heavens! O Earth! O Seas of Father Neptune! is this wisdom?

*Sim.*  Or according to quality: and 't is so as long as there 's Euphony or grace. In Euphony, again, six considerations arise—length, shortness, ponderosity, lightness, the fineness of the string, & the freedom of the mouth.

*Pol.*  Would Heraclitus weep, or Democritus[51] laugh?

*Sim.*  I 'll conclude by defining the thing metaphysically, and as is fitting to the philosophick mind.

*Pol.*  Have done with this vile nonsense, thou she-ass!

*Sim.*  Thou dost not comprehend, peradventure?

*Pol.*                    Nimis altum sapis.
Quid?  Egone ut feram hujusmodi ineptias?
Nec patiar nec feram, nec inultus sinam.

                                         [*Exit.*

*Sim.*  (*canit solus*)

| Personatus ego, | Esse merum pecus, |
| Sic meipsum tego, | Et qui credit secus, |
| Vosque meæ veſtes, | Fallitur, hiho, hiho, |
| Eſte mihi teſtes, | Fallaturque semper, io! |

*Pol.*  Think not so much on high things! What? Shall I
suffer trifling of this sort? I 'll not suffer 't, I 'll not bear
it, I 'll not allow it.

[Exit Polumathes.

*Sim.*  (*Singing alone*)
   Now I 'm a masquerading knave,
   And thus I hide my ſtation;
   Ye and my beard & gown so grave,
   Do lend me confirmation.

   The people are but cattle dumb,
   And who will not agree, Sir,
   Is but a fool, O teedle, tum,
   A fool for aye, you see, Sir!
   O hi ho, he ho, hi, ho, hum,
   He o, he o, io.

### SCENA PRIMA

PANTOMAGUS.     POLUPISTOS.

*Pantomagus.*

 TTENDAS, duæ sunt rationes vertendi
             rerum species,
        Altera brevis, sed quæ plus habet peri-
            culi,
        Et hanc artifices curtationem vocant,
        Altera longa, sed quæ longè tutissima,
        Et hanc longationis verbo exprimunt.

*Pol.*    Dic bonâ fide, tune hanc longationem tenes?

*Pant.*    Exactè, et ad unguem.
*Pol.*                  Quibus expensis opus?
*Pant.*    Mille coronatis.
*Pol.*             Non refert de pecuniis,
    Modo fiat aliquando, et confidas arti tuæ.
*Pant.*    Confidam? dubitas?
*Pol.*             Sed quibus interim opus?
*Pant.*    Habere primum debemus specus subterraneos,
    Furnellos rectos, apertos, clausos, patulos,
    De vitris arboreis, et de Mercurio philosophico,
    Ad exercitium majoris et minoris operis.
*Pol.*    Prægnans animus aurum parturit mihi.
*Pant.*    De rege Antimonii, et luto sapientiæ,

# ACT IV

## SCENE I

PANTOMAGUS.    POLUPISTOS.

*Pantomagus.*

OW, good Sir, heed well: There be two methods of changing the species of things —one short, but far more hazardous, and this the artificers call "curtation"; t' other is more complicated, but far out the safer, which they describe as "longation." [52]

*Pol.*  Prithee, tell me true, doſt thou underſtand this "longation"?

*Pant.*  Perfectly, Sir, down to a hair's breadth.

*Pol.*  What 's the coſt of this method?

*Pant.*  One thousand crowns, Sir.

*Pol.*  The money 's of no account; let it be made somehow, and if thou doſt rely upon thine arts . . . .

*Pant.*  If I rely? Doſt thou miſtrust me?

*Pol.*  But betimes, what 's required for this work?

*Pant.*  Firſt we should have dens 'neath the earth, proper ovens, some open, some closed, some exceeding wide, for the accomplishment of the Greater & Lesser Works, the Cryſtal Tree & the Mercury of the Sages.

*Pol.*  His pregnant soul bringeth forth the gold for me.

*Pant.*  From the Regulus of Antimony & the Clay of the

Et ad artem pertinentes aquas duodecim.

*Pol.*   His paratis quænam est auri confectio?

*Pant.*   Scire debes quod fumus albus, citreus, rubeus,
    Leo viridis, Almagra, et mortis immunditia,
    Limpidum, sanguis, æruca, et terra fœtida,
    Azar, Ozizambe, Azinabam, Dautin, Euticen,
    Almazidor, Uffi, Tuffi, Marchoni, Tincar et Laton,
    Cum Borregor, et Azon, sale et Anatron,
    Juxta præceptum Caleb filii Ezegid Medoia,
    Sunt ingredientes ex quibus fit aurum purissimum.
*Pol.*   Ut hoc verbum auri exhilarat cor meum!
*Pant.*   Jam tu jurabis per præsidem Mercurium,
    Ne cui unquam secretum hoc dixeris.
*Pol.*   Men' times? egone quid dixero? juro Jovem.

*Pant.*   Credo: sed numera pecuniam.
*Pol.*                 Quam?
*Pant.*                     Rogas?
    Ad fornacem philosophicam præparandam benè,
    Ad mercandos carbones, ollas, vitra, patinas.
*Pol.*   Quantum vis?
*Pant.*          Numera quadringentos aureos.
*Pol.*   Habe quingentos.
*Pant.*        Probè curabuntur omnia.
                           *[Exit Pant.*

*Pol.*   Dii immortales, homo homini quid interest!
    Quam verè prudens hic, quam cordatè loquitur!
    Me quod attinet, statim ac hoc aurum habuero,
    Princeps ero, et ædes ædificabo magnificas,

Sages and on to that Art which pertaineth to the Twelve Waters.[53]

*Pol.* With these preparations in order, what is 't that maketh the gold?

*Pant.* Thou shouldst know by means of the white, citronate, and red fumes, the Green Lion, the Almagra & the Immund of Death, clean, sanguine, rusty & fœtid Earth, Azar, Ozizambe, Azinabam, Dautin, Euticen, Almazidor, Uffi, Tuffi, Marchoni, Tincar & Laton, together with Borregor & Azon, Salt & Anatron, following after the directions of Caleb, of the sons of Ezegid Medoia, these be the ingredients from which cometh the purest gold.[54]

*Pol.* The very name of gold delighteth mine heart!

*Pant.* Now shalt thou swear by Mercury the Protector, that at no time thou 'lt betray this secret to any man.

*Pol.* Dost doubt me? What, pray, could I have told? I swear by Jupiter.

*Pant.* I believe thee; but pay me ready money.

*Pol.* How now?

*Pant.* Canst thou ask? For the proper preparation of the philosophic furnace, for the purchase of coals, flasks, glasses, bowls.

*Pol.* How much dost thou require of me?

*Pant.* Count out four hundred in gold.

*Pol.* Take five hundred.

*Pant.* All shall be well arranged.

[*Exit Pantomagus.*

*Pol.* Immortal gods! How one man doth exceed another!
How discreet is this man, how sagely he speaketh!
For my part, of this gold I 'll forthwith make use,
I 'll be a prince, and shall build a palace grand,

Immo totas civitates mihi cognomines,
Cum suis Theatris, Balneis, et Peristyliis,
Gerontotrophiis, Pædotrophiis, et Nosocomiis.
Nec tam privatis quam publicis operibus
Illustre nomen erit, et decus meum.
Alpes complanabo, et sylvam Hercyniam,
Desiccabo deinde Paludem Mœotidem,
Projiciendo in eam montes Hyperboreos.
Desertum Lop et Zin prata erunt uberrima,
Mons Atlas frugifer, et arena Lybica
Producet sumptu meo decuplum, centuplum.
Loquuntur idiotæ, et vulgus hominum,
De ponte Trajani, et stupendis operibus
Romanorum, Theatris, et Mausoleis tumulis;
At hæc si ad nostra conferantur opera,

Nulla futura.  De vivo saxo pontes condam duos,
In ornamentum Europæ, et stuporem Oceani.
Primus erit a Caleto ad Doroberniam,
Alter ad fretum et fauces Euxini Maris,
Ubi Xerxes olim trajecit exercitum.
Faciamque piscinam de Mari Mediterraneo,
Cum infinitis aliis, quæ nunc in mentem non veniunt.
Hoc solum addam, si cui vestrum præbibero,
Sive sit ex auro, argento, aut gemmâ poculum,
Cyathum ebibens secum domum auferat;
Atque hæc fient a pecuniis et auro novo.
Regali fastu vivam, luxuque splendido,
Delicatè agens, et ditescens supra omnem fidem.

Yea verily, whole cities shall be called by my name,
Along with their theaters, baths, and cloisters,
Almshouses, orphanages, & hospitals.
But not so much by private as by public works
Shall be made my fame & glory great.
I 'll cast down Alps, and raze Hercynian Forest,
Then I 'll make dry the Mæotidian Fens[55]
By flinging down therein the Hyperborean Mountains.
Desarts of Lop & Zin I 'll turn to fertile fields,
Mount Atlas fruits shall bear, Libyan sands shall flow'r
Ten, yea an hundred-fold, at my expense.
Fools & all that vulgar rout, do prate aloud
Of Trajan's Bridge & stupend labors of the Romans,
Of their theaters great & of that Mausolus' Tomb;
But these, compar'd with works of ours, are less than
    naught.
From living rock I 'll carve out bridges twain
For Europe's glory, and the wonder of Oceanus.
The very first will be from Calais unto Dover,
T' other cross that narrow inlet of the Euxine Sea,
Where once the great Xerxes led his mighty armies.
Out of the Mediterranean a fish-pond I shall fashion—
And many other toys that come not now to mind.
This alone I 'll add: after I 've pledg'd a man's health,
He shall bear off the emptied cup to 's own home,
Though the cup be of gold, or silver, or precious stone;
All this by means of my new gold shall come to pass.
In royal state & glowing pride I 'll live and thrive,
Faring gently and waxing rich beyond belief of man.

## SCENA SECUNDA

POLUPRAGMATICUS.        SIMON ACUTUS.

*Polupr.*   Ambitus terræ secundum Eratoſthenem
Eſt quadraginta mille ſtadiorum et dimidii,
Cum sesquiplâ, oĉtavâ superpartiente sesquidecimâ.


*Sim.*   Quis hic qui de cœlis tam magnificè loquitur?
Secum supputat, attendam.
*Polupr.*                            Auscultat hic aliquis.
Secundum Alfraganum lunæ concavæ semidiameter
Semidemetientes triginta tres terræ continet,
Cum quadruplâ sesquialterâ, duplâ sesquitertiâ.
*Sim.*   Interpellabo, salve vir grandistrepe!
*Polupr.*   Simon Acute quid agis?
*Sim.*                            Te rebar Tychonem illum
        celebrem,
Tam sublimia fulminabas.
*Polupr.*                       Ego te vulgarem Academicum.
*Sim.*   Sed quorsum hic tam insanus habitus?
*Polupr.*                                   Ne roges.
Sed quæ fama tua jam?
*Sim.*                         Hoc ipsum a te volo,
Quì fiam illuſtris, dynastis, heroibus, ipsi duci
Æque ac tu notus, familiaris, et socius.
*Polupr.*   O Simon, Simon, rem petis arduam,
Magni laboris opus; quia sic ardes tamen,
Docebo te ad famam viam conpendiosissimam.
Disputandum eſt frequenter in scholis publicis
Magno impetu.
*Sim.*                 Hoc feci, et cessit infeliciter.

## SCENE II

POLUPRAGMATICUS.        SIMON ACUTUS.

*Polupr.*   According to Eratosthenes,[56] the circuit about the
Earth containeth forty thousand and one-half ſtadia, with
one-and-a-half times as much again, with one-eighth superpartient to one-and-a-tenth.

*Sim.*   Who is this who speaketh so grandly of the Heavens?
I 'll pay heed whilſt he reckoneth with himself.

*Polupr.*   Someone overheareth this business. According to
Alfraganus,[57] the semi-diameter of the bended Moon,
measuring the half thereof, compriseth thirty-three of the
Earth's, three-halves fourfold, four-thirds twofold.

*Sim.*   I 'll interrupt 'im: God save thee, thou great windbag!

*Polupr.*   Simon Acutus, what doeſt thou?

*Sim.*   I 'm reckoning thee the great Tycho, thou wert ful-
minating so magnificently.

*Polupr.*   I 'm reckoning thee a vulgar Academick.

*Sim.*   But what is the objeſt of this mad deportment?

*Polupr.*   Ask me not. But what now is thy renown?

*Sim.*   'T is this very thing that I require of thee, how I may
be a man of renown, e'en as thou art, known to potentates,
noblemen, the Duke himself, a familiar friend & fellow.

*Polupr.*   O Simon, Simon! what thou seekeſt is an hard
matter to come by; there 's need of great labor; for that
thou 'rt so intent upon 't, however, I 'll teach thee the
shorteſt road to fame. 'T is oft debated at the public dispu-
tations with great violence.

*Sim.*   I 've done that, and it fell out miserably.

*Polupr.*   Agendum in theatris, in publicis comitiis;
    Perorandum, ubi te tota Academia, tota regio,
    Tum possit videre, tum proloquentem audiat,
    Aut coram ipso Duce.
*Sim.*                    Orator sum valde tenuis.
*Polupr.*   Non refert quis sis, saltem amicum habeas
    Cujus operâ utaris, tu tantum proferes.
    Benè veſtitus super omnia viris illuſtrissimis
    Associare te debes.
*Sim.*                    Hæc forsan præſtare potero.
*Polupr.*   Vel sic, cude suppositiones, orationes, epiſtolas,
    Prælectiones, animadversiones, quicquid in buccam venit,
    Prosâ an versu non refert, bis anno quolibet,
    Et ad Francofurtanas plerumque nundinas.
*Sim.*   Laboriosum nimis hoc, at enitar tamen.
*Polupr.*   Hoc obiter.  Si scriptoris cujuspiam mentionem
        feceris,
    Epitheton adjicias.  *Mulus mulum scabit.*
*Sim.*   Intelligo.
*Pol.*            Vel edes alienum opus tuo nomine
    Cum notis quibusdam, vel adjectiunculis.

*Sim.*   Inhoneſtum.
*Polupr.*            Librumque inscribes heroi alicui,
    In cujus laudem insurges supra omnem fidem,
    Licet ille bardus sit.  *Obsequium amicos parit.*

*Sim.*   Prudenter hoc.
*Polupr.*            Operumque tuorum scribe ipse cata-
        logum,
    Vitamque tuam præfiges.

*Polupr.*  Thou shouldst speak in theaters, in publick assembly; pleading to the very end, where the entire University, the whole region round about, e'en the very Duke himself, may be able to see thee, as well as hear thine eloquence.

*Sim.*  I am an exceeding poor orator.

*Polupr.*  'T mattereth not what thou art; at least thou hast a friend whose works thou mayest use, greatly enlarging on 'em. Fitly clad, thou shouldst, above all else, associate thyself with the most famous men.

*Sim.*  This, perchance, I may be able to accomplish.

*Polupr.*  E'en so, pound out the counterfeits, orations, epistles, lectures, criticisms; whatever cometh to mind, prose or verse, it mattereth not; take anything thou wilt to the Frankfurt Marts twice a year.

*Sim.*  A mighty task, this; howbeit I 'll do my best.

*Polupr.*  Note this, by the way: Shouldst thou make mention of any writer, apply a word of praise. "Mule scratcheth mule." [58]

*Sim.*  I understand.

*Polupr.*  Or thou canst publish the work of another man in thine own name, with certain marginal notes, or trifling additions.

*Sim.*  'T is a dishonorable practice.

*Polupr.*  And thou shouldst inscribe a book to some other great man, in whose praise thou 'lt overshoot thyself beyond all belief, although he may be a numskull. "Flattery begetteth friends." [59]

*Sim.*  Wisely spoken.

*Polupr.*  Make a catalogue of thine own works & prefix to it thy Life.

*Sim.*                    Hoc esset vanissimum.

*Polupr.*    At hoc crebro fit. Si quem noris scriptorem celebrem,
     Huic te opponas; quicquid ait, nega;
     Convelle, carpe, explode, sugilla, exsibila.


*Sim.*    Hoc ambitiosum.

*Polupr.*             Vel novam sectam instdtues,
     Habebisque statim sectatores innumeros.

*Sim.*    Opinor.

*Polupr.*        Nostin' paradoxum absurdum aliquod?
     Explosum renovabis, aut finges aliud de novo,
     Moveri terram, stellas et lunam incoli, et hujusmodi.

*Sim.*    Ridiculum.

*Polupr.*        Utcunque, defendes per Jovem,
     Qui possit vel ausit, carpat opus tuum.

*Sim.*    At qui defendam si quis in me scripserit?


*Polupr.*    Contemnes, irridebis, cujuscunque sit ordinis,
     Qui sugillârit doctum et generosum opus tuum.
     Et licet ei dignus, quod aiunt, præstare matellam
     Non sis, vilipendes—infra iram tuam—tu leo leporem?


*Sim.*    Hoccine totum quod vis?

*Polupr.*            Concludo breviter,
     Si vis insignis et primus haberi philosophus,
     Par est ut sis acutus, ferox, audax, impudens,
     Leno, parasitus, vanus, vulpes, simia,
     Redargutor superbus, jactator omniscius,
     Irrisor sublimiloquus, omnium horarum homo.
     Ditesces ita et inclaresces quam ocyssimè.

                                            [*Exit.*

*Sim.*  'T would be the height of vanity.

*Polupr.*  But 't is commonly done. Shouldſt thou know any
famous writer, attack him; whatsoever he asserteth, deny
it; confute him, find fault, disapprove, defame, detract,
blacken, hiss him out of the place.

*Sim.*  'T is a far-reaching plan.

*Polupr.*  Or, found a new sect, and thou 'lt have, in the wink
of an eye, innumerable disciples.

*Sim.*  I quite believe 't.

*Polupr.*  Doſt thou know some silly paradox? Rub up one
that 's been rejected, or create a new one—earth is shift-
ing; moon & stars are inhabited, & matters of that sort.

*Sim.*  All out absurd.

*Polupr.*  However that may be, defend it, by Jove; let him
who can, or dares, carp at thy work!

*Sim.*  But how am I to defend my views, supposing anyone
writes against me?

*Polupr.*  Ridicule him; whatever be his rank, mock any man
who 'll defame thy noble work & learning. And even
though thou 'rt not fit, as the saying goeth, to hand him his
chamber-pot, yet hold him cheap; treat him as beneath
thy resentment; art thou, the lion, to ſtoop unto an hare?

*Sim.*  Is that all you propose for me to do?

*Polupr.*  I 'll add this word more: If thou doſt yearn to be
held a famous & pre-eminent Philosopher, 't is meet thou
shouldſt be witty, courageous, bold, shameless, a pimp, a
parasite, a fox, an ape, a vain fellow, an arrogant opponent
in argument, a boaſtful pretender to omniscience, pouring
out scorn in grandiloquent language: "*a man ready at all
affairs.*" [60] In this fashion thou 'lt wax both rich & famous
in the wink of an eye.          [*Exit Polupragmaticus.*

*Sim.*  Recte suades; dabo operam pro virili meâ,
  Et pro eo quo sum imbutus ingenio,
  Producam ex hoc capite novem Tomos illicò.
  Dicam libro primo Lunam esse habitabilem,
  Idque leporibus et cervis.  At quid inquis ita?
  Quoniam cum indefessi latrent ad lunam canes,
  Probabile eſt videre illic currentes lepores.
  Secundus aget de Thaumaturgicis operibus,
  Tertius de Zilphis, Pygmæis, et spiritali animâ.
  Quartus de Subpolaribus, et politiâ Antipodum.
  Quintus de condylomatis, rhagadibus, et morbo Gallico.
  Sextus de Erebo, et arcanis quibusdam magicis.
  Nonus contra Vallam de reciprocatione *sui* et *suus.*
  De rebus aliis admirandis libris in reliquis
  Audacter disputabo, contradicam liberè.
  Vos auditores parate saltem versiculos,
  Præfigendos in laudem authoris et operis,
  Reliqui ad coemendum parate pecunias,
  Proſtabunt Francofurti, proximis nundinis.


SCENA TERTIA

Antonius et Tibicines.

Æquivocus *cum lucernâ.*

*Ant.*  Æquivoce!
*Æq.*          Quis me vocat?
*Ant.*                        Quid hic tibi negotii,
  Hoc noctis cum lucernâ?
*Æq.*                  Herum quæro.

*Sim.* Right well haſt thou advised me: I 'll lay hold of the business to the beſt of mine ability, and, in accordance with inſtruction, I 'll produce from this mine head nine volumes on the spot. In the firſt book I 'll prove that moon 's inhabited, and that by ſtags & hares.

Doſt thou ask me, *why?*

For that when hounds, unwearied, bay the moon, 't is like that they behold thereon the running hares.

The second book telleth of magick works; th' third of sylphs, pygmies & the elemental spirits of the air. The fourth book 'll treat of the region under the Poles and the polity of the Antipodes. The fifth, of the swol'n fundament, sores, & the French pox. The sixth 'll speak of Hell and of the moſt secret practices of magick. The ninth 'll be againſt Valla[61] on the reflexive pronouns, *sui* & *suus.*

Concerning the other wonders in the remaining books, I 'll reason boldly, and contradict with freedom. Get ye ready, disciples, at leaſt the little verses in praise of the author & his work; the reſt, for ready money, they 'll sell to the Frankfurt-folk, come next market-day.

### SCENE III

#### ANTONIUS & FLUTE-PLAYERS.

#### EQUIVOCUS, *with a lantern.*

*Ant.* Equivocus!

*Eq.* Who calleth me?

*Ant.* What business haſt thou with a lantern at this time o' night?

*Eq.* I 'm seeking the Maſter.

*Ant.*                                    An hac abiit?

*Æq.*   Hac abiit inquis? quâ non abit? huc, illuc, ubique,
　　　Per omnes vicos urbis noctivagus repit
　　　Ad horas omnes noctis, nunc virili habitu
　　　Nunc muliebri incedens, omnes formas induens,
　　　Lenæ, obstetricis, interdum vero militis.
　　　Proteus opinor non est illo mutabilior,
　　　Nec vulpes mage versipellis, aut versutior.
　　　Sed quo tu cum fidibus?

*Ant.*                         Ad amicam.

*Æq.*                              Intelligo.

*Ant.*   Sed heus, dum hi ludunt, tu canes.

*Æq.*                              Quando ita vis volo.

*Ant.*   Atque eccum prope sumus, hæc ni fallor domus,
　　　Atque hoc cubiculum, ubi Camæna mea cubat,
　　　Hæc fenestra, ludatis jam si lubet.


　　　　　　　　　　　　[ *Tibicines ludunt.*


*Æq.* (*canit.*)     Morpheu Deorum summe,
　　　　　　　　Et insomniorum Deus,
　　　　　　　　Portas aperi corneas,
　　　　　　　　Claude sed eburneas.


　　　　　　　　Camænamque seu a dextrâ,
　　　　　　　　Sive cubat a sinistrâ,
　　　　　　　　Sive cubat hæc supina,
　　　　　　　　Tegat Morpheus a ruinâ.


　　　　　　　　Pungens procul esto pulex,
　　　　　　　　Cantans procul esto culex,

*Ant.*   Hath he gone out this way?

*Eq.*   Hath he gone out, say you? At what hour doth he not go? Hither, thither, everywhere, through all quarters of the city, a night-prowler, he creepeth forth at all hours, now clad as a man, now mincing along like a woman, assuming all shapes: bawd, midwife, sometimes e'en as a soldier. Methinks Proteus himself is not more changeable than that man, nor fox more sly & crafty. But whither doſt thou go with flutes?

*Ant.*   To see a friend.

*Eq.*   Ha! I underſtand.

*Ant.*   But hark'ee, whenas these men play, thou shalt sing.

*Eq.*   Seeing that 't is thy wish, I will.

*Ant.*   Behold, we are quite near at hand; this, an I miſtake not, is the house, & this the bed-chamber wherein my Camena lieth. Here 's the window. Ye may play now, an ye please.

> [*The Flutiſts play.*

*Eq.* (*sings*) Morpheus, great God, who art the King
>         Of dreams that fade with dawn,
>         Bind faſt the ivory gates, and fling
>         Full open those of horn.

>         Camena may on the right side lie,
>         Or on her left side sleep,
>         Perchance upon her back she 'll sigh:
>         The god her safety keep!

>         The vexing flea muſt keep away,
>         The buzzing gnat muſt go;

Funeſtus absit incubus,
Magus absit et veneficus.

Et quando aperit ocellos,
Pulchrè scintillantes illos,
Graves procul absint curæ,
Seu præsentes, seu futuræ.

Adsit amor, et delitiæ,
Dolor absit, et triſtitiæ,
Moveatur vel requiescat,
Loquatur vel conticescat.

Attendat musicus sonorus,
Atque gratiarum chorus,
Suaveolentes et odores,
Et gratissimi colores.

*Ant.*   Salve Camæna, salve Tarentilla, salve vetula!
Eamus jam si placet, illucescet enim illicò.


### SCENA QUARTA

POLUPISTOS.          PANTOMAGUS.

*Pol.*   Narravi amicis multis consilium meum
De conditione hâc inter me et medicum,
Dehortantur, faſtum putant consilio malo.
Non refert quid dicant, prudentiores forent modo.

Foul Incubus may here not ſtay—
Sir Wizard, get below!

And when her eyes she opes at laſt,
Shining like cryſtals clear,
All heavy cares from her be caſt,
And aught that bringeth fear.

May Love lie close, and all delight,
Sadness, and grief go hence;
In speech, abroad, or hid from sight,
Be thou her providence.

May she music hear—a rapturous tune—
And songs in praise of her name,
With fragrance may her senses swoon,
And Beauty salute her fame.

*Ant.*   God keep thee, Camena; farewell, Tarentilla; good-
night to thee, old woman! An ye please, we 'll now depart,
for the light of day 's upon us.

## SCENE IV

POLUPISTOS.          PANTOMAGUS.

*Pol.*   To many friends I have related my intention concerning
this covenant 'twixt me and the physician; they advise
againſt it, they think 't is a sorry business. 'T mattereth not
what they say; they 've been more prudent with their
means.

*Pant.*   Polupiste!                                              [*Intrat.*
*Pol.*                Quid vis? quî succedit negotium?
*Pant.*   Ex voto, sed interim opus est auro novo.


*Pol.*   Cui usui?
*Pant.*                Donum mittendum est præsidi Mercurio,
Ars enim sacra est.
*Pol.*                        Cape votivam pecuniam.
*Pant.*   Benè est, sed opus etiamnum viginti minis
Ad coemendos carbones abiegineos.
*Pol.*   Etiamne molestus?
*Pant.*                        Ne graveris impendere,
Uncia quælibet auri, quam insumis hoc opere,
Meâ fide ter centum mille rursus dabit.
*Pol.*   Cape quod vis.
*Pant.*                Probè curabuntur omnia.

                                                          [*Exit.*

*Pol.*   Insumpsi jam quadringentos aureolos,
Sed ad rem: sic inquit, auri quælibet uncia
Ter centum mille dabit—si sic, quid quadringenta dabunt?


                                          [*Supputat in tabulis.*
Subduco rationem arithmeticè, et statim proveniunt
Tercentum mille, mille, millionum myriades.
Sic est in tabulis, subduxi rationem benè,
Pergo per æquationem proportionis continuæ,
Et mille minæ dabunt tres plenos modios,
Quindecim modii complebunt doliolum,
Per tot modios quadringenta multiplicata dolia
Implebunt ad tectum usque totam hanc cameram,
Ædes meæ non continebunt, parabitur horreum.

*Pant.*    Polupiſtos!                                    [*Pantomagus enters.*

*Pol.*    What wilt thou? How goeth the business?

*Pant.*    According to promise, but meantime there 's need for more gold.

*Pol.*    For what use?

*Pant.*    A gift muſt needs be sent to Mercury, bespeaking his favor; for 't is in sooth an holy art.

*Pol.*    Take then what money 's needed for the vow.

*Pant.*    Well done; but besides this there 's need for another sixty pound, for the buying of wood-coals.

*Pol.*    What, more troubles?

*Pant.*    It should be no tax to spend an ounce of gold; for any ounce thou doſt expend upon this work, 'pon my faith, 't will give thee back three hundred thousand more.

*Pol.*    Take what thou wilt.

*Pant.*    Sir, all things will be arranged in good order.

[*Exit Pantomagus.*

*Pol.*    I 've now put forth four hundred pieces of gold, but back to the business in hand: any given ounce of gold, saith he, will yield three hundred thousand—an that be true, what will four hundred yield?

[*He computes on a tablet.*

I calculate that according to arithmetic, and lo there are at once three hundred thousand thousand,—ten-thousand millions. So 't is on paper, I 've calculated the matter carefully. I proceed by equal proportion through comparative relations, and behold a thousand minæ will yield three full pecks; fifteen pecks will fill a little barrel; from so many pecks multiplied, four hundred wooden casks; they 'll fill this entire vault to the very brim! This house of mine will not hold so much; a storehouse muſt be made.

## SCENA QUINTA

THEANUS.　　PEDANUS, *cum famulo.*

*Th.*　Unde tu tam sublimis rediisti nobis tam gravis?
　　Et cum famulo? quid? annon dignaris nos aspicere?
　　Unde hic pulcher habitus? mirari satis non queo.

*Ped.*　Annon videtur admiratione dignum?
*Th.*　　　　　　　　　　　　　　　　Maximè equidem.
　　Sed quæ causa?
*Ped.*　　　　　Ipsa felicitas.
*Th.*　　　　　　　　　　Quid ais?
*Ped.*　Ter beatum, divitem, honoratum, me vides.

*Th.*　　　　　　　　　　　　　　　　Adeo brevi?
*Ped.*　Atque admodum.
*Th.*　　　　　　Quæso repete totum ab initio?
*Ped.*　Nosti qualis eram, pauper alumnus, servus tuus.

*Th.*　Benè novi.
*Ped.*　　　　　Hinc profectus rus rectâ fui,
　　Incidi in ædes aurati cujusdam equitis,
　　Pædagogus futurus, et capellanus simul.

*Th.*　Quid inde?
*Ped.*　　　　　Nactus inde honores, opes, titulos,
　　Et, quod magis mirere, binum sacerdotium,
　　Omissis iis quæ mercatus sum.
*Th.*　　　　　　　　　Græcâ fide.
*Ped.*　Fortasse.
*Th.*　　　　Sed unde honor tuus?

## SCENE V

THEANUS.                 PEDANUS, *with a servant.*

*Th.* Whence, as haughty as thou art grave, hast thou re-
turned unto us? And is that thy servant with thee? What?
Dost vouchsafe to recognize us or no? Whence this handsome raiment? by my faith I can't admire 't enough!

*Ped.* Doth it seem worthy of admiration or not?

*Th.* Truly, of the highest worth. But what 's the occasion?

*Ped.* Success itself.

*Th.* What sayest thou?

*Ped.* Thou beholdest me thrice blessed, rich and honored.

*Th.* All that in this so short a while?

*Ped.* And beyond all believing.

*Th.* I beg thee to tell me all, from the very beginning.

*Ped.* Thou knowest well the sort of man I was, poorly bred,
thy servant.

*Th.* I know 't full well.

*Ped.* Setting out from this place I went forthwith to the
country, where I happened upon the house of a certain
knight, set out with gold, sithen which I 've been both
tutor and chaplain.

*Th.* What then?

*Ped.* Having then got honors, wealth, titles, and, what may
astonish thee more, two Benefices—not to mention those
which I have bought.

*Th.* For ready money?

*Ped.* Peradventure.

*Th.* But whence came thy honor?

*Ped.*                                        Sequitur divitias.
Irenarcha sum apud meos, et sacellanus Ducis.

*Th.*    Mira narras.

*Ped.*                      Ita eſt.

*Th.*                                   Sed quorsum nunc venis?

*Ped.*    Ad accumulandos gradus.

*Th.*                                      Quos demum gradus?
Doctorne futurus, an Sacræ Theologiæ Baccalaureus?

*Ped.*    Uterque, si Diis placet, et his proximis comitiis.
Sed jam festino.

*Th.*                      Quò tandem?

*Ped.*                                     Ad ducem propero.

*Th.*    Quam ob causam?

*Ped.*                           Ob bonum reipublicæ,
Timeo ne occidione occidant omnes populi.

*Th.*    Dii melius! unde timendum? an a peſtilentiâ,
Fame, bello, diluviove?

*Ped.*                           Certiora affero.
Nam viden'? noſtin' apud villas in singulis domibus
Magnum esse numerum gallorum septennium?
Hos compertum eſt anno quovis septimo parere,
Enascique ex eorum ovis basiliscos, serpentum genus,
Quorum obtutu solum homines infecti pereunt;
Et si non ſtatim a Duce prospectum fuerit,
Actum erit a Ducatus hujusce incolis.

*Th.*    Quid ergo suades?

*Ped.*                      Ut in singulis oppidis
Quidam deligantur qui gallorum cædem faciant,
Ne quid inde Respublica detrimenti capiat.

*Th.*    Prudenter sanè.

*Ped.*                      Pleraque alia sunt etiam

*Ped.*   'T followeth riches. I 'm a justice of the peace 'mongst
my people, and chaplain to the Duke.

*Th.*   'T is a marvelous tale.

*Ped.*   'T is a true one.

*Th.*   But for what purpose hast thou now come hither?

*Ped.*   For the purpose of accumulating degrees.

*Th.*   Just what degrees, pray? Dost intend to be a Doctor?
or a Bachelor of Sacred Theology?

*Ped.*   Both, God willing, and at the very next Congregation.[62]
But now must I make haste.

*Th.*   Where, pray?

*Ped.*   I speed me to the Duke.

*Th.*   For what reason, pray?

*Ped.*   For the good of the State; I fear lest, through calamity,
all mankind may perish.

*Th.*   God save us! What 's this dreadful business? th' plague?
famine? war? floods?

*Ped.*   I 'll shew thee more particularly. Hast thou not marked,
dost not know 'mongst the farms at every house there 's a
vast number of seven-year dung-hill cocks? It hath been
discovered that these lay eggs in the seventh year all over
the earth, and from these eggs are hatched the basilisks,
a tribe of serpents, at whose mere glance man dieth of in-
fection. And if at once 't is not prevented by the Duke, 't
will be all up with the people of this duchy.

*Th.*   What then dost thou counsel to be done?

*Ped.*   That in every town certain men be chosen who may
destroy the cocks lest the State suffer harm from them.

*Th.*   A wise precaution, indeed.

*Ped.*   There are a great many others also who strive exceed-

Quæ maximè spectant ad Reipublicæ bonum,
De quibus singulis certiorem Ducem faciam.

*Th.*    Benè fit: prævideo te futurum Episcopum.
Sed Pedane, dic sodes, pro veteri amicitiâ
Quî possim et ego tui similis evadere?

*Ped.*    Quî possis? neque manendo in Academiâ,
Neque studendo, licet omnem Encyclopædiam crepes,
Ipsum superes Augustinum, aut Chrysostomum
Morum probitate ad unguem exprimas,
Haud curat patronus si nihil afferas,
*Si nihil attuleris ibis Homere foras.*
Dum vos hic per annos aliquot famelici
Legatis Divum Thomam, et J. Duns Scotum,
Pallentes studiis, nos indulgentes genio
Expiscamur interim opima quæque sacerdotia.

*Th.*    Quid vis ergo faciam?

*Ped.*                            Rus ite singuli,
Sunt ibi patroni, proceres, reliqua omnia.                [*Exit.*

*Th.*    Rus ite singuli. Sequar hoc salutare consilium.
Meditabor de verbis hisce noctes et dies.
Et me accingam mox ad officinam proximam,
Inde parabo vestes, et reliquum viaticum,
Rus iturus illicò. Quid enim? semperne vixero
Solus, delirus, macer, et melancholicus,
Cogitabundus de genere, et specie, et de prima materia,
Cachexiæ, dentium dolori, et catarrhis obnoxius?
Scote vale, Thoma vale, genus et species
Valete, et Musarum mystæ omnes simul!

Valete Academici,
Et combibones optimi,

ing well for the good of the State, concerning each of
whom I shall inform the Duke.

*Th.*    Well said: I predict thou 'lt be a Bishop. But Pedanus,
in behalf of old friendship, tell me, I pray thee, how I,
likewise, may attain to greatness.

*Ped.*    What fitness dost thou possess? neither abiding in the
Academy, nor studying therein, though thou mayest boast
an encyclopedia of the arts, surpass an Augustine, or body
forth to a nicety the character of Chrysostom, if thou hast
not produced somewhat, the patron will not respect thee;
"if he brought nothing, e'en Homer would be shown the
door." [63] Whilst here you starvelings, through some years,
read the Divine Thomas[64] and Duns Scotus, pale from
much study, we, cockering ourselves, fish out betimes the
fat Benefices.

*Th.*    What wouldst thou, then, that I do?

*Ped.*    Get thee to the country alone; there are the patrons,
governors, and all the rest.                  [*Exit Pedanus.*

*Th.*    Get to the country alone. I 'll follow this wholesome
advice. I shall meditate upon these words both night and
day. And I shall equip myself anon at the nearest shop,
wherein I 'll get the garments & whatso is needful for the
journey. I 'll hie me to the country at once. Why forsooth?
Shall I forever live alone, doting, lean, and melancholy?
pondering about genus and species, and the primal substance? subject to cachexy, toothache, and the rheum?
Farewell Scotus, farewell Thomas; genus & species farewell; farewell all ye who minister to the Muses, farewell!

    Farewell, ye Academic louts,
    And toss-pots of dear drinking bouts,

Osunensesque reliqui
     Et nunc et in perpetuum!

Valete coci et lanii,
Sutores crepidarii,
Propolæ, proletarii,
     Et nunc et in perpetuum!

Sancte Petre in occidente,
Sancte Petre in oriente,
Cum Mariâ mediante,
     Et nunc et in perpetuum!

Longum vale Catherina,
Longum vale Thomasina,
Et quot estis in sutrinâ
     Et nunc et in perpetuum!

Valedicturus ego sum,
Et discessurus pannis cum,
Valete multum et usque dum,
     In sæcula sæculorum!

Si quis vestrum venit rus,
Et vos forte sim visurus,
Bibetur plenus cantharus,
     In gratiam amicorum.

*Sic ubi fata vocant, udis abjectus in herbis,*
*Ad vada Mæandri concinit albus olor.*

Valete ad unum omnes, et si sapitis sequimini!

Townsfolk, and all who heard our shouts,
    Both now and evermore!

Farewell ye cooks and butchers fat,
And ye who make our shoes so flat,
The huckster's cart and dizzard's brat,
    Both now and evermore!

To old Saint Peter-in-the-West,
To Peter on the Eastern crest,
With Holy Mary 'twixt the rest,
    Both now and evermore!

Farewell for aye, my buxom Kate,
And Thomasin, thou jade sedate,
And all who ply their needles late,
    Both now and evermore!

I 'm now about to take my leave,
And I 'll decamp with bags this eve;
Farewell, I 'm gone and shall not grieve,
    Until our time doth end!

If any seek my country fair,
And I by chance do see ye there,
We 'll drink a cup that 's full, I swear,
    And thus our friendship mend.

"Thus, where the Fates call, down 'mid the damp
reeds, near the shallows of the Meander, a white swan
singeth." [65]
    Farewell to one and all, an ye be wise ye 'll follow
me! [66]

## SCENA SEXTA

STAPHYLA.      TARENTILLA.      CAMÆNA.

*St.*  O fortunatum et verè diem aureum,
      Quo mihi contigit Osunam accedere!
      Quoties enim vitæ anteactæ recordor meæ,
      Quam vilis olim, pauper, quam lacera fui,
      Inter squalorem et sordes quam miserè ætatem habui,
      Contenta pane mucido et tenui cerevisiâ;
      Et quam ornatè jam, quam jovialiter agam,
      Quam omnigena supellex, lautæ exoticæ dapes,
      Cunctaque fere habeam, et ad animum meum;
      Tam felix derepente tam fortunata videor,
      Ut fortunis meis superaddi nihil queat,
      Ut si quis deus optionem daret mihi,
      Non esset omnino quod optarem amplius.
      O me beatam ter et filiolas meas!
*Cam.*   Felicioresque futuras, si quod tuum est ageres.
*St.*  Quid vultis? vesperi cubatis, mane surgitis
      Quando libet, quousque placet, itis reditis etiam
      Ad libitum quo vultis, victum et vestitum, omnia
      Habetis. Quid deest?


*Cam.*               Ædes angustæ nimis.
*St.*  Parabimus ampliores.
*Tar.*             Sed nec victus placet.
*St.*  Quos vultis cibos?
*Tar.*           Hortulanos carduos,
      Pisces marinos, bene conditas cochleas,
      Vinum generosum, et purissimum pollinem.

## SCENE VI

### STAPHYLA.    TARENTILLA.    CAMENA.

*Sta.*  O most happy and golden day that brought me to
Osuna! How oft I recall my life before that time, how
worthless then, a pauper; how ragged was I; 'mid squalor
and filth, what a wretched life I 've had, content with
mouldy bread and such beer as I could get: and now how
tricked out, how merrily I live, with household stuff of
every sort, dainty foreign dishes—I may have them all to
my heart's desire: such sudden success, so fortunate am I,
that naught can add to the sum of my happiness, so that
e'en though a god should offer me my choice I could not
ask for more. O thrice blessed am I, and my darling
daughters!

[duty by 'em.

*Cam.*  Who would be happier still an thou wouldst do thy

*St.*  For what dost thou wish, I pray? Thou liest down at
eventime, and in the morning whenas it liketh thee well
thou dost arise as thou dost desire; thou 'rt at liberty to
go out and return again at will, whithersoever thou wishest
to go, thou 'rt fed, clothed; all manner of things thou
hast. What, pray, is lacking?

*Cam.*  The house is much too small.

*St.*  We 'll buy a larger one.

*Tar.*  But the food doth not please me.

*St.*  What food dost thou desire, wench?

*Tar.*  Artichokes, seafish, nicely seasoned snails, a noble wine,
and the finest flour.

*Cam.*   Famulumque unum et alterum.

*St.*                                    Quidquid vultis dabitur.

                                              [*Exit Staph.*

*Cam.*   Jam solæ sumus.  Dic mihi bonâ fide, soror,

   Quæ tam diversos experta es tam innumeros procos,

   An amasium malles scholarem academicum,

   An oppidanum, rusticum, an aulicum?

*Tar.*   Tu dic prior.

*Cam.*                          Auscultat opinor hic aliquis.

*Tar.*   Nemo, solæ sumus.

*Cam.*                          Cavendum tamen,

   Sunt enim oculatæ turres, aurita mœnia.

*Tar.*   Scias inæqualem esse furorem hominum,

   Aliter uruntur adolescentes, aliter senes;

   Aliter cives, aulici, pauperes, divites.


*Cam.*   Sed unde discrimen?

*Tar.*                          Pauperes obsequio

   Placere putant, at divites muneribus,

   Conviviis, pompâ, ludis, et spectaculis.

   Civis amare nescit absque zelotypia,

   Oppidanus amando fit omnino stultior,

   Dives profusis rebus fit sapientior,

   Aulicus ob amicam magna quævis aggreditur,

   Nil audet civis.

*Cam.*                   At quem interim probas?

*Tar.*   Aulicum ego.

*Cam.*                      Ego scholarem academicum,

   Et inter scholares unicum Antonium.

*Tar.*   At quam ob causam?

*Cam.*                          Quam quæris? multiplicem.

*Cam.*   And a servant or two.

*Sta.*   Whatsoever ye wish will be granted ye.

[*Exit Staphyla.*

*Cam.*   At laſt we are alone. Tell me in sooth, siſter, which 'mongſt thy many and differing suitors haſt thou approved thus far? doſt prefer a University ſtudent for a lover, or a townsman? a ruſtic swain, or a courtier?

*Tar.*   Speak firſt thyself.

*Cam.*   Methinks someone here liſteneth.

*Tar.*   Nay, we are alone.

*Cam.*   Nathless be on thy guard, for there be towers with eyes and walls with ears.

*Tar.*   Thou shouldſt know that the passions of men are of varied sorts: Young men burn in one way, old men in another; common citizens, courtiers, poor, and the rich are all moved in a different degree.

*Cam.*   But wherein lieth the difference?

*Tar.*   The poor think to please by flattery and compliance; but the rich man by gifts, banquets, display, merriment, public shows. A common citizen knoweth not how to love without display of jealousy; the townsman loveth like a fatuous fool; the rich man's more discreet in his extravagance; the courtier attempteth for his miſtress any mighty enterprise whatsoever; the common citizen ventureth naught.

*Cam.*   But which, meanwhile, doſt thou approve?

*Tar.*   I prefer the courtier.

*Cam.*   The Academick for me; and, 'mongſt all the ſtudents, Antonius alone.

*Tar.*   But for what reason, pray?

*Cam.*   Thou queſtioneſt that? There be many reasons. There

Sunt ingeniosi scholares, ornati, nobiles,
Juvenes plerumque, blandi, benigni, faciles,
Jocis et cantilenis adoriuntur amasiam,
Dant quicquid habent, supra modum et facile amant.

*Tar.*   Quidni et oppidanos?

*Cam.*                          Fœtent de allio,
Hircum et canem olent, vultus habent horridos,
Duri, deformes, agreſtes, nasuti, indigi,
Nec curant puellam nisi cum sint ebrii,
Carent argento, et fere omnes uxorem timent.

*Tar.*   At quem locum præfers?

*Cam.*                          Hunc ego singulis.

*Tar.*   Eundem ego. Vale Roma, valete Venetiæ,
Sena, Pisa, Mediolanum, civitatesque Italæ!
Regiones habitare mallem Acheronticas.
Hic portus meus, hic forum quæſtuarium,
Sint Osunenses meæ delitiæ.

*Cam.*   Mihi præ cunctis placent Academici,
Hæc mea sedes, hic sunt amores mei.

### SCENA SEPTIMA

PANTOMAGUS.     POLUPRAGMATICUS.
LODOVICUS PANTOMETER.     SIMON ACUTUS.
FIDICEN.     PROMUS.

*Pant.*   Proh Dii immortales! quis me fortunatior,
Qui ex obscuro, bardo, et impolito homine,
In hunc honorem evasi, et tam cito?

                                   [*Intrant reliqui.*

are witty scholars, well set out, noble, young moſt part, flattering, bountiful, easy of entreaty, and they approach their fancy with quips and songs; they give of aught they have, and make love beyond all bounds.

*Tar.*   And why not the townsmen?

*Cam.*   They reek of garlic, they ſtink like unto a goat or a dog; their faces are all over briſtles, rough, foul, boorish, big-nosed and barbarous; they pay a girl no heed save when they 're drunk; they lack money, and well-nigh all of 'em are afraid of a wife.

*Tar.*   But where doſt thou prefer to dwell?

*Cam.*   This place alone.

*Tar.*   I the same.  Farewell Rome, farewell Venice, Siena, Milan, and all ye gentle Italians!  I 'd sooner live in Hell! Here 's my haven, here 's the money-mart; may the men of Osuna be my darlings.

*Cam.*   Bar none, the Academicks please me beſt; here 's my habitation, and here are my loves.

### SCENE VII

PANTOMAGUS.     POLUPRAGMATICUS.     SIMON ACUTUS.
LODOVICUS PANTOMETER.     LUTE-PLAYER.
A DRAWER.

*Pant.*   Oh immortal gods!  Who is more blessed than I, who, from an obscure, blockish, and rude fellow have risen to this honored position, and that so quickly?

    [*The reſt enter; except Lodovicus Pantometer.*

*Polupr.*   Cuja vox hæc quæ tam prope nos sonat?

*Sim.*   Pantomage quid agitur?

*Pant.*                              Optimè, optimè.

Omnes opinor Dii mihi benefactum volunt.

Etenim præter spem in virum quendam incidi,

Qui me ditavit abunde, et supra omnem fidem.


*Sim.*   Cur tu tam tristis?

*Polupr.*                    Nostin' Æquivocum meum?

*Sim.*   Tanquam te.

*Polupr.*                    Nosti ergo circulatorem et furem.

*Sim.*   Quì sit?

*Polupr.*          Compilavit mihi scrinium,

Aufugitque, immo ne drachmam fecit reliquam.

*Sim.*   Fallere fallentem non est fraus.

*Pant.*                              Heus bone vir!

Artem imponendi non surripuit tibi.

*Polupr.*   Non, nisi me unà auferat.


*Pant.*                    Quid ergo dolet?

Damnum leve; superest dum fraus, supererit pecunia.

                              [*Intrat.*

*Lod. Pant.*   Amici et socii mei, jamdudum vos sequor.


*Sim.*   Eccum Lodovicum! Unde venis, ut vales?


*Lod. Pant.*   Id ipsum volebam a vobis percontarier.

Rure ego.

*Sim.*          Quoniam jam rursus convenimus,

Et jam soli sumus, memorare quisque occipiat

Quid egerit, aut quì Spartam adornarit suam.

*Polupr.*   Who 's that I hear speaking so near at hand?

*Sim.*   How doth my noble Pantomagus?

*Pant.*   Excellent well, the beſt of everything. Methinks the gods are minded to prosper me. In sooth I 've prospered beyond expeĉtation through a man I 've lately fall'n in with, who hath enriched me abundantly, and that paſt all belief.

*Sim.*   Why, then, art thou caſt down?

*Polupr.*   Did'ſt know mine Equivocus?

*Sim.*   Aye, e'en as well as thee.

*Polupr.*   Then thou 'ſt known a mountebank and a thief.

*Sim.*   What hath he done?

*Polupr.*   He pilled and robbed a cheſt for me, and took to 's heels and fled: aye, marry, and he left me not a penny of 't.

*Sim.*   To deceive a deceiver 's not deception.

*Pant.*   So ho! my good fellow! he hath not ta'en from thee the art of cozenage.

*Polupr.*   Nay, not that, unless he had borne me off at the same time.

*Pant.*   Why, therefore, grieve? 't is a slight loss: whilſt deceit aboundeth, money will abound.

[*Enter Lodovicus Pantometer.*

*Lod. Pant.*   My friends and fellows, for a long while now I 've followed ye.

*Sim.*   Behold, here 's Lodovicus! Whence comeſt thou? How 's thy health?

*Lod. Pant.*   I was about to ask thee this very thing. As for me, I 've come from the country.

*Sim.*   Now good gentles, whereas we 're together once more, and now that we 're alone, each man shall report what he hath accomplished, or how he hath furnished his eſtate.[67]

*Pant.*   En vobis hoc aurum.
*Polupr.*                         Quid illud?
*Pant.*                                         Indicium.
*Sim.*   En vobis has literas.
*Polupr.*                     Quas? cui usui?
*Sim.*   Ad me missas a tribus diversis Academiis.
*Lod. Pant.*   Quam ob causam?
*Sim.*                               Ob professorem publicum.
*Polupr.*   Itane Simon?
*Sim.*                           Sed et vir magnus audio,
    Si quando vel in publicum apparuero,
    Certatim ab omnibus ad me curritur,
    Velut ad visendam noctuam reliquæ aviculæ,
    Dicentes *hic ille Simon Acutus, summus philo-*
        *sophus.*
*Lod. Pant.*   Idem ubicunque de me ferè prædicant.


*Sim.*   Molesti sunt mihi, orant, ambiunt, obsecrant,
    Videre ut liceat, ad se accersi jubent
    Magnates, heroes; ut se et filios suos
    Docere digner, ut præceptis imbuam,
    Alter ut hunc vel illum locum interpreter,
    Respondere ut velim, et in viam dirigere.
    Nimia est miseria doctum esse hominem nimis.


*Pant.*   Hoc ipsum ferè etiam contingit mihi,
    Mane surgo, pulsat statim aliquis fores;
    Quis? tuum consilium? mox succedit alius,
    Patritius, senator, aut femina nobilis.
    Vix suspiro, en anhelantem e rure aliquem.

*Pant.*   Behold! this gold's for ye.

*Polupr.*   Why that?

*Pant.*   A token.

*Sim.*   Behold these letters for ye.

*Polupr.*   Those? For what end?

*Sim.*   Sent to me, sirs, by three different Academicks.

*Lod. Pant.*   For what reason?

*Sim.*   As a public acknowledgment.

*Polupr.*   Really, Simon?

*Sim.*   Aye, and I'm known as a great man, as well. Whensoever I've made a public appearance, they tear away
from all else and run to me, e'en as other birds flock about
an owl, crying "Here's Simon Acutus, the greateſt of
philosophers!"

*Lod. Pant.*   They are saying almoſt identically the same
things of me.

*Sim.*   They vex me greatly; they beseech me, they compass
me round about, intreat me piteously, whether they may
be permitted to see me; they burn to invite me before them,
the grandees, the noblemen: to learn whether I deem them
and their sons worthy of inſtruction, that I may furbish
them out with wise saws; another desireth that I judge
this place or that, or whether I'm willing to decide for
'em, and to direct 'em in the right way. Sure 't is a mighty
plague to be too wise a man![68]

*Pant.*   This same vexation hath also fall'n upon me: I rise
of a morning, and lo, someone knocketh upon the doors:
"Who is it, pray?" "Thine advice, an you please?" In the
wink of an eye here cometh another, a patrician, a senator,
or an high lady. I can scarce take breath when behold

Accersor. Eo. Absolutum me censeo.
Statim alius, receptum fratri aut patri.
Juvo omnes. Hæc fere est vita mea,
Hæc ars, plus lucror quam medici decem.

*Lod. Pant.* Ego per villas incedens, rudemque plebeculam,
Superstitiosum vulgus, et imprimis mulieres,
Abundè victum habeo. Nunc a Geomantiâ,
Nunc a stellis docens, nubilibus viros
Promitto, mares gravidis, prolemque sterilibus,
Ægris salutem, et si quæstum non interciperent
Fratres quidam Chiromantici, supra modum ditescerem.

*Polupr.* Me censet vulgus plus quam Thaletem sapere,
Doctum, divinum, de cœlo delapsum hominem.
Dux honorat, proceresque, et vos scitis probè.
Sed quorsum hæc? quasi nos inter nos non norimus.
Amici cavendum nobis est, idque seriò.

*Sim.* Quid ita?
*Lod. Pant.* Obsidemurne?
*Pant.* Cœlumne ruet?
*Polupr.* Verendum ne quis prudens Academicus
Nos prodat aliquando, et fucum suboleat,
Si quis has artes in apertum proferet,
Miserè periimus, actum de nobis erit.
Maturâ deliberatione opus est, nam quod aiunt
Fortuna nunquam perpetua est bona.
*Lod. Pant.* Quid ergo vis?
*Sim.* Quid suades?

here's another puffing in from the country. I'm summoned. I hie me out. I think my business is finished. At
once there's another appointment, for the brother, or the
father. I help them all. This craft is all my life: I take
more gain than half a score of Doctors.

*Lod. Pant.* I, Sirs, moving about 'mongst the farmhouses,
fare abundantly at the hands of clods, dolts, the common
people, the superstitious herd, and, above all, the women.
Now counselling by means of geomancy, now advising by
the stars: to the marriageable I promise men; to them that
are big with child I predict a male, and to the barren an
issue; to the ailing, health: and if certain necromantic
friars did not encroach upon my profits, I'd grow rich
beyond measure.

*Polupr.* The commoners reckon me to know more than
Thales, a scholar, a seer, a man come down from heaven.
The Duke respecteth me, and so also the governors, as ye
well know. But what's the end of all this? as if, 'mongst
ourselves we did not know it. Friends, we must have a
care, and that in good earnest.

*Sim.* Yea, but why, Sir?

*Lod. Pant.* Are we watched?

*Pant.* Will the sky fall on us?

*Polupr.* 'T is to be feared lest some knowing Academick find
us out on a day and smell out the deceit. If any should lay
bare these doings, we're miserably undone; 't will be the
end of us. A timely consideration is needful, for, as they
say, good luck tarrieth not long.

*Lod. Pant.* What, then, dost thou wish us to do?

*Sim.* Yea, Sir, what is thy counsel?

*Polupr.*                            Eamus hinc ocyus.

    Pervagandum puto ad reliquas Academias.

*Pant.*   Quasi perspicaces æquè non essent alibi.

*Sim.*   Quo tandem?

*Polupr.*             Friburgam Brisgoæ, aut Hafniam Daniæ,

    Pragam Bohemorum, aut Anglorum Oxoniam.

*Lod. Pant.*   Cavesis edico ut appellas Angliam, ni lupum,

    Vulpem, aut ursum, adjungas comitem.

*Polupr.*   Quid ita?

*Lod. Pant.*        Ob frequentes molossos qui sunt ibi.

*Polupr.*   At cur ursum aut lupum vis adjungam comitem?


*Pant.*   Ut te relicto ruant molossi in eorum aliquem.


*Polupr.*   Nugaris. Vultis visitare Academias Italas?


*Sim.*   Non.

*Polupr.*     Quare?

*Sim.*            Sunt ibi doctiores nobis mulieres.

*Polupr.*   Quî sit?

*Sim.*           Ob frequentem fratrum, et theologorum

    concubitum,

    Qui rorem instillant his, et inspirant quendam spiritum.

*Polupr.*   Vultis Salamancam?

*Sim.*                Illic nobis non est opus.

*Lod. Pant.*   Habent plures fortasse nobis non absimiles.

*Polupr.*   Si plures, tunc nobis securis esse licet.

*Lod. Pant.*   Sed minus lucrandum.

*Pant.*               Disceptabimus alias,

    Cessabit quisque nunc ominari malè.

*Polupr.*  Let us get hence quickly. Methinks we muſt needs wander out amongſt the other universities.

*Pant.*  As if they were not equally acute elsewhere!

*Sim.*  Whither, pray, shall we go, when all 's done?

*Polupr.*  To Freiburg in Breisgau, or to Hafnia[69] in Denmark, Prague in Bohemia, or Oxford in England.

*Lod. Pant.*  I charge thee to take care, an thou bringeſt up in England, that thou 'rt accompanied by a wolf, a fox, or a

*Polupr.*  And why, pray?                                    [bear.

*Lod. Pant.*  By reason of the maſtiffs that abound there.

*Polupr.*  But why doſt thou advise me to be accompanied by a bear or a wolf?

*Lod. Pant.*  So that forsaking thee, the dogs may pursue one of them.

*Polupr.*  Pish! thou deal'ſt in trifles. Wouldſt visit the Italian academies?

*Sim.*  Nay.

*Polupr.*  And why, pray?

*Sim.*  The women there are more skilled than we.

*Polupr.*  Why is that?

*Sim.*  By reason of the vaſt numbers of swiving friars & divines, who ſtir the moiſture in 'em, and spur 'em to boldness.

*Polupr.*  Doſt thou propose Salamanca?

*Sim.*  There 's no business there for us.

*Lod. Pant.*  Peradventure they have many like unto us.

*Polupr.*  If there are many, then sure 't is safe for us.

*Lod. Pant.*  But there 's less profit in the business.

*Pant.*  We 'll arbitrate this affair at another time; each of us, under these circumſtances, will loiter about to make evil prophecy.

*Sim.*    Congratulabimur hunc nobis felicem diem,
Et si vultis ad proximam tabernam unà ibimus.
*Pant.*    Quin evocamus cauponem huc? Heus puer!

*[Intrat.*

*Promus.*    Quis vocat?
*Lod. Pant.*                Insterne mensam sine morâ.
Affer huc vinum et cyathos, et qui fidibus canat.
Intendam vires omnes, et me strenuum potando geram,
Laus enim nunc est. Sed congerrones accumbite.

*[Accumbunt.*

Simon, quod faustum felixque sit, poculum præbibo tibi.

*Sim.*    Accipio, sit salus! Heus, tibi totum hunc cyathum.

*Promus.*    Fidicen adest.

*[Intrat Fidicen.*

*Sim.*                Intende nervos, bone vir!
Et exhilara nos facetâ cantiunculâ, si quid potes.
*Polupr.*    Vereor ne lusus hic in luctum desinat.
*Sim.*                                    Tace.
*Fidicen.*        Phœbus dum pererrat orbem,        *[Canit.*
                Lustrans quæque, præter spem
                Martem videt et Venerem,
                Sine thalamo cubantem,
                At nec Phœbus visum celat,
                Sed Vulcano rem revelat.

*Omnes. (Canunt.)* Ex Diis quidam tum facetè,
                O utinam vidisset me,
                Cubantem sic cum Venere.

*Sim.*   Nay, we 'll rejoice, and count this a lucky day for us;
   an 't is your good pleasure, we hie us to the nearest tavern.
*Pant.*   Why not call hither the inn-keeper?  Ho, boy!

*[A Drawer enters.*

*Draw.*   Good gentlemen, who calleth me?
*Lod. Pant.*   Sirrah, cover the table without delay.  Fetch
   hither wine & cups[70] and the fellow who plays the lute.

   I shall lay abroad full strength, and support myself
stoutly for the drinking, for 't is now deemed a laudable
deed.  But sit ye down, my merry fellows.
(*They sit*)

   Simon, forasmuch as thou 'rt a lucky and prosperous
fellow, I 'll drink this cup to thee.
*Sim.*   I pledge thee, thy health!  Ho, there, this cup to all
   o' ye!
*Draw.*   Good gentlemen, the lute-player 's here at hand.

*[Enter a Lutist.*

*Sim.*   Stretch the strings, my good man! make us merry with
   a witty song, an thou 'rt able.
*Polupr.*   I fear lest this sport 'll end in sorrow.
*Sim.*   Hold thy peace!        *[The Lutist plays and sings.*
*Lutist.*        As Phœbus swept along his way
            Replacing friendly night with day,
            He spied where Mars and Venus lay;
            They clip't upon a couch defiled,
            So Phœbus peeped and, lo! he smiled,
            Then sped for Vulcan to betray.


*All* (*Sing*)    One of the gods then merrily cried:
            Would that he had seen but me,
            Bedded thus at Venus' side!

*Fidicen.*        Vulcanus fecit illicò,
                Rete quoddam de metallo,
                Invicem se complexantes,
                Et nil tale cogitantes,
                Quod ligavit tanto nodo,
                Ut non solvant ullo modo.

*Omnes.*         Ex Diis quidam tum facetè,
                O utinam ligasset me,
                Cubantem sic cum Venere.

*Fidicen.*       Postquam sic ligasset eos,
                Vocat simul omnes Deos,
                Et ostendit concumbentes,
                Sese mutuò foventes,
                Hærent casse obvoluti,
                Sunt in risum Dii soluti.

*Omnes.*         Ex Diis quidam tum facetè,
                O utinam risissent me,
                Cubantem sic cum Venere.

*Pant.*   O utinam risissent me, cubantem sic cum Venere.

*Sim.*   Profecto benè: tu jam ludes, nos canemus invicem,
Incipiam si lubet, vos autem sequimini.
                                        [*Canit.*

                Exultemus et ovemus,
                Pergræcemur et potemus
                Simul et amicè.

*Lutiſt.*      So Vulcan at his smithy sweat
           To forge him faſt a metal net,
           And bind the lovers, sans regret.
           The heedless pair now helpless lie,
           Within a knot they can't untie,
           Their clasped limbs are sore beset.

*All.*         One of the gods then merrily cried:
           Would that he had bound but me,
           Bedded thus at Venus' side!

*Lutiſt.*      When he had snared them thus complete,
           He called the gods to view the feat,
           And shewed the pair with love replete:
           In vain they ſtrove to hide their shame,
           But, sans a sheet, all saw the game,
           The laughing gods enjoy'd the treat.

*All.*         One of the gods then merrily cried:
           Would that they had laughed at me,
           Bedded thus at Venus' side!

*Pant.*  O that they had laughed at me, bedded so at Venus'
side!

*Sim.*  Bravo! an thou 'lt play now, we 'll sing by turn: I 'll
begin, if ye will, and ye all may follow.
   (*Sings*)
          Let us revel and rejoice,
          Let us drink and sing,
             Let 's resound with lifted voice,
             Together let it ring.

*Pant.*

Sed quis vinum ministrabit,
Sed quis potum præsto dabit,
 Multum sitienti?

*Lod. Pant.*

Vos evocate puerum,
Cognoscentem bonum vinum,
 Idque primo visu.

*Pant.*

Euge, puer optime,
Græcè bibens et Latinè
 Tuum fac officium.

*Omnes.*

Hæc est illa bona dies,
Unde nobis tanta quies
 Facta fuit hodiè.

Nullus metus, nec labores,
Nulla cura, nec dolores,
 Sint in hoc symposio.

*Sim.*

Omnes fortes sunt vinosi,
Et potantes animosi,
 Dicit Aristoteles.

*Pant.*      But who will serve the wine, my lad,
           And who will pour the ale,
                Yea, who will make our gullets glad,
                Quench thirsts that never fail?

*Lod. Pant.* Call the lad who tends the tap,
           And knoweth wine the best,
                He 'll fetch the drink without mishap,
                And quickly serve the guest.

*Pant.*      Well done!  Thou art a noble youth,
           Drinking in Greek and Latin,
                Perform thy duty swift forsooth,
                And thou shalt surely fatten.

*All.*       'T is a day the gods ha' blest,
           Whereon we play and sport, Sirs;
           It is a day of peace and rest,
           For Sack and honest Port, Sirs.

           Toil is done, there is no fear,
           Down then with care and sorrow,
           Now at our feast there 's not a tear,
           We take no thought of morrow.

*Sim.*      All topers are of courage full
           Brave toss-pots, men of bottle,
                Stout knights are they who stoppers pull,
                Saith wise old Aristotle.

*Polupr.*            Ubi nemo veſtrûm sapit,
                     Sed vos omnes vinum capit,
                        Quid sequetur illíco?

*Omnes.*            Bibe, bibe, bibe, bibe,
                     Tu qui sapis bibe, bibe,
                        Dum Lyæus imperat.

*Promus.*          Sed vos rogo, dum potatis,
                     Ter quaterque videatis,
                       Ne frangatis cyathum.

*Pant.*              Dulce dulci misceatis,
                     Ex hoc in hoc effundatis,
                       Ut potemus melius.

*Polupr.*           Sed jam potrix turba tace,
                     Ne pro veſtrâ tantâ pace
                       Bellum fiat arduum.

*Omnes.*            Ergo tandem desinamus,
                     Et potantes abeamus,
                       Canentes hilare.

*Polupr.*     Where there's no man who's kept his wit,
              But all pour wine so free, Sirs,
                  What follows fast before they quit,
                  In what plight will they be, Sirs?

*All.*        Drink, O drink, ye merry knaves,
              The wise do drink esteem;
              The sober louts are canting slaves;
              Drink! Bacchus is supreme.

*Draw.*       But I beg ye, whilst ye drink
              So oft for thirst to slake, Sirs,
                  And whilst the brimming glasses clink,
                  My cups ye will not break, Sirs.

*Pant.*       Mix ye sweet wine for bellies sweet,
              From this pour into this, Sirs,
                  For guzzle-guts it is no cheat,
                  But makes way for greater bliss, Sirs.

*Polupr.*     Thou drunken wench bide now thy peace,
              Lest by thy leave we'll hold thee still,
                  And if our 'bibing do not cease,
                  The bout will do thee ill.

*All.*        Now at length we call a halt,
              And drunken stagger out, Sirs;
              The feast was sure without a fault,
              So we will sing and shout, Sirs.

## SCENA PRIMA

SORDIDUS.     CORNUTUS.     RUBICUNDUS.

*Cornutus.*

ME infelicem et miserum! quid agam? quid
    querar?
Apud quos? ubi?
*Sord.*                 Hem, Cornute, quid
    agis?
Quid id eſt quod te tam sollicitum tenet?
Salva domus, uxor salva, salvi liberi,
Dives es, sanus es, liber es—et quid dolet?

*Corn.*   Dolet, et si non vidissem his ipsis oculis.

*Sord.*   Quid vidiſti, larvam, lemures, an Gorgoneum caput?

*Corn.*   Non, sed cornigerum caput.
*Sord.*                Doletne caput?
*Corn.*   Dolet caput.
*Sord.*           Apagesis cum tuo capite,
An tu primus, an tu solus in hoc oppido?
Quod convenit omni ferè et semper, quid te dolet?
Annon heroes, duces, ipsi reges cornigeri?

*Corn.*   Emat, vendat, rem familiarem coquat,
Propinet, pytisset, usque in diem cubet.
Probare possem, et probo, at hoc tamen.

184

# ACT V

## SCENE I

SORDIDUS.    CORNUTUS.    RUBICUNDUS.

*Cornutus.*

WRETCHED & unhappy man that I am! What shall I do? For what shall I make complaint? Before whom? Where?

*Sord.* How now, Cornutus, what's this thou sayest? What is 't that keepeth thee in such disquiet? Thy home's safe, all's well with thy wife & children, thou 'rt rich, sound of health, and a freeman—so what aileth thee?

*Corn.* It tormenteth me; would that I had not seen it with these mine eyes!

*Sord.* What hast thou seen? A ghost? An hobgoblin, or a Gorgon's head?

*Corn.* Nay, but an head with horns.

*Sord.* Doth the head afflict thee?

*Corn.* Aye, the head tortureth me.

*Sord.* Fie! begone with thy head! Art thou the first man, the only man to be caught up with horns in this town? For 't is a thing that o'ertaketh well-nigh all mankind; why then art thou cast down by 't? Are not heroes, Dukes, & e'en Kings themselves cuckold?

*Corn.* That head buyeth, selleth, meddleth with the household affairs; it drinketh, spitteth, lyeth a-bed all day long. I can test it, and I do—nathless, there 't is.

185

*Sord.*  Hoc nihil.

*Corn.*            At ipse vidi, et in ædibus meis.

*Sord.*  Certus es id tibi contigisse in individuo,

    Quod convenit omnibus oppidanis in genere.


*Corn.*  At a scholari factum.

*Sord.*                Non refert a quo fiat modò.


*Corn.*  Ero ludibrium.

*Sord.*          Quibus ludibrium?

*Corn.*              Civibus.

*Sord.*  Clodius accuset mœchos—sed, Cornute, sanum con-
    silium

    Amplectere amici, et quod vides, non vides,

    Et quod scis, nescis, tu pol si sapis, atque ita

    Pacatus vives, et fortasse quæstum uberem facies.

    Ego sic soleo. Sed non omnibus dormio.      [*Intrat.*

*Rubic.*  Amici, populares, concives, homines,

    Ferte opem innocenti.

*Sord.*          Quis hic, Rubicundus furens?

*Corn.*  Is ipsus.

*Rubic.*       O caput, O costas, O cranium!

*Sord.*  Quid vis? quid agis?

*Rubic.*            Me miserum! scholares duo

    Omnes dentes labefecerunt mihi,

    Colaphisque tuber fecerunt totum caput.

*Corn.*  Itane? ubi?

*Rubic.*       Meis ipsius ædibus.

*Sord.*  Quâ de causâ?

*Rubic.*        Quod totum propinanti cyathum

    Ego tantum ebiberam dimidium.

*Sord.*  'T is naught.

*Corn.*  Yea but I 've seen it myself, & that in mine own house.

*Sord.*  Aye, certes this thing hath fall'n upon thee in especial, since it hath already fall'n upon the commonality of townsmen!

*Corn.*  But to be made thus by a mere student!

*Sord.*  It mattereth not by whom 't was done, since now 't is done.

*Corn.*  I 'll be mocked.

*Sord.*  By whom?

*Corn.*  By the citizens.

*Sord.*  "The devil rebuketh naughtiness!" [71] But Cornutus, take the sound advice of a friend; if thou 'rt wise, see not what thou seest; what thou knowest, know it not: thus thou 'lt live at peace, and, peradventure, thou mayest once again wax fat. Thus 't is with me. But I 'm not asleep for everyone.     [*Enter Rubicundus.*

*Rubic.*  Friends, countrymen, fellow-citizens, gentlemen, help ye an upright man!

*Sord.*  What 's this, is Rubicundus raging mad?

*Corn.*  'T is he himself.

*Rubic.*  O my head! O my ribs! O the skull of me!

*Sord.*  What dost thou want? For what dost thou plead?

*Rubic.*  Alack, miserable wretch that I am! Two o' th' scholars ha' loosened every tooth I 've got, & bang'd my head till it 's all one big bump.

*Corn.*  Is that indeed true? Where was this?

*Rubic.*  In mine own house.

*Sord.*  What was the occasion for this?

*Rubic.*  Because in reply to one drinking a whole cup to my health, I emptied scarce a half.

*Corn.*   Grave facinus.

*Sord.*            Quo telo?

*Rubic.*                   Pugnis suis,
   Et crebris poculis ita sævierunt in caput.

*Corn.*   Ita videtur.

*Sord.*            Sed ubi læsus interim?

*Rubic.*   Non sum omnino læsus, sed quod sursum pedes
   Volent aliquando, et deorsum caput,
   Ligârunt omnes sensus magicis carminibus.

*Corn.*   Magnis credo poculis.

*Sord.*                Tu verberatus quidem,
   Sed audi, tu te domum quam primum conferes,
   Ibique te pronum in lectum conjicies,
   Præ te ferens verberatum, læsum graviter.

*Corn.*   Quem ob finem non video.

*Sord.*               Obsecro taceas.
   Uxor primo mane querelam deferat ad ducem,
   Læsum civem, et conjugem semimortuum.
   Nos interim per omne dissipabimus oppidum,
   Civem verberatum, et in ipso foro.
   Tu sis lecto æger, amici te visitent.

*Corn.*   Quid tum sequetur?

*Sord.*             Audi totam fabulam.
   Scholares hoc audito solvent quidvis, ne quid gravius
   Contingat, rem componentes cum uxore tuâ.
   Aut si non, coram ipso Duce causam agent.

*Corn.*   Placet hoc consilium.

*Rubic.*           Et fiet illicò.

*Sord.*   Tu te verberatum fortasse lætabere.

*Corn.*   A serious offense, that.

*Sord.*   With what weapons did they this?

*Rubic.*   With wine-cups & their fists they did repeatedly vent their rage upon mine head.

*Corn.*   So it appeareth.

*Sord.*   But where 's the wound?

*Rubic.*   I 'm not altogether hurt, but forasmuch as they bewitched all my senses with magick songs, sometimes my feet went one way, whilst my head went another.

*Corn.*   Methinks 't was by vast cups 't was done.

*Sord.*   Thou'st indeed been severely beaten, but harkee, betake thyself home as soon as thou 'rt able, and, once there, throw thyself upon thy bed, shewing thy lashes and acting as one severely wounded.

*Corn.*   I perceive not the intent of this business.

*Sord.*   Be silent, I beseech thee. At break of day let thy wife make complaint unto the Duke: a citizen 's been wounded, her husband 's half kill'd, &c. In the meantime, we 'll spread abroad the news, over all the town, that a citizen hath been set upon, ay, marry, in th' Forum itself. Thou 'lt be sick-a-bed, with friends visiting thee.

*Corn.*   What, prithee, will follow next?

*Sord.*   Mark well the whole story. After this tale's been heard, the Scholars will pay thee whatsoever thou askest, lest somewhat of graver import may hap, settling the matter with thy wife. Or, happen not, they 'll plead the case before the Duke himself.

*Corn.*   This plan pleaseth me mightily.

*Rubic.*   And 't will be executed without delay.

*Sord.*   Mayhap thou 'lt rejoice that thou wert so soundly beaten!

## SCENA SECUNDA

ANTONIUS. ÆQUIVOCUS.

*Ant.* Quam nunquam secundus amor est, vel ad exitum
  Lætum perveniat, quin hunc excipiat dolor illicò,
  Malo meo demens hoc ipsum intelligo.
  Compressi virginem, et ducturum me fidem dedi,
  Quæ res me sic excruciat ut nihil magis.
  Tanquam navis jactor pelago, et ad crucem
  Statim adigor infelix vel ad insaniam.
  Ut nubam cogit lex, pietas, æquitas, amor,
  Fides, religio, at stat e contra pater,
  Durus pater qui me præcipitem dabit.
  O vos beati qui procul ab his vinculis
  Neptunum a terrâ videtis furentem procul.
  O fallaces mulieres quæ non secus ac canes feræ
  Prosequuntur, apprehensum mordicus tenent.
  O perfidum Æquivocum, pessimum omnium mortalium
  Qui mihi malum hoc machinatus es, hanc perniciem.
  Sed lupus in fabulâ, subducam me attendens quid ait.
                [*Intrat.*

*Æq.* Sudore diffluo, ita me pondus auri premit.
  Herum compilavi, et Pantomagum medicum
  Furtivas claves ementiendo circumveni graviter.
  Sed et Antonium fraudavi hâc sicâ et chlamyde,
  Et jam nunc equum, et bajulum servum peto,
  Qui me levent hoc onere, sed et artificem
  Statuarium, statuam enim mihi fieri volo.

*Ant.* En tibi servum et bajulum, qui te levabit hoc onere,
  Artificemque qui parabit tibi pro statuâ crucem,
  Perfidissime!

## SCENE II

ANTONIUS.          EQUIVOCUS.

*Ant.* Love 's never favorable; e'en though it cometh to an
happy consummation, grief followeth hard on its heels.
This evil, I know well, is through mine own folly. I 've
deflower'd a maid, and pledg'd my word that I would
marry her—a thing that rends me beyond endurance. E'en
as a ship, toss'd by the sea am I, & headed straightway to
destruction, driven to misery or to madness. The law,
piety, justice, love, good faith, & religion constrain me to
marriage, but my father 's set against it; a hard father,
who 'll cast me out. Blessed are ye who are far removed
from these fetters! Ye see Neptune raging far beyond the
land. O beguiling women who pursue their prey so close,
like unto wild dogs seizing fast with their teeth! O treach-
erous Equivocus, vilest of mortals, who wrought for me
this evil, this dread calamity! . . . . But, like the wolf in
the fable,[72] I 'll steal away, paying good heed to what he
saith.

*[Enter Equivocus.*

*Eq.* I 'm all a-sweat, the burden of this gold weigheth upon
me so. I 've pill'd and poll'd my master and Doctor Pantomagus; by counterfeiting the keys I 'd slipped away, I 've
grievously deceived 'em. But I 've also filch'd from
Antonius this short sword and cloak! now for an horse &
a carrier-servant to ease me of this load—but I seek also a
sculptor; I desire a statue to be made for me.[73]

*Ant.* Behold thy servant & porter who 'll relieve thee of thy
load, a craftsman who 'll raise no statue to thee, but a
gibbet, traitorous knave!

*Æq.*          Antoni suavissime, per Jovem,
   Joco feci.
*Ant.*          At seriò pœnam dabis.


### SCENA TERTIA

POLUPISTOS.          STEPHANIO.

*Pol.*   Qui ubi sunt, fuerunt, aut futuri sunt asini,
   Stulti, stolidi, buccones, blenni, fatui,
   Ego longè anteo omnibus stultitiâ.
   Pudet. Perii. Me hoccine ætatis hominem
   Ludum bis factum esse, quo magis id repeto,
   Magis uror: excoriavit me totum medicus,
   Decoxit rem totam familiarem mihi,
   Auro usque attondit doctis indoctum dolis;
   Hoc est quod dolet, quod peracescit modò
   Me hoc ætatis ita ludificari hominem,
   Vix sum compos animi, ita ardeo iracundiâ.
   Sed quid sto? quidni queror? scelestum quidni persequor?
                              [*Exeunti convenit.*

*Steph.*   Polupiste, quo tam citus?
*Pol.*                    Stephanio, ut vales?
   Osunam ego.
*Steph.*          Quid succenses, quid frontem caperas?
*Pol.*   Quo tu demum? aut quid te tam sollicitum tenet?


*Steph.*   A filio nuper allatæ sunt mihi literæ,
   In quibus scribit se civis vitiasse filiam,
   Et ut ducat in uxorem jam cogi a legibus;
   Hoc me torquet; illuc tendo ut subveniam

*Eq.*   Moſt beloved Antonius, by Jove, I did but jeſt.

*Ant.*   But in earneſt thou 'lt be soundly punished.

SCENE III

Polupistos.          Stephanio.

*Pol.*   Of all them that are or have been or will be asses, fools, dolts, dizzards, cullys, dunces, and idiots, I exceed 'em all in folly. I 'm all over shame. I 'm undone. For a man of my years to 've twice been made a laughing-ſtock oppresseth more heavily the more I call it to mind. The Doctor hath completely ſtript me; he hath consumed my whole eſtate: the ignorant knave hath fairly eaten my gold with subtile guile. This it is that grieveth me, what hath sour'd me so; at my ripe age to be made the butt of jeſts, so that I 'm nigh out o' my wits, I burn so hot with rage.[74] But why do I tarry here? Why not make complaint? Why not prosecute the knaves?

[Going out he encounters Stephanio.

*Steph.*   Polupiſtos, whither away so suddenly?

*Pol.*   How art thou, Stephanio? I 'm off to Osuna.

*Steph.*   Why art thou raging? why the knitted brow?

*Pol.*   Where, in sooth, goeſt thou? and why art thou so troubled?

*Steph.*   Letters have of late been fetched me from my son, wherein he saith that he hath deflowered the daughter of a citizen, so that now by law he 's forc'd to wive her: 't is this that wringeth my heart: I haſte me thither that I

Si fieri possit, et pharmacum adhibeam.

Sed nihil etiamnum audis de tuâ filiâ?

*Pol.*   Nihil præter incertos rumores quod Osunæ siet,

Proficiscor illuc jam.

*Steph.*                           An ob hoc negotium?

*Pol.*   O Stephanio, sed inter eundum rem totam dicam tibi.

### SCENA QUARTA

#### POLUMATHES.    PHILOBIBLOS.

*Phil.*   Polumathes quid? invenisti sapientem adhuc?

*Polum.*   Quærendus alibi sapiens.

*Phil.*                           Itane?

*Polum.*                                     Ita.

*Phil.*   At invenisti, opinor, doctos innumeros.

*Polum.*   Divites plures, paucos doctus, sapientem neminem.

*Phil.*   Non intendis fortasse.

*Polum.*                       Conveni, consului,

Summos, infimos, cujuscunque ferè ordinis.

*Phil.*   Quos demum probas? de vulgo quid existimas?

*Polum.*   Sunt benè vestiti, et quoad barbam conspicui,

Incessum, vocem, vultum, humani plerumque et graves,

Stipati famulis nonnunquam, et pulchro satellitio,

Præ se ferentes gradus, titulos, insignia:

Jurares ad unum omnes sapientes, doctissimos.

may lend my aid, an I am able, and apply some remedy.
But art thou still without news of thy daughter?

*Pol.*   Aye, save doubtful rumors that she dwelleth in Osuna.
I go there now.

*Steph.*   Goest thou on account of this trouble?

*Pol.*   O Stephanio! but as we journey I 'll tell thee the whole
affair.


### SCENE IV

POLUMATHES.          PHILOBIBLOS.

*Phil.*   What ho, Polumathes? Hast thou found a wise man
yet?

*Polum.*   The wise must be sought elsewhere.

*Phil.*   In sooth?

*Polum.*   In sooth.

*Phil.*   But thou hast met, methinks, learned men without
number.

*Polum.*   Many rich, a few learned, but not one wise man.

*Phil.*   Perchance thou hast not sought diligently.

*Polum.*   I 've met with & consulted 'em all, from the lowest
to the highest, men of every rank and station.

*Phil.*   Whom, then, dost thou approve? Concerning the common run, what thinkest thou?

*Polum.*   They 're neatly gowned and are notable as to beards,
stately carriage, manner of speech, impressive countenance,
and, most part, ponderous; sometimes compassed about
with servants, a handsome guard, showing off their station,
titles, & insignia: thou 'd take oath that, to a man, all of
'em were wise and very learned.

*Phil.*    Quales vero sunt?

*Polum.*             Nostin' templum Ægyptiacum?

*Phil.*    Capio quid vis, tu vero dic apertè et liberè.

*Polum.*    Sunt ob majorem partem Cumani asini,
     Infantes, aridi, jejuni, steriles, straminei,
     Plumbei, caudices, bardi, fungi, stipites,
     Inertes, idiotæ, somno gulæque dediti,
     Illiterati, arrogantes, larvati, philologi,
     Armati solum barbis et impudentiâ.

*Phil.*    Tu mirus præco mirum encomiasten agis,
     Incensus fortasse in omnes hanc iram evomis.

*Polum.*    Et quidni incensus? quis æquo animo ferat?

*Phil.*    Peregrinus quum sis tu conticescas tamen.

*Polum.*    Egone feram tot impostores proletarios,
     Semipaganos, philosophastros, nugivendulos?
     Faxo sciant, et si possum pœnas ferent.

*Phil.*    At quid in omnes inveheres?

*Polum.*                 Malè capis.
     Habet Osuna viros undiquaque doctissimos,
     Suspiciendos omni scientiarum genere,
     Quos ego veneror, admiror, amplector, exosculor,
     At hic plures tamen pistrino digni asini,
     Ex harâ producti, de Gothicis hisce loquor.

*Phil.*    Rectè sentis; sed tu nimis acerbus interim;
     Non habent omnes fortasse disciplinas Encyclias,
     Sed in singulis præcellunt, quisque non est Hippias.

*Phil.*   Nay, but what are they truly?

*Polum.*   Doſt thou know Egyptian temples? [75]

*Phil.*   Aye, marry, I know well what thou meaneſt; in sooth speak plainly and freely.

*Polum.*   They 're, most part, Cuman asses, infants, outsides, phantaſtick shadows, barren mannikins, ſtraw men, clods, dolts, sots, dullards, giddy-heads, lazy-bones, idiots, slaves of bed and belly, ignorant dizzards, puff'd-up clowns, mummers, babblers, whose whole equipment consiſteth of venerable beards and shameless impudence.

*Phil.*   Thou 'rt a ſtrange cryer, spreading ſtrange encomiums; inflamed, peradventure, by all this, thou doſt pour out thy wrath.

*Polum.*   And why not inflamed, prithee? who beareth affliction with an even temper?

*Phil.*   Nathless since thou 'rt a ſtranger thou 'lt keep ſtill.

*Polum.*   Nay, shall I endure all these cozening proletaires, country-clowns, philosophaſters, dealers in toys & trifles? I 'll show 'em what they are, and if I 'm able they 'll be soundly punished.

*Phil.*   But why shouldſt thou inveigh againſt them all?

*Polum.*   Thou takeſt me amiss. On every side Osuna hath her moſt learned men, held in high eſteem by all for their learning, men whom I revere, eſteem, love heartily, and full oft salute; but there are more of 'em that are better fitted to be asses in a workhouse, litter from a pig-ſty: 't is about these Goths that I have spoken.

*Phil.*   Thy reasoning 's sound; but betimes exceeding sharp: they have not, mayhap, all the learning in the world, but have exceeded in some single thing; every man is not a Hippias.

*Polum.*   Nec ego quæro tam multiplicem scientiam,
Si vel in unâ mediocres, satis superque foret.

*Phil.*   At sunt sophiſtæ.
*Polum.*                     Si quis altum vociferet in scholis
Libros vulgares, et deliramenta quædam glossematica
Legat et effutiat, summum habent philosophum,
Si togatus ambulet, insignem peripateticum.

*Phil.*   Insignes fortasse grammatici?
*Polum.*                     Fortasse quidem.
Si quis emergat poetaſter, vel criticus
Qui notas fecerit aut animadversiones aliquot,
*Deleatur d, alii legunt sic, codex meus sic habet,*
Phœbus audit, literarum decus, sidus, oraculum.
*Phil.*   Profeſto rem tenes, et hoc malo meo didici,
In grammatiſtam quendam incidi, qui me conviciis
Oneravit, quod inter loquendum *marcesco* excideret.
Satis habui incolumi pallio me inde proripere,
Et hunc opinor Rhetoricâ præsertim præcellere.

*Polum.*   Præcellunt sanè, si quis hic inde flosculos
Consarcinare possit, aut quasdam sententiolas
Ad ornandam orationem, orator audit optimus.
Artes plerumque negligunt, hoc solum votis habent
Opimum sacerdotium, hoc habito habentur omnia.
*Phil.*   Ergò dant operam Theologiæ, idque unicum
Elaborant, consilio non malo; sed quales erant?

*Polum.*   Vidi Theologos per annos triginta Academicos.
*Phil.*   Tanto doſtiores.

*Polum.*   Nor do I seek for such encyclopedian knowledge; if
e'en in one measurable matter they knew aught, 't would
more than suffice.

*Phil.*   But they are Sophists.

*Polum.*   If some great notable sets out to his disciples the common sort of books, and some doting critic readeth and
gusheth forth a fount of words, lo they have the most lofty
philosophy; if he struts abroad in toga clad, 't is the mark
of a Peripatetic.

*Phil.*   Peradventure 't is the mark of a grammarian?

*Polum.*   Peradventure, indeed! If any poetaster or critic
cometh forward, who hath made footnotes, or a few com-
ments such as, *"Omit so and so," "Some read it thus,"*
*"My Ms. hath it so,"* [76] he is called a very Phœbus, the
glory, the constellation, the very oracle of letters.

*Phil.*   Thou dost indeed understand the matter; I learnt it
to my cost. I 've fall'n in with a grammarian of late who
hath o'erwhelmed me with abuse for that, in the midst of
our converse, the word *marcesco* slipped out. I considered
myself fortunate to get off with my cloak; and yet methinks that in Rhetoric this man surpasseth all.

*Polum.*   Aye, surely they surpass all; if from every hand they
're able to patch together flowery words or wise saws for
tricking out a speech, they 're hailed as the best of orators.
Most arts they contemn; a rich Benefice 's the one thing
to which they pay their devotions:[77] this gain'd, all 's well.

*Phil.*   To this end they apply themselves to theology & for it
alone do they take pains, with no bad judgment: but what
manner of men are they?

*Polum.*   I 've known academick theologians for thirty years.

*Phil.*   Such learned men!

*Polum.*                Tanto crassiores asinos,
  Gulæ devotos, somno ventrique deditos,
  Qui suggeſtum æquè ac piſtrinum fugiunt.
  Sed his parco.

*Phil.*            Quales vidiſti medicos?

*Polum.*   Pudet dicere, mittoque medicinæ carcinomata
  Quibus hoc tempore nihil putidius,
  Passim quod medicorum eſt nunc anus bajula,
  Olidus balneator, vel tonsor audaculus,
  Verbosus Paracelsita, aut ignavus Empiricus,
  Lucellum captans impoſturis agit.

*Phil.*   Soli reſtant Jurisperiti.

*Polum.*                Mitto illorum ulcera,
  Si videres iſtorum in dicendo arrogantiam,
  Jurares præter liter nihil esse reliquum
  Præter os et frontem, licitumque[78] latrocinium.

*Phil.*   Stupenda narras.

*Polum.*                Vera, ita me Deus amet.
  Hi sunt quos inseƈtor, quos odio semper habui,
  Et sanciendam legem curarem aliquam
  Quæ tam enormem frænaret licentiam,
  Et quicunque sunt cordati philosophi
  Favebunt, sat scio, huic inſtituto meo.

*Phil.*   Quod ego laudo, et reformarem libentius
  Si mei juris esset. At quid agendum mones?


*Polum.*   Quærendum eſt ad eos, et quorum intereſt
  Academiarum præfeƈtos, et in hoc summo duci,
  Qui mox ad tribunal hoc aderit.


*Phil.*                Do me comitem, si lubet.

*Polum.* Such stupid asses! vow'd to gluttony, slaves to bed
and belly, who avoid alike both desk & drudgery. But I 'll
say no more.

*Phil.* What manner of Physicians hast thou known?

*Polum.* I 'm ashamed to say, & I forbear to mention the noxious plague of physick, than which, in our time, naught is
more loathsome, scatter'd all abroad by these Physicians—
now by some nasty old woman, now by a stinking bath-
keeper, now a brazen barber, a wordy Paracelsian, or a
lazy empirick, seeking petty profits through base imposture.

*Phil.* The Doctors of Law are all that 's left.

*Polum.* I pass over their corruptions: if thou didst but hear
their vaunting speeches, thou 'dst swear that nothing 's left
save only lawsuits, impudence, audacity, & legal robbery.

*Phil.* 'T is a stupend tale thou tellest.

*Polum.* As God loveth, 't is true. These whom I inveigh
against, I 've ever hated: would that I might cause some
law to be enacted that would curb such exceeding wickedness, and all sensible Philosophers will, I 'm sure, support
this plan of mine.

*Phil.* The which I applaud, & would the more willingly
amend, had I the power. But what dost thou advise to be
done?

*Polum.* It must be inquired into in the behalf of those I 've
named, & those Prefects of the University, and, more than
all, in behalf of the Duke, who, anon, will hie him to this
Tribunal.

*Phil.* If thou 'lt have me, Sir, I 'll appoint me thy disciple.

SCENA QUINTA ET ULTIMA

INTERLOQUUTORES FERÈ OMNES.

*[Intrat Dux cum supplicibus in manu libellis,*
*et multis querelas deferentibus, &c.*

*Dux.*   O quam deceptus fui! quis unquam crederet
   Sub hâc togâ tantam latere nequitiam!
*Eu.*   Fronti nulla fides.
*Crat.*                  Neque credendum alicui.
*Dux.*   Sed qualis fuit qui te tantis affecit injuriis?

*Steph.*   Quod ad professionem, Jesuitam præ se tulit,
   Ex voce, gestu, habitu, vir doctus et probus,
   Sed O in hostem me potius contingat incidere
   Quam talem! præter bibendi et artem mentiendi benè
   Natum meum docuit omnino nihil.
   Deceptus ab eo cujus fidei commiseram
   Inter lenam et meretrices absorpsit pecuniam.

*Dux.*   Inter lenam et meretrices? quas, quales, ubi?

*Steph.*   Habitant non procul hinc in suburbanis hortulis.
*Dux.*   Lictor accerse. Nosti hominem si videris iterum?

*Steph.*   Plus satis, damno meo.
*Dux.*                  Esto animo bono,
   Pœnas dabit tanto dignas facinore.
*Eu.*   Tu bis delusus, an ab eodem homine?

*Polupist.*   Non, sed diversis.
*Crat.*                  Quibus artibus?

SCENE V, & THE LAST

NEARLY ALL THE SPEAKERS IN THE PLAY

> [*The Duke enters, and many persons*
> *preferring complaints, accusations, &c.*

*Duke.* Alas, how I 've been deceived! Whoever would believe that beneath the gown such knavery could be hid!

*Eubulus.* There 's no trusting outward show.[79]

*Cratinus.* Nor can I credit any man.

*Duke.* But what manner of man was he who inflicted such
injury upon thee?

*Stephanio.* As to public profession, he called himself a Jesuit;
by his speech, carriage, and apparel he seemed a learned
and upright man; but, oh, I 'd rather 't were my fate to
fall into an enemy's hands, than those of such a man! He
hath taught my son nothing whatever save the arts of
tippling and cozening. Having been deceived by him
whose honor I 'd trusted, he now wasteth my money
'mongst whores and on an old bawd.

*Duke.* Amongst whores and a bawd, sayest thou? Which
ones? Of what kind? Where dwell they?

*Steph.* They dwell in a little suburban garden near by.

*Duke.* Sergeant, fetch them hither. Wouldst thou know this
man, an thou didst see him again?

*Steph.* Aye, marry, more than well, to my loss be 't said.

*Duke.* Be of good cheer; he shall pay dearly for such a
heinous crime.

*Eu.* Thou hast been twice deceived, peradventure by the same
man?

*Polupistos.* Nay, they differed widely.

*Crat.* In what way?

*Polupiſt.*   Alter suaviloquus, et quoad barbam conspicuus,
   In magiâ jaĉtabat singularem peritiam,
   At plenus erat præſtigiarum, deceptionis, mendacii.

*Eu.*   Idem fortasse qui huic alteri imposuit.

*Polupiſt.*   Alter Spagiricus tantam verborum ambrosiam
   Effudit, ut persuaderet se posse penitus
     Aurum conficere, quibus ego faĉtus velut ebrius
     Credebam illi fortunas meas, at ille nebulo
     Insignis pro auro carbones reliquit mihi.

*Crat.*   Mirum eſt hoc præ cæteris impoſturæ genus.


*Eu.*   A quo læsus tu?

*Rub.*             Verberatus gravissimè.

*Dux.*   Per quos?

*Rub.*           Duos scholares ebrios in foro.

*Dux.*   O execrandum facinus, verberare civem et senem,
   Et in ipso foro.

*Eu.*           Quod damnum tuum?

*Corn.*   Damnum sed pudet dicere.

*Crat.*              At illum non puduit facere.

*Corn.*   Legas si placet.

*Eu.*         Quid tu quereris?

*Sord.*   Civis sum si placet, et hic in viciniâ
   Villam habui cultam pro more ruſtico,
   Sed dum scholares habitârunt hoc oppidum,
   Nec ædes, nec villa, nec quid mihi reliquum.

*Dux.*   Quid ita?

*Sord.*         Suffurati sunt pæne omnia,
   Lignum, gallinas, fruĉtus, anates, anseres,
   Agnos, oves, nil cuſtodimus, equum gradarium
   Alter a me nuper conduĉtum occidit.

*Polupiſt.*   One was fair-spoken, with a venerable beard: he
boaſted great skill in magick, but he was full of trickery,
deceits, and lies.

*Eu.*   The same, no doubt, who cozened this other man.

*Polupiſt.*   'T other fellow was an Alchemiſt who poured out
such delightsome speech that he fully persuaded me he
could make real gold, at the which I was e'en as one drunk,
believing my fortune made; but that damned knave, inſtead of gold, left me naught but charcoals.

*Crat.*   By compare with 't other trickeries this is moſt marvellous.

*Eu.*   By what means wert thou injured, my good man?

*Rub.*   I was badly beaten, Sir.

*Duke.*   By whom?

*Rub.*   By two drunken scholars, at the Forum.

*Duke.*   O damnable villainy, to beat a citizen, an aged man,
in the Forum itself!

*Eu.*   My good man, what 's thy grievance?

*Corn.*   'T is wrong'd I am, Sir, but I blush to name it.

*Crat.*   Ha, but he who did thee wrong blush'd not to do it.

*Corn.*   Thou mayeſt read the complaint, an thou wilt, Sir.

*Eu.*   What 's thy complaint?

*Sord.*   I 'm a citizen, please your worships, and in this vicinity
I had a provision-farm, after the cuſtom of the country;
but sithen the scholars have dwelt in this town, neither
house, farm, nor anything else hath been left for me.

*Duke.*   How so, my good man?

*Sord.*   They 've privily filched well-nigh every thing a man
could name: fire-wood, hens, fruit, ducks, geese, lambs,
sheep—we 've preserved nothing; one of my two pacing-
horses, but lately hired, hath been done to death.

*Steph.*    Propter irruptiones etiam ferè continuas
    Nos qui habitamus ad sextum abhinc lapidem
    Nec aves defensamus, nec damas protegimus,
    Nec leporem in arvis, neque piscem in aquis.

*Dux.*    Hine venatores?

*Steph.*                  Et piscatores etiam.

*Dux.*    O calones! O verberones!

*Sord.*                 Audi gravissimum.
    Ignarus medicus suis virulentis pharmacis
    Uxorem interemit mihi carissimam.

*Rub.*    Utinam occidisset meam!

*Corn.*              Et, si placeret Diis, meam!

*Dux.*    Proh Deûm atque hominum fidem! tot scelera,
    Tam abhorrenda, quis audivit a talibus tam brevi?
    Quod tam atrox factum quod non commiserint?
    Quæ fraudes, imposturæ, furta, cædes, adulteria,
    Luxus, ebrietas, turpe quod crimen, fædum facinus,
    Quod non designârint? hi fructus ingenii?
    Hoc illud bonum quod persuaserunt mihi?
    Ipsa barbaries nihil produxit immanius.
    Hic si Musarum profectus, eradicabo memoriam
    Et nomen Academiæ, reditus et latifundia
    Redibunt in fiscum, in milites et aulicos
    Impertientur, et in usus bellicos.

*Eu.*    Laudo summè hanc proboque sententiam,
    Hoc enim cedet in lucrum mihi.

*Crat.*              Ni fallor et mihi.

*Philobib.*    Procella gravis, quamprimum effare Polumathes.

*Steph.*  Because of these frequent incursions, we who dwell near the sixth mile-ſtone henceforward preserve not the birds, nor the fallow-deer, nor the hare on the fields, nor the fish in our waters.

*Duke.*  Are these fellows huntsmen?

*Steph.*  Aye, Sir, and fishermen also.

*Duke.*  Ah, the varlets! Ah, the knaves!

*Sord.*  Hear, prithee, gentlemen, a tale moſt grievous. An unskill'd tyro of a doctor with his noxious drugs hath kill'd my deareſt wife.

*Rub.*  Oh, would that he'd kill'd mine!

*Corn.*  Mine also, please God!

*Duke.*  Oh, faith of God and man! such villainy againſt all reason, who hath heard such like in so short a while? Since such monſtrous deeds have been already done, to what length might they not have gone? What snares, impoſtures, pilferings, murthers, adulteries, riots, drunkennesses—what base crime or filthy act is there which they have not perpetrated? Is this the fruitage of genius? Is this that excellence by means of which they prevailed upon me? The barbarians themselves have done nothing more cruel. Here, so be the Muses have departed, I shall root out both the remembrance and the name of this University, reſtoring the eſtates, and will turn back the moneys into public revenue, where they shall be beſtowed upon soldiers, courtiers, & for use in war.

*Eu.*  Sire, I moſt highly commend this speech, and approve thy judgment; for 't will yield a profit to me.

*Crat.*  And to me if I be not deceived.

*Philobib.*  A moſt grievous calamity! speak up quickly, Polumathes.

*Polumath.*   Ne sic, O benigne princeps! revoca sententiam,
     Nimis severam, injuſtam, et duram nimis;
     Parce, parce, parce, precamur te singuli.
*Eu.*   Qui vos tandem?
*Polumath.*               Duo peregrinantes philosophi.
*Crat.*   Nugatores: abite.
*Philobib.*               Audi loquentem prius,
     Serenissime Princeps!
*Dux.*               Æquum petit, eloquere.
*Polumath.*   Sponte facis, quod nos ipsi petituri fuimus,
     Ut judicares hanc corruptam Academiam.


*Dux.*   Quid ergò deprecaris ut revocem sententiam?


*Polumath.*   Ne simul cum malis exularent etiam boni,
     Aut ars malè audiret ob abusum artificis.
     Habet Osuna viros doctos, illuſtres, graves,
     Qui verè et sincerè colunt philosophiam,
     Atque horum causâ, Princeps serenissime,
     Obnixè oravi ut revocares sententiam.


*Dux.*   At qui demum sunt in quos inveheris?


*Polumath.*   Quos tu rebaris dignos Academicos,
     Et admittebas prius in hanc scholam tuam,
     Fungi plerumque erant, idiotæ, asini,
     De fæce plebis balatrones circumforanei.
     Jam si vis benè mereri de republica literariâ,
     Coerce errores iſtos, fæcem hanc amove,
     Atque horum vice viros subſtitue bonos,
     Statuta nova sancias, leges novas,

*Polumath.*   Nay, not so, O moſt gracious Lord; prithee recall this exceeding hard, unjuſt, and severe sentence;
gently, gently, gently, we beseech thee.

*Eu.*   Who be ye, pray?

*Polumath.*   Two wandering scholars, Sir.

*Crat.*   Triflers! Away with ye!

*Philobib.*   Moſt juſt and noble lord, I pray thee hear firſt
what he hath to say.

*Duke.*   He sueth for a fair hearing: speak, Sir.

*Polumath.*   Thou 'rt executing of thine own accord what we
ourselves were about to petition: that thou shouldſt try
this corrupt Academy.

*Duke.*   Why, therefore, doſt thou make plea that I revoke
the sentence?

*Polumath.*   Leſt peradventure the good be banished along
with the evil, or the Faculty be of ill report by occasion of
the abuse of these crafty ones. Osuna hath her learned men,
noble in renown, discreet men, who truly & honeſtly serve
Philosophy, and for sake of these, moſt gracious lord, I beseech thee with all my might and main to the end that thou
mayeſt revoke thy decision.

*Duke.*   But who, when all 's said, are they againſt whom thou
wouldſt inveigh?

*Polumath.*   Those whom thou reckoneſt worthy Academi-
cians, and, in former time, admitted into this thy school;
moſt part dullards, idiots, asses, all out from the dregs of
the commonality, circumforean rogues. An thou shouldſt
desire to deserve well of the republic of letters, check
these errors, banish these dregs, and in their place put
good men; eſtablish new ordinances & new laws; thus
thou 'lt become the pride of learning, the father of thy

Sic eris Musarum decus, pater patriæ,
Et nomen tuum Musæ in æternum canent.

*Dux.* Cordatè loqueris, et jam revoco sententiam.
Sed quî diftinguam probos hosce ab improbis,
Philosophaftros a veris?

*Polumath.* Dicam breviter.
Promulgari ftatim curabis per omnem Academiam,
Ut qui jaftârit se philosophum, poteritque
Latinè saltem loqui, aut syllogismum conficere,
Ad diftributionem mox in arcem veniat,
Singulis enim minæ dabuntur duæ.

*Dux.* Laudo hoc commentum. Liftor, promulga ftatim.

*Philobib.* Hoc promulgato mox turmatim ruent
Inhiantes famæ et lucro, at boni interim
Cordatique contemnent, Musis addifti suis.
Sic eos agnosces, et turba supplicantium
Coram videns impoftorem designabit suum.

*Polumath.* Videbis ftatim, velut ad prædam lupos,
Jamdiu devorantes hoc aurum animis,
Huc concurrentem turbam præcipitem.

*Eu.* Sed eccum philomusas!

*Dux.* Quales hæ fæminæ?

*[Intrat lena cum filiabus.*

*Staph.* Honefta materfamilias, atque hæ sunt filiæ meæ,
Sumusque, si placet, sutrices Academicæ.

*Crat.* Vel quod verius meretrices Academicæ.

*Staph.* Hæc eft illa lena, et meretrix vetula,
Compofta ex vulpe, leone, et simiâ,

country, and the Muses will praise thy name throughout
all time.

*Duke.* Discreetly spoken: and I herewith revoke the sentence.
But how, pray, shall I distinguish the men of honor from
these base fellows, the philosophasters from them that are
truly wise?

*Polumath.* I 'll shew thee in a few words: proclaim thou
forthwith o'er all the University that whosoever hath
vaunted himself as a philosopher and is able to speak
plainly, or to explain a syllogism, may come anon into the
castle, for that two pounds will then be divided amongst
them severally.

*Duke.* I commend this devising of thine. Sergeant, publish
the proclamation at once.

*Philobib.* With this proclamation made, they 'll fly thither
in bands, with mouths agape for fame and fortune; but in
the meanwhile the wise and good men, wholly given to
their Muses, will pay no regard to this business. By this
token thou 'lt know them, & in the presence of this crew
of suppliants, each man will point out his own villain.

*Polumath.* And thou 'lt see them all together in a mad rout,
dashing hither at once, as wolves to their prey, spending,
in their own minds, the whiles, the golden coin.

*Eu.* But behold the she-lovers-of-the-Muses!

*Duke.* What manner of women are these?

　　　　　　　*[Enter the Bawd with her Daughters.*

*Staph.* An honest housewife, and these be my daughters; we
are, an ye please, the seamstresses of the University.

*Crat.* Or, more exactly, the University whores.

*Staph.* This is that bawd, that old strumpet, compounded of
fox, she-lion, and ape, who hath baited and debauched my

Quæ inescavit et corrupit filium meum.
Et hæ sunt Eumenides, hoc illud barathrum,
In quod obligurivit, et profudit opes meas.
*Polupist.*  Hem! quid video? meamne filiam an alteram?
Quam ego jamdiu credideram demortuam,
Nata mea ut vales?

*Cam.*              Pater ignosce, veniam peto.
Seducta ab hâc anu hunc in modum delitui,
Per annos aliquot.
*Polupist.*        At quis te fecit gravidam?
*Cam.*  Antonius, Stephanionis hujusce filius unicus.
Atque eccum opportunè adest.

             *[Intrat Antonius cum Æquivoco, et auro.*
*Ant.*              Salvete judices!
Præsento vobis furem.
*Polupist.*        Et impostorem eximium.
Hic ille magi servus, et medico a consiliis,
Qui me supplantavit.
*Steph.*       Et qui corrupit filium meum.
*Dux.*  Cujus hoc aurum?
*Polupist.*       Meum, quod a me medicus
Surripuit, ille forsan a medico.

*Æquiv.*          Ita est, judices.
*Dux.*  Aurum tuum tibi restituo.
*Polupist.*       Deus benefaxit tibi.
*Dux.*  De hoc videbitur alias, rectâ nunc ad carcerem eat.

*Eubulus.*  Sed heus adolescens, tune hanc fecisti gravidam?

son. And these be the Furies, this that bottomless pit into which he wasted and poured out my fortune.

*Polupist.* Oh, strange! What's this I see? Is't my own daughter or some other? My daughter whom for this long while I had believed dead! My own daughter in sooth, art thou well and sound?

*Cam.* Father, forgive me; I implore thy pardon. Having been seduced by this old hag, I have in this manner hid myself away for these years.

*Polupist.* But who got thee with child?

*Cam.* Antonius, Sir, the only son of this Stephanio; and lo, here he cometh in good season.

   [*Enter Antonius fetching Equivocus and the gold.*

*Ant.* God save ye, Judges! I fetch before ye a thief.

*Polupist.* And a choice trickster he is. This is the lackey of that wizard and counsellor in physick who trick'd me so.

*Steph.* And who debauched my son.

*Duke.* Whose gold is this?

*Polupist.* 'T is mine, Sir, which the physician stole from me; that man, peradventure, stole it in turn from the physician.

*Equiv.* Yea, 't is e'en so, Judges.

*Duke.* I restore thy gold unto thee.

*Polupist.* May God reward thee!

*Duke.* Care will be taken of this at another time; let him be off straightway to prison.

*Eubulus.* But ho there, young man, hast thou got this wench with child?

*Steph.*   O scelus, ut ſtas! ubi pudor? ubi verecundia?
    Quid ad hæc ais?

*Ant.*           Vis dicam verbo? reus sum.
    Pater da veniam quæso, obsecro ignoscas pater.

*Steph.*   Et fateris te vitiasse hanc virginem?

*Ant.*                  Fateor.

*Polupiſt.*   Et in uxorem duces hanc?

*Ant.*              Ducam lubens.

*Steph.*   Ut ducas meretricem? egone ut ad hæc annuam?

*Cam.*   Non sum meretrix, pudicè et probè me habui
    Ad reliquos omnes, hunc unum si excipias.

*Ant.*   Sine te exorem pater.

*Eu.*          Lex hoc ipsum petit.

*Dux.*   Stephanio, iniquus nimis es, æquum uterque poſtulat,
    Ut ducat lex jubet.

*Steph.*        Quando ita leges volunt,
    Age ducat habeatque, quum tibi sic visum fuerit.

*Ant.*   O lenissimum patrem!

*Polupiſt.*       Et dotis loco
    Totum hunc thesaurum do.

*Eu.*         Laudo faĉtum tuum.
                 [*Intrant Philosophaſtri.*

*Dux.*   En gregem!

*Crat.*        Papæ! ut erumpunt inſtar apum;
    Impletur arx multitudine impellentium.
    Veſtrumne quisquam novit horum aliquem?

*Steph.*   Hunc accuso, hic eſt ille impoſtor celebris,
    Jesuitam præ se ferens, qui natum corrupit meum.

*Polupiſt.*   Eundem ego pro mago. Sed hic ille
    Qui me emunxit argento.

*Steph.*　O profligate that thou art! Where's thy shame? where thy modesty? What dost thou say to this?

*Ant.*　Wilt thou that I tell thee a word? I am guilty. Father, forgive me, I pray; I beseech thee to forgive me, father!

*Steph.*　And dost thou confess having deflower'd this maid?

*Ant.*　Father, I confess it.

*Polupist.*　And wilt thou marry her?

*Ant.*　I'll wed her with pleasure.

*Steph.*　How now, thou'dst marry a whore? How should I agree to this?

*Cam.*　I'm not a whore, Sir; I conducted myself modestly and honestly to all other men, save this man alone.

*Ant.*　Father, permit me to persuade thee.

*Eu.*　The law itself requireth this.

*Duke.*　Stephanio, thou'rt exceeding hard; what they both ask is fair enough; the law requireth that he marry.

*Steph.*　Seeing that the laws so require, let him take her off and keep her, since to thee it seemeth right.

*Ant.*　O most tender father!

*Polupist.*　And in the stead of a dowery, I bestow upon ye this entire treasure.

*Eu.*　I applaud thine action.

　　　　　　　　　　　　　　　*[Enter the philosophasters.*

*Duke.*　Behold the motley crew!

*Crat.*　O marvelous sight! they burst forth like unto bees, forcing their way into the castle in multitudes. Know ye any of these?

*Steph.*　I charge this fellow, he's that famed impostor, the self-styled Jesuit, who corrupted my son.

*Polupist.*　I charge the same rogue for's black magick. But here's the one who hath defrauded me of my money.

*Rub.*                Hic ille juvenis
  Qui me verberavit.
*Sord.*           Hic conduxit equum meum.
*Corn.*  Hic nepos uxori meæ tam gratus, hic nebulo.

*Polumath.*  Hi sunt impoſtores et execrandi hypocritæ,
  Qui nos omnes affecerunt hâc injuriâ,
  Quorum causâ Musæ et artes malè audiunt,
  Sed jam capti aliquando pœnas dabunt.

*Philobib.*  Exuite hos habitus, ut plane cognoscamini.
                              *[Detegit.*
  En frontes novas!
*Dux.*            O impoſturam egregiam!
*Phil. (Scrutatur.)*  Quid hic?
*Æq.*              Pera.
*Phil.*                At quid in eâ latet?
*Æq.*  Libri.
*Phil.*      Quid hic? peċten, unguentum, speculum.
*Polumath.*  Quid hic? piċtæ chartæ, cultelli, tali, tesseræ.
  Quid tu circumfers cantilenas, pocula?
  Hæ musæ tuæ?
*Phil.*          Hæc veſtri exercitii viatica?
*Eu.*  O profanum gregem!
*Dux.*            Quod dignum supplicii genus
  Excogitabimus?
*Polumath.*       Illud incumbat mihi.
*Dux.*  Quod vis fac, committo rem totam arbitrio tuo.

*Polumath.*  Sic ſtatuo, quatuor hisce sycophantis egregiis,
  In exemplum et terrorem reliquorum omnium,

*Rub.*   Here's the young rascal that gave me a beating.

*Sord.*   This one hired mine horse.

*Corn.*   Here's the spendthrift who's so welcome to my wife, the vile knave!

*Polumath.*   These be the impostors and cursed hypocrites who have tainted all of us beyond our deserts, for which cause the Muses and the Arts are ill bespoke; but now that they've all been taken, they shall suffer punishment to the full.

*Philobib.*   Strip off those robes, that ye may be clearly known.

　　　　　　　　　　　　　　　　　　*[He uncovers them.*

Behold the new faces!

*Duke.*   Oh, what rare deceit!

*Phil.*   (*Examining*) What's this?

*Eq.*   A pouch, Sir.

*Phil.*   But what's hid within?

*Eq.*   Books, Sir.

*Phil.*   How now, what's this? a comb, ointment, a mirror?

*Polumath.*   And what have we here? cards, little knives, dice, tokens. Why dost thou carry about song-books & wine-cups? Be these thy Muses?

*Phil.*   Is this travel-money for thy use?

*Eu.*   O wicked crew!

*Duke.*   What fitting punishment shall we devise?

*Polumath.*   Let that, Sir, be my duty.

*Duke.*   Do what thou wilt; I commit the whole matter to thy judgment.

*Polumath.*   Thus, then, I decree: these four outstanding sycophants here before us I desire to be branded on either

Utramque genam ſtigmate inuri volo—
Sit vero deuſtionis figura vulpes, aut simia—
Deturbari dein gradu, et expelli Academiâ.

*Lictor.*   Statim fiet.

*Eu.*                    Divinator cur non hoc ante prædixeras?
                        [*Philosophaſtri exeunt inurendi,*
                                    *et mox intrant.*

[*Polumath.*]   Hi vero reliqui, quod sit delictum minus,
      Et quod præ se ferant quandam indolem,
      Abrasis primum barbis tragicâ novaculâ,
      Relegentur per annum unum ad Anticyras;
      Ubi poſtquam nugis, solœcismis, et ineptiis
      Purgati fuerint, reſtituantur ad locum suum.

*Eu.*   De lenâ quid fiet?

*Crat.*                    Ducatur ad carcerem,
      Ubi per dies aliquot macerata cum fuerit,
      Aquam cœnosam, et panem depascens plebeium,
      Circumducatur curru per omnes plateas,
      Atque inde flagelletur ex Academiâ.

*Eu.*   Una supereſt muliercula.

*Crat.*                         In medium profer.

*Dux.*   Commiseratione digna videtur ob formam suam.

*Crat.*   Poenitetne vitæ anteactæ tuæ?

*Tar.*                         Seriò poenitet.

*Dux.*   Age verò, quis horum tecum rem habuit?

*Tar.*   Omnes.

*Dux.*          Itane? ex omnibus unum elige
      Quem virum malles, atque erit vir tuus.

*Tar.*   Hunc volo.

cheek with an hot iron, as an example and a warning to all
the others—aye, marry, it may be the shape of a fox or
an ape, deeply burned. After that they're to be thrust
forth, and ejected from the University.

*Sergeant.*   It shall be done at once.

*Eu.*   Prophet, why didſt thou not forsee this aforetime?

> [*The philosophaſters go forth
> to be branded, and anon enter.*

*Polumath.*   These remaining, for that they've committed
lesser crimes, and because they reveal a certain toward-
ness, firſt shave off their beards with cruel razor, then
they're to be banished to Anticyra for the space of a year;
after that they've been purged of fopperies, incongruities,
& folly, they may be reſtored to their places.

*Eu.*   What should be done concerning the bawd?

*Crat.*   She may be clapt in prison, whence, after the course of
a few days, feeding on mouldy bread, ſteeped in filthy water, she may be drawn about through all the ſtreets at th'
cart's arse; yea, also she may thereafter be whipped out of
the Academy.

*Eu.*   One harlot's left.

*Crat.*   Fetch her hither.

*Duke.*   Judging by her shape, she's deserving of pity.

*Crat.*   Doſt thou repent thy former life?

*Tar.*   I do repent indeed.

*Duke.*   Tell me sooth, which of these men had conneſtion
with thee?

*Tar.*   All of 'em, my lord.

*Duke.*   Indeed, is it so?  From out them all choose what man
thou wilt, and he shall be thy husband.

*Tar.*   I wish this one, my lord.

*Dux.* Tibine placet conditio?

*Pant.* Placet.

*Dux.* Benè sit nuptiis et feliciter.
 Qui inuruntur reliqui, exulent illicò.
 Utque in posterum occurratur hisce nequitiis,
 Volumus, ordinamus et per præsentes statuimus,
 Ut omnes popinæ munus necessariæ
 Tollantur illicò, malorum omnium initia.
 Præesse volumus in posterum viros duos,
 Virtute et morum probitate conspicuos,
 Annuatim eligendos publicis suffragiis,
 Qui vicatim inambulantes noctu et interdiu,
 Plectant auctoritate suâ, et curent hæc fieri.
 Vos autem duo primam hanc vicem gerite,
 Et honoris ergo hunc habetis habitum.

*Eu.* Probo hoc inventum.

*Crat.* Placetque edictum mihi.

*Dux.* Vos ergo quibus hoc mandatum est officium,
 Et quos ego elegi fideles ministros meos,
 Curate munus vestrum, et exercete sedulò.

*Polumath.* Serene princeps, mandatis tuis obsequentissimi
 Hoc munus nostrum exequemur illicò,
 Operamque dabimus ut, quod in nobis siet,
 Longum efflorescat Osuna Academia.

*Dux.* Laudo paratum animum, et si quid deest
 Secus corrigendum, vestræ committo fidei.

         *[Exit Dux, et consiliarii.*

*Polumath.* Sic restauratâ in longum Academiâ,
 Tamque auspicatò rebus compositis,
 Hymnum canamus in laudem philosophiæ.

*Duke.*    Is this agreeable to thee?

*Pant.*    'T is agreeable, my lord.

*Duke.*    May the marriage be a happy one! The others who are branded may be banished at once. And to the end that such knaveries may be prevented in the future, we will ordain and in this presence decree that all unnecessary taverns, the breeding-grounds of all mischief, be at once disestablished. We decree that after this time two men, noted for manhood and morals, have charge; they are to be chosen each year by ballot; they're to walk up and down the streets both night and day; they shall attend to whatsoever is needful to be done, and may administer punishment in their own right. But ye twain first bring order into this place, and keep, therefore, its conduct free from reproach.

*Eu.*    I approve of this arrangement.

*Crat.*    The edict pleaseth me also.

*Duke.*    Ye, therefore, for whom this mandate is an official duty, and whom I've selected as my faithful ministers, look well to your tasks, and press on with diligence.

*Polumath.*    Fair my lord, to thy charge we'll set about this our office most obediently and with despatch, and we shall endeavor to the utmost, whatsoever we are able to do, that the Osuna University may long flourish.

*Duke.*    I commend thy skill'd judgment, and if aught be wanting, see to it that it's remedied; I commit the whole affair to your good faith.

*[Exit the Duke and his advisers.*

*Polumath.*    Thus at length the University hath been new-made, and all affairs are now in so prosperous a state that we may well sing a hymn in Philosophy's praise. And ye

Vos autem cives, quondam malè habiti
Ab execrandis hisce pseudo-academicis,
Læti et jucundi celebrate hunc diem,
Canentes nobiscum unà, et unanimi lætitiâ.

(*To the tune of Bonny Nell*)

[*Unus canit solus.*

Magiſtri, Baccalaurei,
Tirones, Abecedarii,
Doctores, Academici,
Et juvenes dupondii—
*Omnes.*     Cantate serenissimæ
Triumphum philosophiæ.

*Unus.*     Philosophantes, medici,
Studentes, et philologi,
Rhetores, causidici,
Magi, et Mathematici—
*Omnes.*     Cantate serenissimæ
Triumphum philosophiæ.

*Unus.*     Vos Scotiſtæ, vos Thomiſtæ,
Vos Poetæ, Grammatiſtæ,
Oratores, et Sophiſtæ,
Et qui sunt Musarum Myſtæ—
*Omnes.*     Cantate serenissimæ
Triumphum philosophiæ.

citizens that heretofore have been so ill-used by those damned, pseudo-Academicks, now jocund & merry, let us celebrate this day, all together singing in happy concord.


(*To the tune of Bonny Nell*)

[*One sings.*

Masters, Bachelors, gather round,
Ye Freshmen, tyros, swell the sound,
Academicks, Doctors—without spleen—
And two young asses, all out green—

*All.*        Merrily together sing
             Let Philosophy's triumph ring.


*One.*    Sages, men who physick give
          Students and Scholars who here live,
          Rhetorick's lords, and Lawyers too,
          Wizards, Mathematicians true—

*All.*        Merrily together sing,
             Let Philosophy's triumph ring.


*One.*    Ye Scotists, Thomists, subtile crew,
          Grammarians and Poets few,
          Orators, tricksters, band of knaves,
          And ye the Muses' faithful slaves—

*All.*        Merrily together sing,
             Let Philosophy's triumph ring.

*Unus.*        Europæi, Asiani,
               Afri, et Americani,
               Continentes, insulani,
               Lauti cives oppidani—
*Omnes.*          Cantate serenissimæ
                  Triumphum philosophiæ.


*Unus.*        Vos Germani, vos Hispani,
               Vos Insubres, vos Britanni,
               Cimbri, Sardi, et Siculi,
               Poloni, Mosci, et Itali—
*Omnes.*          Cantate serenissimæ
                  Triumphum philosophiæ.


*FINIS.*

*Plauserunt*
Feb. 16to.
1617.

*One.*        Europeans and Asian clans,
               Africk's blacks and Americans,
               Continentals and island-folk,
               Citizen rayed in fashion's cloak—

*All.*         Merrily together sing,
                 Let Philosophy's triumph ring.


*One.*        Ye Germans, Spaniards of the Main,
               Lombards, Britains, join our refrain,
               Cimbrians, all from southern isles,
               Italians, Poles, and all exiles—

*All.*         Merrily together sing,
                 Let Philosophy's triumph ring.


*THE END*

*They Applauded*
*Feb. 16th*
1617

## EPILOGUS

Sortita finem eſt longa tandem fabula,
Nullis referta jocis, nec aspersa salibus,
Quæ in aliorum fabulis haberi solent;
Fatemur, et capax subjeċtum non fuit.
Si quid aberratum, aut obsoletum quid nimis
Offendat aures, præmonuimus ab initio
Undecim abhinc annis hanc scriptam fabulam.
Moleſtiores æquo si forsan fuimus,
Non noſtra culpa eſt, iis hanc culpam imputent
Quorum malignitas hoc in scena petiit.
Asperius in quem si quis hic putet invehi,
Is demum impudentes, non bonos, carpi sciat.
Si quid moleſtum ſtylo aut subjeċto fuerit,
Emeritus poeta veniam petit.
At nos de grege si quid forsan aberravimus—
Aliis utcunque, vobis opinor non imposuimus—
Voce aut manu si quid erratum fuerit,
Date veniam, non hiſtriones sumus.
Sed non veremur veſtrum favorem, judices,
Benignitatem et gratiam; fremat frendat licet
Unus et alter læsus, bonus quisque dabit
Jam renovatæ plausum Academiæ.
Longum efflorescat Osuna Academia!
Et quo quisque veſtrûm Musis amicitior
Erit, is tanto plausum alacriorem dabit.

*Plauserunt*
*Feb.* 16*to.*
*Æde Chriſti*
1617

226

# EPILOGUE

At last our lengthy play its end doth reach,
Not stuff'd with jests, nor spic'd with witty speech
Such as old custom hath in tales of other men;
The fault we freely own: it suited not our pen.
If aught amiss hath been, what's staled by age
Offend keen ears, we warned ye from this stage,
That eleven years agone this comedy was writ.
And if, perchance, we 've griev'd ye much with it,
Not ours the fault, turn then on them thy rage
Whose evils fetch'd this to our stage.
Supposing any here shall think himself defamed,
Know ye, not honest folk, but wantons here are blamed.
If aught hath vext in subject or in style,
The quondom Poet begs that ye forgive the while.
But say, forsooth, our troop of actors err'd
(On ye we 've not imposed, though others we have spur'd);
In voice or gesture we may have been arraign'd:
Pray overlook the fault; we are not actors train'd.
But we doubt not, O Judges, your acclaim,
Your bounty, & your praise.  One after t'other, all aflame,
May rage and gnash 's teeth, but honest men will praise
The University, re-formed before your gaze.
Let Osuna's University flourish ever! sans abuse,
And those of ye more friendly to the Muse
More lustily will plaudits yield, & bays.

*THE END*

*They Applauded*
*Feb. 16th*
*At Christ Church*
*1617*

# NOTES

## ARGUMENT

**Page 5, note 1.** *Lapithæ:* The Lapithæ were a people of Thessaly, celebrated in mythology as having had a contest with the Centaurs. Pirithous, one of the Lapithæ, was married to Hippodame. The Centaurs were invited to the wedding feast, where one of them got drunk and carried off the bride. The banquet ended in a brawl. See Ovid, *Metamorphoses*, Book XII, lines 210–530.

**Page 13, note 2.** *Vertumnus:* Matthew Gwinne's play, was acted in Christ Church, Oxford, in 1607.

## ACT I

**Page 25, note 3.** *Algorism:* From al-Khowarazmi, the surname of an Arabian mathematician, Abu Ja'far Mohammed Ben Musa (ninth century); Algorism is equivalent to the decimal system of numeration.

**Note 4.** *Zanze:* An African drum-like musical instrument. The *Zinzizanzizenique* defies research at present, and is probably nonsense.

**Note 5.** *elami:* The note E, sung to the syllable *la* or *mi*, according as it occurred in the hexacord.

**Page 27, note 6.** *Scotus:* Duns Scotus (1274–1308).

**hæcceity:** *Hæcceity* is equivalent to "thisness," that is to say, the principle of individuality or the difference of individuals. In the history of philosophy the names of Scotus and Thomas of Aquin are inseparably linked.

**Note 7.** *Gabrielites:* An Anabaptist sect founded by Gabriel Scherling in 1513.

**Note 8.** *paramirum:* "Paramirum" is a term used by Paracelsus in two of his medical works—*Paramirum de quinque entibus omnium morborum* and *Opus paramirum secundum*, issued at Cologne in his collected works (1589–1590); it seems to have been an unguent or elixir taken from dead for living bodies.

**Mumia:** *Mumia* was bitumen or pitch, taken from mummies, in the belief that it would prolong life. It was freely used in six-teenth- and seventeenth-century medicine.

**Note 9. reverberated:** These metallurgical terms were em-ployed by alchemists and referred to the processes used in refining or changing the metals. *Saturn* = lead; *Venus* = copper; *Jupiter* = tin. *Iron saffronated* = "crocus of iron" or "iron sulphate." *Rever-berated* refers to heating in what was called a reverberating furnace.

**Page 29, note 10. Rufflers:** Swaggering vagabonds. The term occurs in *Henry VIII* and in Dekker's *Belman of London*.

**Note 11. Agyrta:** Mountebank.

**Page 31, note 12. Hippias of Elis:** A contemporary of Socra-tes. He was reputed to have excelled in all arts and crafts.

**Page 33, note 13. I excel as grammarian . . . . :** A quotation from Juvenal's *Satires*, iii . 76–77.

**Note 14. stenography:** On the assumption that the word *stenographia*, which is used in the Roxburghe text, is correct, the word may be taken to mean a system of shorthand. It was so used by John Willis in 1602. But Mr. Buckley suggests that the word may have been either "*stereographia*" (the art of representing solid bodies on a plane), or "*steganographia*" (cipher-writing).

**Bial, Hartumim, Jedoni:** Familiar spirits.

**Page 35, note 15. A poet's next-door to an orator:** See Cicero, *De Oratore*, i . 16 . 70.

**Note 16. whatso I 'tempt to say . . . . :** An imitation of the words in which Ovid confesses to have been always dropping into verse when he tried to write prose (Ovid, *Tristia*, iv . x . 25, 26).

**Note 17. Alcala de las Henares:** The birthplace of Cervantes.

**Medina-Sydonia:** The dukes of this Spanish town had long been famous.

**Page 39, note 18. As well expect agreement amongst Philos-ophers . . . . :** See Seneca, *Ludus de Morte Claudii*, chap. ii, sec. 3.

**Page 51, note 19. Cardinal's "mules":** Concubines. In the *Fabyan Chronicle* (*ca.* 1494), VII, ccxxix, 259, "Ye Cardynall made sharpe processe agayn prestys, yt noresshed Cristen-moyles [mules]."

**Page 53, note 20.** *held by chains:* Chained-books in the library.

**Page 57, note 21.** *Philip:* Father of Alexander the Great. King Philip, writing to Aristotle, is said to have expressed joy, not so much over the birth of his son as that he was born in the days of Aristotle, who he hoped might educate the boy.

**Note 22.** *Entrust the sheep to the wolf:* See Terence, *Eunuchus*, line 832.

## ACT II

**Page 59, note 23.** *"Quoniam necessaria est, . . . .":* This passage, from Porphyrius' Introduction to Aristotle's *Categories*, receives reckless commentary from Simon Acutus, who imagines the vocative of the man's name to whom Porphyrius addresses his work is a verb, derived from the Greek *Chrusos* and the Latin *orare!*

**Page 61, note 24.** *major:* Major premise. See Shakespeare's *Henry IV*, Part One, II . iv . 544.

**Page 63, note 25.** *drive me mad:* Terence, *Adelphoe*, line 111.

**Page 67, note 26.** *The Court o' the Sun, . . . . :* The four lines are quoted from Ovid's *Metamorphoses*, II . 1–4.

**Page 69, note 27.** *Calepino:* Ambrogio Calepino, an Augustinian monk (1435–1511), compiled a huge polyglot dictionary, issued at Reggio in 1502.

**Page 71, note 28.** *permission from his mother:* Professor Edward Bensly recalls in this connection a passage in Joseph Hall's satires (*Virgidemiarum*, Lib. II, Sat. vi, 12–14). This book, a copy of which was in Burton's library (the 1598 edition) contains a satire describing the conditions under which a "Gentle Squire" hires a "trencher-Chaplaine" to instruct his sons. The last condition is:

> "Last that he never his yong master beat,
> But he must ask his mother to define,
> How many ierkes she would his breach should line."

**Note 29.** *without punishment:* See Pliny, *Naturæ Historicæ*, xxix . 1(8) . 18.

**Page 73, note 30.** *essentification:* Making into an essence.

**Page 77, note 31.** *"Qui nescit dissimulare nescit vivere":* This line occurs also in Burton's *Anatomy* (Part I, Sec. II, Mem. 3,

Subs. 15), and is said to have been a favorite maxim of the Emperor Frederic Barbarossa.

**Page 81, note 32.** *Pons asinorum:*   The Bridge of Asses. In *Euclid*, Book I, Prop. 5. Equivalent to saying, "A bridge difficult for stupid young things to cross."

**Note 33.** *Fracastorius:*   Hieronymus Fracastoro (1484–1553), astronomer, geologist, physicist, poet, and physician. This great Veronese genius was one of the most notable and versatile men of his time. His *Homocentrica* (Venice, 1538) was a valuable contribution to astronomical science.

**Helisæus Roeslin:**   Helisæus (Eliseo) Roeslin, German astronomer and scholar of the sixteenth century, lived at Frankfort, and, among other things, wrote *Theoria nova cœlestium Meteoron* (Strassburg, 1578).

**Patricius:**   Franciscus Patricius, or Patrizi (1529–1597), lived at Caieta, Italy, and wrote several works on history, mathematics, and astronomy mentioned in *The Anatomy of Melancholy* ("Digression of Air").

**Thaddeus Haggesius:**   According to a note in *The Anatomy*, Thaddeus Haggesius wrote a book on *Metoposcopy*, about 1578.

**Page 83, note 34.** *Falcidian Law:*   P. Falcidius, Roman tribune under Augustus, 40 B.C. The law related to proportionate inheritance.

**Papinianus:**   A Roman jurist under Septimus Severus, *ca.* A.D. 212.

**Page 87, note 35.** *the weight of words:*   An imitation of Ovid, *Heroïdes*, III . 4, and *Fasti*, 1 . 182.

**Note 36.** *Achilles Tatius . . . . The kiss of a lover . . . . :* The translation here is taken from the text of Robert Burton's brother, William Burton. This translation was done in 1597 and has recently been edited and republished under the supervision of Mr. Stephen Gaselee (Shakespeare Head Press, 1924).

**Note 37.** *"I yearn not, . . . .":* Amphimacer's speech is quoted from Palingenius, *Zodiacus Vitæ*, Book V, lines 1–4.

**Note 38.** *"to do thy bidding, . . . .":* Virgil, *Aeneid*, i . 76–77.

**Page 89, note 39.** *"Be kind to me, . . . .":* Ovid, *Fasti*, 1 . 17–18.

**Note 40. *Anticyra:*** A town in Italy, made famous by reason of its supply of Hellebore, a remedy then used for madness and melancholy. "Go to Anticyra!" was the equivalent of "You 're crazy!"

**Page 91, note 41. *a pair of my Hedio's buskins:*** "Hedio" is not in the play. The word is obviously a misprint. Professor Bensly suggests that it was intended for "Hegio," a character out of the *Adelphoe* of Terence, where also is a slave named *Dromo* (see *Adelphoe*, III . iii . 84). Burton drew frequently from Terence, and his audience would appreciate the reference when Dromo speaks of "my Hegio."

**Page 95, note 42. *Whatever Juno whispereth:*** For the origin of this line see Plautus, *Trinummus*, lines 207, 208.

**Note 43. *Aspire not to high things:*** Romans xi:20.

**Note 44. *he hath given him a bone to gnaw:*** See Terence, *Adelphoe*, lines 227–228.

**Page 97, note 45. *Thy face is not far from misfortune:*** See Plautus, *Bacchides*, line 595.

## ACT III

**Page 107, note 46. *'T is evident from the piss:*** Burton is here satirizing the water-prophets of his time, who claimed the ability to diagnose all ailments from looking at the urine. An interesting volume, published at London in 1637, by Dr. Thomas Brian, bears this title: *The Pisse-Prophet, or, Certaine pisse-pot lectures. Wherein are newly discovered the old fallacies, deceit, and jugling of the Pisse-pot Science, &c.*

**Page 121, note 47. *splendesco, liquesco, tabesco, . . . . :*** These are inceptive verbs, and are used to denote the beginning of an action. Properly, they have no present stem. Pedanus, the quibbling grammarian, took issue with Philobiblos on account of the word *marcescere*, here translated "to get slack."

**Page 123, note 48. *So hath Apollo delivered me:*** Horace, *Satires*, i . ix . 78.

**Page 125, note 49. *Mammotrectus:*** The *Mammotrectus super Bibliam* was a famous Biblical glossary in the fifteenth century, compiled by Joannes Marchesinus. In the *Colloquies* of Erasmus it is sometimes referred to as the *Mammothreptus*, and Erasmus speaks

slightingly of the book. The earliest printing I have noted is that
by George Husner, at Strassburg, in 1473. The *Catholicon* was likewise a dictionary, done by Joannes Balbus de Janua, and issued by
Gutenberg, at Mainz, in 1460. It was compiled in 1286. The Latin
words, beginning with *arx* (tower), are either "mixed *i*-stems," or
Greek derivatives, with which the pseudo-grammarian had some
difficulty.

Page 131, note 50. *Harmonic Apotome:*   In Pythagorean mu-
sic, a semitone, expressed by the vibration ratio $\dfrac{2187}{2048}$ ; but in the mind
of this philosopher it comes to mean nothing.

Note 51. *Democritus:*  In *The Anatomy of Melancholy*
("Democritus to the Reader," page 48 of the Dell–Jordan-Smith
edition), Burton enlarges upon the Latin, *Fleat Heraclitus, an rideat
Democritus*, in this fashion: "Would this, think you, have enforced
our Democritus to laughter, or rather made him turn his tune, alter
his tone, and weep with Heraclitus . . . . ? "

## ACT IV

Page 135, note 52. *"longation," "curtation":*  See the Col-
*loquies* of Erasmus (available in Nathan Bailey's translation [Glas-
gow, 1877], page 206), from which Burton probably took a hint or
two.

Page 137, note 53. *Twelve Waters:*  An Oxford manuscript
of the thirteenth century bears the title, "On the Twelve Waters of
the Secret River," and, like many another ancient work of alchemy,
is attributed to Aristotle.

Note 54. *purest gold:*  *Almagra* = red earth; *Almazidor* =
verdigris; *Tincar* = borax; *Laton* = brass; *Azon* is probably azoth,
or mercury; *Anatron* = saltpeter; *Tuffi* = a porous stone, or, perhaps, *tutia* = zinc oxide. If the reader will search through a score
or more alchemical books of the sixteenth and seventeenth centuries
he will be rewarded by finding these terms used in widely different
ways; therefore I take refuge in quoting a footnote from W. R.
Thayer's *Best Elizabethan Plays* (Boston, 1890), dealing with a similar passage from Jonson's *The Alchemist*, pages 159–160: "It
would be time wasted to rummage the old works on alchemy for an
explanation of all these terms, which were doubtless as strange to

the majority of play-goers in Jonson's time as they are to us." According to *Dictionnaire Mytho-Hermétique* (Paris, 1758), *uffituffi* is the odor emanating from "Sages' Mercury," and *Azinibam* is the sediment of the Pure Matter of the Sages.

**Page 139, note 55. Hercynian Forest .... Mæotidian Fens, ....:** See *The Anatomy of Melancholy* (Dell–Jordan-Smith edition, page 81), where in "Democritus to the Reader," Burton speaks of draining the "Mæotian Fenns" and cutting down "those vast Hercynian Woods."

**Page 141, note 56. Eratosthenes:** A mathematician and astronomer, born at Cyrene, 270 B.C. He taught that the circumference of the earth equaled 250,000 stadia.

**Note 57. Alfraganus:** Arabian astronomer, ninth century.

**Page 143, note 58. "Mule scratcheth mule":** From Ausonius.

**Note 59. "Flattery begetteth friends":** From Terence.

**Page 145, note 60. "a man ready at all affairs":** "*Omnium horarum homo,*" from Quintilian.

**Page 147, note 61. Valla:** Lorenzo Valla, famous humanist, reformer, and philologist of Italy (1407–1457). His *De Elegantiis Latinæ Linguæ* passed through fifty-nine editions in less than seventy years and was paraphrased by Erasmus.

**Page 157, note 62. Congregation:** This is the term used at Oxford for the meeting at which degrees are conferred.

**Page 159, note 63. "if he brought nothing, e'en Homer, ....":** From Ovid's *Ars Amatoria,* Book II.

**Note 64. Divine Thomas:** Thomas Aquinas.

**Page 161, note 65. "Thus, where the Fates call .... a white swan singeth":** From Ovid.

**Note 66. an ye be wise, ....:** Probably from Plato's *Phædo,* 61, the message of Socrates to Evenus, by Cebes.

**Page 169, note 67. or how he hath furnished his estate:** *aut qui Spartam adornarit suam.* From an ancient proverb.

**Page 171, note 68. Sure, 't is a mighty plague .... too wise a man:** See Plautus, *Miles Gloriosus,* line 68.

**Page 175, note 69. Hafnia:** Copenhagen.

**Page 177, note 70. Fetch hither wine & cups:** An echo of Horace, *Epodes,* ix . 33–34.

## ACT V

**Page 187, note 71.** *"The devil rebuketh naughtiness":* Burton's Latin, *Clodius accuset mœchos,* means, literally, "Clodius accuseth adulterers." P. Clodius, enemy to Cicero, was a notorious adulterer: he was free to accuse others of the same sin, but he was caught himself, and lives in the ancient proverb which Burton quotes from Juvenal. The line, *"what thou knowest,* etc.," is borrowed from Terence, *Heauton Timorumenos,* line 748.

**Page 191, note 72.** *wolf in the fable:* "Speak of a wolf and thou 'lt see its tail."

**Note 73.** *I desire a statue,* . . . . : At first sight it may seem rather far-fetched that Equivocus is so elated by his successful theft that he thinks that he deserves the honor of a statue; but Burton is here borrowing a touch from the *Bacchides* of Plautus, line 640, where the slave Chrysalus, congratulating himself on his achievement in robbing his master, says: "this child deserves to have a golden statue erected to him." In the next scene Burton helps himself to a large slice of the same play. Compare *Philosophaster,* Act V, beginning of Scene iii, with *Bacchides,* lines 1087 ff. [Professor Edward Bensly's note.]

**Page 193, note 74.** *I burn so hot with rage:* See Terence, *Adelphoe,* line 310.

**Page 197, note 75.** *Egyptian temples:* The term occurs more than once in Burton's *The Anatomy of Melancholy,* and is taken to mean "fair without but foul within." *Cuman asses,* a few lines below, is also an expression found in *The Anatomy;* it refers to the ass in Æsop that was arrayed in the lion's skin.

**Page 199, note 76.** *Omit so and so,* . . . . : See *The Anatomy of Melancholy* (Dell–Jordan-Smith edition, p. 96), a similar passage.

**Note 77.** *a rich Benefice's the one thing,* . . . . : The Latin, *"hoc solum in votis habens, optimum sacerdotium,"* occurs in *The Anatomy of Melancholy* (Part I, Sec. II, Mem. 3, Subs. 15), and Burton renders it, "A good Personage was their aim."

**Page 200, note 78.** Mr. Buckley, in his list of errata, appended to the Roxburghe edition, gives *licitum* as a misprint, but unfortunately the variant he supplied is likewise *licitum!* Until Burton's MSS are available it will have to stand as printed.

**Page 203, note 79.** *There's no trusting outward show:* From Juvenal, *Satires,* ii . 8.

IACOBI

# AVG · THVANI

## HISTORIARVM

### SVI TEMPORIS

*PARTIS PRIMAE*

Tomus II.

PARISIIS,

Apud AMBROSIVM & HIERONYMVM
DROVART, via Iacobæa, sub scuto Solari.

M. DCIV.

*Cum Priuilegio.*

FACSIMILE OF BURTON'S AUTOGRAPH ON HIS COPY OF *THUANUS*

# BURTON'S PREFACE TO
# RIDER'S *DICTIONARIE*

# EDITOR'S NOTE

This preface (and the verses numbered xix) appeared in the 1617 edition of Rider's *Dictionarie*. It was unknown to Mr. W. E. Buckley, and was first brought to the attention of Burtonians by Professor Edward Bensly, who referred to it in *The Cambridge History of English Literature* (Volume IV, page 565). Through the courtesy of the British Museum it is here for the first time reprinted.

The *Dictionarie*, by John Rider (1562?–1632), later (1612) Bishop of Killaloe, appeared first under the title *Dictionarium Latine et Anglice*, and was printed at Oxford in 1589. Francis Holyoke (1567?–1653) enlarged and revised this work, and it was issued in the revised form in 1606 by Adam Islip. Burton's contribution, however, is to be found only in the editions of 1612 and 1617.

Recte Vives: *esse nonnulla quæ primo quoque;*
*tempore necesse erit evulgari, narrationem rei gestæ ad plurimos*
*viventium pertinentis, tum quæ insectandi criminis in commune*
*noxii, aut depellendæ à nobis calumniæ causâ componantur.*
Quorum ego unum & alterum, quum tibi & libro tuo, falsò
licèt, inustum viderem:

> *Id mihi negoti credidi solùm dari,*

tum ob amicitiam veterem (ut qui sub eadem ferulâ meruimus)
túm ob ipsius causæ bonitatem, ut hisce quibuscunque; calum-
niis, sannis, & ludibriis occurrerem, & te simul & bonos tecum
omnes quam primum vindicarem. Et sanè quod ad susurronem
illum attinet, hujusce scommatis autorem & calumniȩ, aut illius
saltem conductitium rhetorem, qui scurrili quadam procacitate
fretus, nescio quo *supercilioso super suspectâ latinitate judicio,*
*doctis viris risum te sustulisse vult,* & labores tuos verè operosos,
*futilissima Etymologiarum figmenta vocet,* & barbare ludens,
*avaris & lucripetis* litem intendat: quod ad illum, inquam,
attinet, Atheniensium more mulctatum vellem. Nam, quod
optimê Cardanus, *Si per hos sycophantas impunè licet oppedere*
*probis viris, qui opes & operam pro studiis impendunt: ludi-*
*brie mox habebuntur artes & disciplinæ, simul cum ipsis qui*
*eas profitentur, viris.* Sed quibus ille verbis calumniatorem
suum affatus est, iisdem & tu tuum alloquaris; *Dii dabunt ut*

*faba hæc in suum caput recudatur,* qui tam liberè censuram agat, ipse tamen deteriora his quæ reprehendit, admittat. Verùm hæc aliis fortassè, non tibi; *lucripetis & avaris,* quum tu longè absis à sorde: novit ingenuum animum tuum, & verè liberalem; de grege suo Typographos perstringit. At qui alterum incusat probri, ipsum se intueri oportet *Omnia quæ vendicâris in altero* (inquit orator,) *tibi ipsi vehementer fugienda sunt.*

*Et si enim illi hæc contumeliâ digni sunt,*
*At ille indignus qui hæc diceret tamen.*

Vel quod apud Æsopum, frendens aper respondit irridenti asino, si illi *poenâ digni, at ille indignus qui ab his poenam sumat.* Et, quod illi in aurem dictum sit, si lucrum in causa non fuisset: nec tibi, nec illis litem hanc intendisset. Nec ego interim hunc hominum gregem excusatum habeo. Nam, ut quod res est cum Vernamo dicam, questui magis & avaritiæ, quàm literarum profectui student: &, quod appositè *Rainoldus, ad lucrum attentiores quàm ad officium, solùm curant, non ut maximo cum legentium fructu, sed ut suo minimo cum sumptu rem expediant.* Quòd si itaque horum aliqui frustraneum hunc laborem, & molem inutilem objiciant securè contemnas. Nam & ii ipsi qui sic arguunt, nugas omnium nugacissimas, modò sint in rem suam, ingentes ineptiarum tomos, interdum fastidiosè protrudunt. At æquiùs ferendum foret, si de grege hoc quispiam solummodo vellicaret. Verùm è doctorum numero sunt, valdè docti (si diis placet) egregiè docti, qui subsannantt hoc opus: qui non tam *futilissimum hoc Etymologiarum figmentum,* sed totum hoc studium Criticum calumniantur ut in utile, aspernantur ut leve; ipso consulente Lipsio Criticorum *Phœbo,* ut ille *ex Albania canis* qui donatus *Alexandro, vindica te ab illis solo contemptu.* Etenim calumnitari, debacchari, derogare, diffamare, rixari, nugari, & obloqui, familiares huic ævo morbi sunt, ingeniorum clades, & pestes Epidemicæ, penè dixeram Academicæ, susurrones ubique sunt; clam palàm irrident; hoc invicem faciunt, *cædimur inquem vicem* &c. hoc bonis æquè ac malis sit: & quod te soletur, hoc optimis sit; hoc, inquam, divinis viris sit,

*O Jane a tergo quem nulla ciconia pinsit,*

Nec refert quam ob causam fiat: si non alia occurrat, hæc latis: unaquæque secta (quod ex Firmiano pulchre notavit Agrippa) *omnes alias evertit, ut se suàmque confirmet: nec ulla alteri sapere concedit, ne desipere videatur.* Improbent ergo illi & obloquantur, rumpantur licèt & maledicant: tu cum Lucilio canas,

*Te paucis malle á sapientibus esse probatum.*

Si qui cordatiores sunt qui studium hoc reprehendant, hisce illustre nomen Varronis, Festi, Isidori, Nonii, e neotericis, Canisii, Perotti, utri usque Scaligeri (quantorum *Europe* luminum!) qui in hoc pulvere sudârunt; ipsius Lipsii, qui salem & solem vocat, opponas. Fremant illi: in rectà pergas ad famam viâ, & quod in Reipub. literariæ bonum, quod fœlix faustumque sit, pergas, Majoris ingenii, doctrinæ, judicii est hoc opus, quàm illorum mille centones.

Neque te moveant interim nasuti quidam Grammatistæ, Rhetores dicaculi æque ac delicatuli, qui tibi nescio quem σολοικισμον ipso statim ingressu, tanto strepitu objiciant, ob casus immutationem horrendum scelus! Perinde ac Antonius ille Iulianus apud Gellium in oratione M. Tullii; *Verbi ab eo mutati argutiam tenuiter & curiose explorent.* Nam si dictionis illius morem hi tam acuti paulò penitiùs rimari velint: nihil ibi

coactum, nihil immutatum, nullum omnino Solœcismum in-
venient, nihil ibi, nisi quod certa ratione, & proba Gramaticæ
disciplina dictum sit, nec aliam dicendi legem assumptam nisi
qua gravissimi priùs autores approbarint, & nil quod non ipsius
exemplo Tullii defendi poterit. sed consulant Gellium lib. 1.,
cap. 7. qui magnam exemplorum & loquutionum talium copiam
prebæt; & cap. 16 ejusdem libri, ubi familiarem hanc & frequentem casuum transpositionem offendent. Legant ejuspem
cap. 14. lib. 10. ubi innumera hujusmodi occurrunt, sibi-
que ipsis satisfaciant. Sed quod stolidis hisce Grammatistis, tum
idìsque magistellis dictum in genere velim: Est imperitum,
dicaculum, imperiosum, &, si quod aliud, arrogans hoc genus
hominum: qui singulos fere allatrant superciliose contemnunt,
quibus nihil magis volupe est, quàm ut in aliorum scriptis
dictisve quid arrodant, ut phrasin aut formulam vellicent,
quando ipsi interim nec quid ausint, nec possint, quod scite
Picus, *Mercurium in lingua, non in pectore gerunt.* Qui si
puerilem in modum, consarcinatis hinc inde flosculis, e the-
sauro phrasium unam aut alteram oratiunculam habuerint, &
pro famâ pollinxerint: deus bone, quantos inde spiritus as-
sumunt quám elati incedunt, solos se peritos, solos eloquentes,
undiquaque doctos, omnem Encyclopædiam, omnem sapien-
tiam se putant assequutos; quàm fastidiunt illicò omnes, qui
non æqueterse ac polite dicant, qui non in omni clausurâ
Ciceronem eaque exprimant, quàm illiteratos habent, quàm
nullos? quando quod loquanter interim non habeant & quod
de lusciniâ dictum ferunt, *Voces sint, præterea nihil, mancipia
pauca lectionis cum sint,* (Scaligeri verbis utor) exangues, aridi,
steriles, inanes, & vix artes à limine salutarint. At sibi quam
diú velint, plaudant: indisertam mavult Cicero prudentiam,
quàm stultam loquacitarem. Et me quod attinet, dispeream, si

non ego quemvis potiùs de plebe philosophum, etiam e Gram-
maticorum caſtris, Sipontinum, Desponterium, Ascentium Ba-
dium, utcunque balbutientem, mille logodædalis, mille simiis,
mille Nizolianis, mille—prætulerim. Sed cum Senensi philoso-
pho concludam. Malo scientiarum fato sit, *ut tempeſtate noſtra
pleriquem omnes, qui linguæ latinæ ſtudent, scientias nullas
norint; contra, qui liberales artes sequuntur eloquentiæ ferè
omnes expertes sint.* Hos ergo tu quales, secure contemnas, &
illorum diċteria flocci pendas. Rideant illi, tu pergas tamen
alacer & erećtus, magni illius exemplo Lipsii, *per medium hoc
calumniantium agmen, adversus omnium linguarum tela, scuto
teċtus veritatis & Candoris. Illi ringantur & liveant: tu canas
epinicia lætus, & avertentia sacra facias* Pallori & Invidiæ.

Vale, E. Musæo quinto Calend Aprilis.

RO. BURTON ex Æde Chriſti.

# BURTON'S POEMATA

## EDITOR'S NOTE

The verses that are here reprinted are, with the exception noted (Verse XIX), taken from Mr. Buckley's edition of *Philosophaſter*, sixty-five copies of which were issued by the Roxburghe Club in 1862. Since copies are exceedingly scarce, so much so as to vex Sir William Osler through twelve years of weary and vain seeking, it is thought well to make them more accessible to the ſtudent. The Latin notes which were in the margin of the Roxburghe edition are referred to the annotated line with an asterisk. Numbered notes in brackets are by the present editor, or by Bensley.

# BURTON'S POEMATA

## I

[From Academiæ Oxoniensis Pietas *erga* Jacobum *Regem*.
Oxoniæ, 1603, quarto, pp. 155–156.]

Vane quid in mediis ſtruis oppugnacula campis,
    Mœnia cur saxo non ruitura facis?
Picticus ille tuus tanto molimine murus
    Structus, et immensus qui fuit agger abit.
Hoſtis abeſt, timor omnis abit, conjunxit in uno
    Fœdere nos unus, nunc manet una salus.
Ergo cadat murus, pateat via, concidat agger,
    Unius imperio dum sine lite sumus;
Unius ob pacem proceres, populusque precentur,
    In quo pax populi, pax procerumque manet.

ROB. BURTON, *Art. Bacc. ex Æde Chriſti*

## II

[From Musa Hospitalis, *Ecclesiæ Chriſti*, *Oxon.*
*Oxoniæ*, 1605, quarto, sign. D 2.]

### DE SOLE, VENERE, ET MERCURIO IN VIRGINE CONJUNCTIS QUO TEMPORE REX ECCLESIAM CHRISTI INGRESSURUS EST.

Soli junĉta Venus, Veneri Cyllenius heros,
    Virginis inque unâ parte, quid esse putem?
Sol Rex, et Venus eſt Regina, Ecclesia Virgo,
    Mercurius Princeps, quid mage perspicuum?
Sic, ô sic veri semper præsagia cœli
    Sidera, venturos significate Deos.
Et quoties fuerit Veneri Sol Virgine junĉtus,
    Atlantis magni Pleionesque nepos:
Dignetur toties tua nos præsentia, et ædes
    Invise has toties (magne *Jacobe*) tuas.
Interea ter gratus ades (ter maxime Princeps)
    Gratior huc hospes nemo venire poteſt.
Officiosa tibi domus hæc devota salutem
    Submissè impertit, mœnia χαῖρε sonant.

ROBERTUS BURTON, *Art. Mag.*

# III

[From Juſta Oxoniensium. *Londini*, 1612, quarto, sign. D 3, pp. 37–38.]

## INFESTUS SYDERUM ASPECTUS, QUI FUIT
## OCTAVÂ HORÂ POMERIDIANÂ, *ANNO* 1612, SEXTO
### *NOVEMBRIS, QUO TEMPORE OBIIT*

### HENRICVS
### *PRINCEPS*

Quâ *Princeps* mundo illuſtris valedixerat horâ,
    Cur quinque è septem sydera mersa latent?
Pernitiosa duo superis remorantur in auris,
    *Saturnus* cœli quid prope culmen agit?
Et *Mars* solus habet cœlum Peregrinus, et exul,
    Quæ stella in terris horrida bella movet.
At cur deseruit mundum *Sol?* mitis in alto
    *Jupiter* occasu, quid vaga *Luna* latet?
*Mercuriusque* celer motu, *Venerisque* salubre
    Sydus de cœlo præcipitanter abit?
An casu hoc dicam fieri? vel sponte seipsa
    Subduxisse polo sydera fauſta putem?
Sponte suâ, ne portentum tam triſte viderent,
    Auguror *Hesperio* delituisse salo.
Scilicet hoc tempus nisi mors vidisset, an ausa
    In charum HENRICI mittere tela caput?
Ausa eſt tale nihil, vires ni occasio reddat,
    Cum terris cœlum nil dare possit opis.
Sic fuit ô superi: sic, sic voluiſtis: ut iſtud
    Luctiferum tempus, flebilis hora, foret.
Sol Diadema illi, et longos promiserat annos,

Æternum, et felix *Jupiter* imperium.

Blanda *Venus* nuptam cum multâ prole, *Diana*
    Jus maris, et *Maiæ* filius eloquium.

Et quia non poterant præstare hæc, forsitan illos
    Detinuit pudor, aut fecit abesse dolor.

Attamen hoc solvunt quod possunt cardine in imo,
    Quando quod vellent hoc sibi fata negent.

Astrigero æternam sedem dat *Phœbus Olympo*,
    Immortale decus, *Jupiter*, inquit, erit.

*Mercurius* famam, et quicquid præstare *Camœnæ*,
    Quicquid et ingenium *Mercuriale* potest.

At tumulum *Venus*, et suaves largitur odores,
    Hymnos, et quicquid nobile funus habet.

Sertum de variis contextum *Cynthia* gemmis,
    Et lachrymis plenum vas, feretrumque dedit.

Ro. Burton, *Mag. Art.*

*Ex Æde Christi*

## IV

[From Epithalamia sive Lusus Palatini.
Oxoniæ, 1613, quarto, sign. D, D 2, pp. 30–31.]

Qui modò lugebant crines umbrante cupressu,
Jam læti recinant redimiti tempora myrto.
Quæque dies tulerat feralis tædia vittæ,
Nunc mutata feret genialis gaudia lecti.
Illuſtris charam ducit FREDERICVS ELIZAM,
    O *Hymenæe* fave, *Venus* alma, et pronuba *Juno*.


Illa *Calydoniæ* nympha eſt celeberrima sylvæ,
*Arctoum* sydus, gentis *Cynosura Britannæ:*
Aſt ille *Herciniæ* decus et laus unica sylvæ
*Germanos* iubar effulgens supereminet omnes:
Ille rosas flagrans, illa autèm cinnama spirans.
    O *Hymenæe* fave, *Venus* alma, et pronuba *Juno*.


Alter *Musarum, Charitum* decus altera; et ambo
Naturæ illuſtres, fortunæ dotibus ambo,
Rélligione pares; annis, atque ignibus ambo,
Ite agite ut *Geryon* corpus coalescite in unum,
Mens eadem licèt in diverso corpore spiret.
    O *Hymenæe* fave, *Venus* alma, et pronuba *Juno*.

Uxori *Poetus,* qualis fuit *Arria Poeto,*
*Tyndaris Iliaco, Veneri* dilectus *Adonis,*
Talis ELIZA tibi, talis FREDERICVS ELIZÆ.
Contingat Vobis concordia turturis, anni
Cornicum, ac eadem genialis gratia lecti.
    O *Hymenæe* fave, *Venus* alma, et pronuba *Juno.*

Ut plantam plantæ producunt, semina semen,
Ut generant aquilas aquilæ: sic *ftemmate ab ifto*
Nascetur regum series, cælestis *Imago,*
Quæ totam *Europam* illustret, *Borealia* terræ
Climata, perque omnes mundi latè imperet oras.
    O *Hymenæe* fave, *Venus* alma, et pronuba *Juno.*

Quamque diù in *Rhenum* gelidas dat *Neccharus* undas,
*Thamisis* inque fretum lucentes volvit arenas,
Parvulus *Auguftâ* ludat *Fredericvs* in aulâ,
*Heydelberga* Tuos videat timeatque nepotes,
Dii faxint; rata sint omnes pia vota precamur.
    O *Hymenæe* fave, *Venus* alma, et pronuba *Juno.*
           RO. BURTON *in Art. Mag. ex Æde Chrift*

# V

[From Justa Funebria Ptolemæi Oxoniensis Thomæ Bodleii.
Oxoniæ, 1613, quarto, pp. 43–44.]

## *IN BIBLIOTHECAM* BODLEIANAM[1]

*Barbara Pyramidum sileat miracula Memphis,*
   Aut olim quicquid *Roma* superba dedit.
Et *Sophiæ* templum Bizantia littora longè,
   Jactare hinc cessent *Justiniane* tuum.
Ostentare suum Veneti, et *Nidrosia* templum
   Desinat, aut *Ædes Escoriale* suas.
*Argentina* suas taceat *Cremonaque* turres,
   *Hispalis* à Mauro coctile celet opus.
Omnis enim nostro cedat structura *Lyceo,*
   *Unum pro cunctis fama loquatur opus.*

## *AD* BODLEIVM

Hic ubi triste Chaos quondam crassæque tenebræ,
   Cum blattis tineæ barbariesque fuit,
Aera per medium pendebat aranea filo,
   Et fœdum visu, et nil nisi squalor erat;
Aurea resplendet nunc trabs, pictumque lacunar,

[1] [Burton refers to the Bodleian Library and its founder, Sir
Thomas Bodley, in *The Anatomy of Melancholy*, pages 457–458 of
the Dell–Jordan-Smith edition (Part 2, Sec. 2, Memb. 4).—P. J.-S.]

Luce novâ illuſtris Bibliotheca nitet.
Conspicui et varii pulchro ſtant ordine libri,
    Disposita in classes quæque *Camæna* suas.
Reddita Musa sibi eſt BODLEIO Præside, fiunt
    *Deliciæ populi quæ fuerant domini.*

### AD EUNDEM

*Quæ tam seposita eſt, quæ gens tam barbara* voce
    Ex quâ non librum *Bibliotheca* tenet?
*Indus, Arabs,* quicquid *Græci* scripsere, *Latini,*
    *Æthiopes,* quicquid *Persa* Camæna dedit,
Aut olium *Hebræi,* aut *Syri,* quodcunque vetuſtas,
    *Galli, Itali, Hispani,* quod nova lingua dedit:
Omnes BODLEIVS Thecam congessit in unam,
    *Mæcenatem* uno te velut ore sonant.
Æternumque tuum resonabunt mœnia nomen,
    Mœnia quæ sumptu sunt rediviva tuo.
Suavis odor famæ totum transibit in orbem,
    Musa nequit myſtæ non memor esse sui.

ROB. BURTON, *Art. Mag. ex Æde Chriſti*

# VI

[From Jacobi Ara. Oxoniæ. 1617, quarto, sign. C, pp. 17, 18.]

DE SCOTIS ET ANGLIS SIBI INVICEM ANTŒCIS, A MURO PICTICO
VELUT ÆQUATORE DIVISIS. SOLE IACOBO MERIDIANUM
UTRIUSQUE GENTIS SIMUL IRRADIANTE, ET DECLINATIONE
SUA CIS VEL CITRA MURUM PICTICUM, VARIAS RERUM
VICES EFFICIENTE.

*Antœci oppositœ* sunt gentes, *dividit* illas
    *Æquator,* partes et facit esse *duas.*
*Culminat* his idem *Sol,* lustrans tempore *eodem*
    Utrosque, et medius *lumen utrique* facit.
Unde his *una dies, nox* est simul *una,* sed istis
    *Æstas opposito* et tempore, *bruma* venit.
Nos sumus *Antœci,* quis enim neget, utraque leges
    Gens habet oppositas, et regimen proprium.
Et velut *Æquator* medios nos dividit *agger,*
    Quos sic divisos *unius* aura fovet,
*Iacobus Rex* qui tanquam *Sol* aureus, ambos
    Lumine stellanti perpetuoque regit:
*Catnesi* fines, *Rutupinaque* littora longè
    Prospicit, hos, illos *irradiansque* simul,
Australes *Britones,* quicquidve interjacet *Arcton,*
    Lustratur radiis inclyte *Phœbe tuis.*
Una *dies* utrisque, simul regnante *Iacobo,*
    *Sole* cadente tuo, *nox* erit *una* simul.
At licèt *una dies* sit nobis una *eadem nox,*

Tristis in *opposito* tempore sævit *hyems.*
Alternæque vices rerum, cœlique Britanni,
 *Obliquis radiis* quas modo *Phœbe* facis.
Experti loquimur, fulgor, vultusque serenus
 Nos ubi destituit, qui fuit ante tuus;
Destituit nos unà *æstas,* cœlumque serenum,
 Et quicquid pulchrum floridus annus habet.
Excepere simul nubes, et squalor, et imbres
 Assidui, et mæstis tristior aura fuit.
Quando illi intereà tua quos præsentia (*Cæsar*)
 Dignata est, festos quot tenuere dies.
Quam suaves epulas, ludos, spectâcla, triumphos,
 Lætitiam, vultus te *radiante* suos.
Verum ubi jam nostras *Phœbus declinat* ad oras,
 Flat Zephyrus, venit et blandior inde tepor,
*Autumnus* quasi *Ver,* nubes pelluntur *Olympo,*
 Jam rursus cœlum gestit, et aura nitet.
En animos nuper dijectos, saucia corda,
 *Aspectu* primum jam rediviva tuo.
Nos ubi te reducem (*Rex*) incolumemque videmus,
 *Salve* quam læto murmure quisque sonat.
Hi donis certant, votis hi, versibus illi,
 Et proceres, et plebs officiosa ruunt.
Illis e contrà, tuo quos *præsentia* liquit,
 E quibus et *radios* subtrahis (*alme*) tuos,
Vastities venit, et torpor *brumæque* rigores,
 Lugent decessum, læti abiere *dies.*
O longùm maneas nobiscum, *hyememque* repellas,
 Perpetuam *lucem* lætitiamque ferens.

Subque tuis *radiis* ut jam læta *Anglia* floret,
    Floreat æternùm *sole micante* precor.
E thalamoque suo *Sol* tanquam *Sponsus* ut errat,*
    Ad cursum exultans, indomitusve *gigas*,
Egredere è solio *fœlix*, et perfice cursum,
    Quem tibi signavit, disposuitque *Deus*.

ROB. BURTON, S.T.B. *ex Æde Chriſti*

* Psalms 19:6.

## VII

[From Academiæ Oxoniensis, Funebria Sacra, Æt. Mem. Ser. Reg. Annæ. Oxoniæ, 1619, quarto, sign. B 3, p. 14.]

### IN OBITUM SERENISSIMÆ ANNÆ ANGLORUM REGINÆ

### CALENDIS MARTIIS, ANNO 1618

*Lampedo* Spartana suo celeberrima sæclo,*
    Inter fœmineum fœmina sola gregem,
Inter fælices et fælicissima quondam,
    Regis enim conjux, filia, mater erat.
*Anna* Britannorum sydus, Junonia proles,
    Diis genita, et Regis filia, sponsa, parens.
Utraque diva parens regum, divina propago,
    Quæ major tamen, hæc sitne, vel illa, petis?
*Quantum lenta solent inter viburna cupressi,*
    Spartanam super hanc extulit *Anna* caput.
Anglorum genti quantumque Laconia cedit,
    Tantùm *Annæ* cedit Nympha Pelasga Deæ.
Tantùm prole subit, tantumque in conjuge cedit,
    Fortunâ, et formâ, et stemmate victa jacet.
Ergò *Annæ* palmam det *Plinius,* omnibus *Anna*
    Præcellit formâ, et dotibus Ingenii.
*Anna* decus gentis, nuptarum gloria, matrum
    Deliciæ, et sexus gemmula sola suæ.
At fuit, heù fuit hæc; neque res neque gratia formæ
    Servare hanc potuit, mors ubi sæva venit.
Occidit, et quæ viva parem non invenit, ecce
    Mortua par cuivis, sic jubet urna, jacet.

    * Plinius, lib. 7, cap. 41.

Occidit, atque iterum terras *Astræa* reliquit,
    *Astræa* hæc *Britonum* lucida stella micat:
Non in Zodiaco velut illa *Astræa* refulgens,
    Non ubi *Calisto* aut *Cassiopæa* nitet,
Non sortita locum sequitur sua plaustra *Bootes*,
    Tardus in occasum, quà sine fine rotans.
Non *Aquila* hanc posuit cælo, aut *Thaumantias Iris*,
    *Mercurius* celer, at prævia stella comans:
Signavitque viam, et scandens super æthera, dixit
    Hàc sequere, en lucem præbeo, chara Comes.
Illa super cœlos sequitur, stellasque relinquens
    Ad superos victrix *Anna Perenna* venit.
*Anna Perenna* venit, quid ni sic *Anna* vocetur?
    *Anna* Dea, et nomen verius istud habet.
*Didonis* soror *Anna* eadem quæ præfuit annis,
    *Numicio* præceps flumine mersa fuit.
Diva habita, et sic dicta olim, quærentibus illam
    Quòd dum sustinuit conscius amnis aquas,
*Ipsa loqui visa est, placidi sum Nympha Numici,**
    *Amne perenne latens, Anna Perenna vocor.*
Idibus hinc *Annæ* festum geniale *Perennæ*
    Martis erat, cui plebs non nisi pota piat.
At Dani soror *Anna* istæc, Martisque Calendis
    Mortem obiit, fato sed meliore tamen.
Dum Britonum imperium durat, dum carmina, vatum
    Ore perenne vigens, *Anna Perenna* viret.
Menseque in hoc Martis nomen dum permanet Anglûm,
    Annua sacra tibi qui dabit, *Anglus* erit.

                  Robertus Burtonus, *Sac. Theol.*
                    *Bacc. ex Æde Christi*

\* Ovid, *Fasti*, III. 653.

# VIII

[From Ultima Linea Savilii. Oxonii, 1622, quarto, sign. B 2, p. 27.]

Suspicio quoties signis variabile cœlum,
    Zodiacum obliquum, ſtelliferumque polum;
Hinc video fera monſtra, illinc animalia, pisces,
    Inde canes, lepores, præſtigiasque hominum,
Informes ursos, aurigas, plauſtra, dracones,
    Ignavum pecus, et *Gorgonis* ora nitent,
Quorsum *Aries* cœlo, quid *Taurus* imagine vaſtâ,
    Quid brutus *Cancer?* quid *Capricornus* agit?
Quo jure? an potuit vatum imperiosa poteſtas
    Tantum audere nefas? hoc, Ptolomææ, feres?
Deturbentur, et in barathrum scelerata propago,
    Quod meruere pati, præcipitanter eant.
*Perseus Alcides, Cepheus,* divinus *Orion,*
    Cum *Geminis Cheiron,* pulcher et *Antinous,*
Quos quondam veteres dignati sedibus illis,
    Stent, olim illuſtres Aſtronomi, et meritò.
At quorsum cœlo, meretrix? quorsum lyra, cignus,
    Quid leo, quid vultur, quid fera monſtra polo?
Descendat vaga turba, locum teneatque propago
    Divina Heroum, et quæ Jove digna cohors.
Alphonsus, Bacon, Ticho, Copernicus alter
    Atlas,[1] Candisius, Drakus et Americus.


[1] [In the *Anatomy* of 1624 (page 37) Burton uses the words, "Copernicus, Atlas his successor, is of opinion the Earth is a Planet" (page 64 of the Dell–Jordan-Smith edition). Mr. Buckley was of the opinion that Burton took the phrase from the foregoing.— P. J.-S.]

Qui Solis quondam comites, quod continet orbis
    Lustrarunt radiis, et vaga signa poli.
Et cœlum amplecti merite ò divine *Saville,*
    Sydus habe, et cœlum sydere dignus habe.
O si aliquis vates nostro floreret in ævo,
    Quem penes arbitrium hoc, si quis Apollo foret,
Qui, ut Naso quondam moribundi Cæsaris umbram
    Transtulit in cœlos, det tibi (Dive) locum.
Non autem Nasone opus est, nec Apolline quovis,
    Æternum nomen nam tibi Musa dabit.
Immortale tuum decus est, dum Luna vagatur
    Cœlo, *Savilli* fama superstes erit.

        ROB. BURTON, S.T.B. *Ex Æde Christi*

## IX

[From Carolus Redux. *Oxon.* 1623, quarto, sign. B 2.]

Mentitus formam quòd Princeps Carolus exit,
    Per freta per montes, itque reditque celer;
Ne mireris; amor jussit; nam Juppiter ipse
    Factus ob hunc olim bos, equus, imber, olor.

        ROB. BURTON, S.T.B. *ex Æde Christi*

# X

[From Camdeni Insignia. Oxoniæ, 1624, quarto, sign. A 4.]

*Marmore de pario ſtatuas si ponere possem,** \
*Pingere vel vultus, vivoque referre colore,* \
*Ducere si possem referentes ære figuras,* \
*Sive viros meritos cælo ſtellisque beare,* \
*Camdenum ſtatuæ, color, æs marmorque referrent,*

In laudem *Aschami Camdenus* talia quondam \
    Scripsit, et in laudes sic ego (Clare) tuas; \
Idque ex ore tuo, verbis et versibus iisdem \
    Te canto, tua quêis Musa beavit eum. \
Dignior et multò es Parium quem marmor honeſtet, \
    Quem pictor, Musæ, et quisque Poeta canat, \
Sydera quem donent cœleſti sede, Lycæi \
    Quem Myſta æternis percolat officiis.

          Rob. Burton, S.T.B. *ex Æde Chr.*

---

\* *In laudem* Aschami *Sylva* Camdeni *Lond.* 1590. *Ep.* Aschami *Præfixà.* Aschamum *habet ille.*

## XI

[From Oxoniensis Academiæ Parentalia. Sacr. Mem. Jacobi.
Oxoniæ, 1625, quarto, sign. A 3, p. 16.]

### *IN TUMULUM* JACOBI *REGIS*[1]

Quis jacet hîc? Rex JACOBUS: Quænam agmina mæstè
    Circumstant tumulum (Dive JACOBE) tuum?
Pax, Musæ, Charites, Clementia. At ille senex quis?
    Europæ Genius. Quæ tamen hæc mulier?
Nympha Britanna. Gemunt omnes; quæ causa dolendi?
    Noster honos, columen, delicium occubuit.
Longùm ergò pax alma Vale: lugete Camænæ,
    JACOBUS Vestro est mortuus exitio.
Æternùmque gemant Britones: Jam pace relictâ,
    Vestram Europæi quærite perniciem.

ROB. BURTON, *Sac. Theol. Bacch.*
*ex Æde Chri.*

---

[1] ["There is a copy of these lines, if it be not the original
draught of them in Burton's hand on the blank leaf of *Oxoniensis
Academiæ Funebre Officium in Memoriam Elizabethæ.* Oxon. 1603,
which Burton gave to the Bodleian Library. In the first line the
manuscript reads 'quæso' instead of 'mæste,' and in the sixth, 'honor'
and 'Delitium.' "—Mr. Buckley's note.]

## XII

[From Epithalamia Oxoniensia. *In* Caroli *et* Henr. Mar. Connubium. Oxoniæ, 1625, quarto, sign. K 3 verso.]

Quos vaſtæ rupes, frendens quos dividit æquor,
    Hos blando suavis fœdere jungit Amor.
Gallam *Hero* pulchram Britonum *Leander* in Anglo
    Littore tutus habes, et *Maria* alta silent.
*Si tibi tale fretum quondam Leandre fuisset,**
    *Non foret* horrisonæ *mors tua crimen aquæ.*

ROB. BURTON, S.T.B. *ex Æde Chr.*

* Ovid, 3, *Trist.* x. 41.

## XIII

[From Britanniæ Natalis. Oxoniæ, 1630, quarto, p. 56.]

Quid sibi vult tantus rumor lætusque susurrus?
    Unde platæa novo quælibet igne micat?
Nascitur Augustus puer. At sic quilibet annus
    Jactavit, Regem quælibet ora tenet.
Sed Rex quotidiè non nascitur: aurea proles,
    Augustus Princeps nascitur (Angle) tibi.
Angle tibi nata est soli Junonia proles,
    Atque novum sydus fulget in orbe tuo.
Ergò læteris fausto Britannia partu,
    Æternùm hoc sydus splendeat orbe precor.
Innumera innumeris cumulentur gaudia sæclis,
    Succrescantque tuis Florida deliciis.

ROB. BURTON, S.T.B.
*ex Æde Chr.*

## XIV

[From Solis Britannici Perigæum. Oxoniæ, 1633, quarto, sign. B 3, p. 21.]

Ut Sol Zodiacum percurrit mensibus æquis,
    Atque Æquatorem bis secat orbe suo.
A tropico Cancri ad Capricornum devius errat:
    Alternum Zonas lustrat utrasque jubar.
Sic Tu percurris gentem (Rex inclite) nostram,
    Numine prospiciens utraque regna tuo.
Æquator murus sit Picticus: Anglia Cancer:
    Scotia sed fines det, Capricorne, tuos,
Et quoniam in Cancro Solis mora longior, Anglis
    Imperii sedes firmior esto tuis.

ROB. BURTON, S.T.B. *ex Æde Christi*

## XV

[From Vitis Carolinæ Gemma Altera. Oxoniæ, 1633, quarto, sign. Ee 4.]

Quam varia hæc vita eſt; totus modo perſtrepit orbis
    De triſti fato et funere (Suede) tuo.
Inde ferox bellum et sævissima mortis Imago,
    O quanti heroes, quot periere duces?
En *nova* tot gemitus inter *gratissima* nobis,
    Regius in noſtro nascitur orbe puer.
Funde merum Genio, veteres cessate querelæ,
    Personet his terris nil nisi dulce melos.

ROB. BURTON, S.T.B.

# XVI

[From Flos Britannicus Veris Novissimi. Oxon., 1636, quarto, p. 6.]

Non habeo argentum, nec enim mihi suppetit aurum,
  Verum quod possum do tibi (Diva) lubens.
Det Diadema tibi Juno, det Cypria formam,
  Det Sophiam Pallas verbaque Mercurius.
Sic precor, et quando fuerit tibi nubilis ætas
  Te dignum exopto Regia Virgo virum.

ROB. BURTON, S.T.B.

# XVII

[From Coronæ Carolinæ Quadratura. Oxon., 1636, quarto, sign. a a a a.]

Vive diu felix virgo, Iove nata Britanno,
  Filia quæ Regis, Regis et uxor eris,
Et Regum mater, Regum matertera, Regum
  Alma parens, Regum stemmata mille feres
Quæ Constantinum superent, Helenamque Britannam,
  Terrarumque orbi Regia sceptra dabunt.

ROB. BURTON, *Theol. B. Æd. Chr.*

## XVIII

[From Death Repealed, *Verses on* Lord Bayning. Oxon., 1638, quarto, pp. 3, 4.]

### IN OBITUM ILLUSTRISSIMI VICECOMITIS
### BAYNING

*Quid voveat dulci nutricula majus Alumno*
   *Quam bona fortunæ, corporis, atque animi?*
*En hæc Heroe hoc simul omnia; quid petat ultra?*
   *Quid potius? Cælum: quod novus hospes habet.*

#### THE SAME ENGLISHED

Can Nurse choose in her sweet babe more to find
Then goods of Fortune, Body, and of Mind?
Loe here at once all this: what greater blisse
Canſt hope or wish? Heaven; why there he is.

ROB. BURTON, *of Ch. Ch.*

# XIX

[From Rider's *Dictionarie Corrected* . . . . By Francis Holyoke. London, Printed by Adam Islip for Thomas Man. 1617, quarto, sign. ¶¶ 2.]

### AD FRANCISCUM DE SACRA-QUERCU

Sacra Jovi quercus, Francisco sanctior olim
　　Nemo fuit, mystis si sit habenda fides.
De Sacra quercu cum sis Francise sacerdos,
　　Atque Jovis summi, nomine réque sacer,
De Sacra quercu quidni Francisce voceris?
　　Rumpatur Momus, sic tibi nomen erit.
Aemula Dodonæ nunc est* Ardenia sylva,
　　Dum sacras quercus, hæc ut & illa ferat:
Quótque dedit quondam quercus Dodonia glandes,
　　De quercúque faber quercea quanta facit;
Tot verbis Etyma & nostros deducis in usus,
　　Verborum egregius non minús ipse faber.
Lexica non solúm comples sed pulpita verbis,
　　Dum populum vera relligione doces.
Perge faber deinceps, pergas sacer, effice verbis
　　Lexica clara tuis, pulpita clara tuis.
Querceto deprome tuo, quod restet in ævum,
　　Quercinum robur, duret ut istud opus.
Déque tua quercu faciat tibi Musa coronam,
　　Aevo sacratam, quam sine fine geras.
Verborum quod monstra domet, veteresque repurget
　　Herculeum nomen Politianus habet.


　　　　* In Com. War. quâ natus F. H.

Sic Ficinus eum verè sic Scala vocavit,
    Herculeus verè nam labor iſte fuit.
Cum tu suſtineas tales tantósque labores,
    Sensum, Etymon verbis reſtituendo suis,
Quid ni ego te dicam Herculeum? qui verba domaſti
    Tot monſtrosa tuæ viᄃta labore manus.
Vel potiùs tibi si speciosa vocabula rident,
    Alter Iolâus tu mihi diᄃtus eris.
Quod verbis Hidrâ oppressis, cariéque peresis
    Tu lucem dederis, prætulerísque facem.
Ergo conveniat quando tibi nomen utrumque,
    Utrius famam, & præmia digna feres.

RO. BURTON, *ex Æde Chriſti*

# ROBERT BURTON'S WILL

## EDITOR'S NOTE

The copy here given is taken from the 1800 edition of Burton's *Anatomy*, with certain corrections suggested by the recent copy printed by the Oxford Bibliographical Society, before cited. The name of Burton's servant is given as Upton in all copies printed prior to 1926; but the Oxford Bibliographical Society gives Oxton in the first place and Upton in the last. This confusion has probably arisen from the present condition of the manuscript.

The original will is in Somerset House, London, Vol. 56, Coventry, Court of Canterbury. The will was proved on May 11, 1640.

IN NOMINE DEI AMEN. August 15th One
thousand six hundred thirty nine because there be so many casu-
alties to which our life is subject besides quarrelling and contention which happen to our Successors after our Death by
reason of unsettled Estates I Robert Burton Student of
Christchurch Oxon, though my means be but small have
thought good by this my last Will and Testament to dispose
of that little which I have and being at this present I thank
God in perfect health of Bodie and Mind and if this Testament be not so formal according to the nice and strict terms of
Law and other Circumstances peradventure required of which
I am Ignorant I desire howsoever this my Will may be ac-
cepted and stand good according to my true intent and meaning First I bequeath Animam Deo Corpus Terræ whensoever
it shall please God to call me I give my Land in Higham
which my good Father Ralphe Burton of Lindly in the County
of Leicester Esquire gave me by Deed of Gift and that which
I have annexed to that Farm by purchase since now leased for
thirty eight pounds per annum to mine Elder Brother William
Burton of Lindly Esquire during his life and after him to his
Heirs I make my said Brother William likewise mine Exec-
utor as well as Heir paying such Annuities and Legacies out
of my Lands and Goods as are hereafter specified I give to my
nephew Cassibilan Burton twenty pounds Annuity per annum
out of my Land in Higham during his life to be paid at two
equall payments at our Lady Day in Lent and Michaelmas or
if be not paid within fourteen Days after the said Feasts to

275

distrain on any part of the Ground on or any of my Lands of
Inheritance Item I give to my Sister Katherine Jackson during
her life eight pounds per annum. Annuity to be paid at the two
Feasts equally as above said or else to distrain on the Ground
if she be not paid after fourteen days at Lindly as the other
*some* is out of the said Land Item I give to my Servant John
Upton* the Annuity of Forty Shillings out of my said Farme
during his life (if till then my Servant) to be paid on Michaelmas day in Lindly each year or else after fourteen days to
distrain  Now for my goods I thus dispose them First I give an
Cth pounds to Christ Church in Oxford where I have so long
lived to buy five pounds Lands per annum to be yearly bestowed on Books for the Library Item I give an hundredth
pound to the University Library of Oxford to be bestowed to
purchase five pound Land per annum to be paid out Yearly
on Books as Mrs. Brooks formerly gave an hundred pounds to
buy Land to the same purpose and the Rent to the same use I
give to my Brother George Burton twenty pounds and my
watch I give to my Brother Ralph Burton five pounds Item
I give to the Parish of Seagrave in Leicestershire where I am
now Rector ten pounds to be given to certain Feoffees to the
perpetual good of the said *Parish* as I have lately done to St.
Thomas's parish Item I give to my Niece Eugenia Burton
One Hundredth pounds Item I give to my Nephew Richard
Burton now Prisoner in London an hundredth pound to re-
deem him Item I give to the Poor of Higham Forty Shillings
where my land is to the poor of Nuneaton where I was once
a Grammar Scholar three pound to my Cousin Purfey of
Wadley my Cousin Purfey of Calcott my Cousin Hales of
Coventry my Nephew Bradshaw of Orton twenty shillings a

---

* The copy given in Oxford Bibliographical Society Papers,
Vol. I, Pt. III, p. 219, says "Oxton."

piece for a small remembrance to Mr. Whitehall Rector of Cherkly myne old Chamber Fellow twenty shillings I desire my Brother George and my Cousin Purfey of Calcott to be the Overseers of this part of my Will I give moreover five pounds to make a small Monument for my Mother where she is buried in London to my Brother Jackson forty shillings to my Servant John Upton forty shillings besides his former Annuity if he be my servant till I dye if he be till then my Servant—ROBERT BURTON—CHARLES RUSSELL Witness—JOHN PEPPER Witness.

An Appendix to this my Will if I die in Oxford or whilst I am of Christ Church and with good Mr. Paynes August the Fifteenth 1639.

I give to Mr. Doctor Fell Dean of Christ Church Forty Shillings to the Eight Canons twenty Shillings a piece as a small remembrance to the poor of St. Thomas Parish Twenty Shillings to Brasenose Library five pounds to Mr. Rowse of Oriel Colledge twenty shillings to Mr. Heywood xxs. to Doctor Metcalfe xxs. to Mr. Sherley xxs. If I have any Books the University Library hath not let them take them If I have any Books our own Library hath not let them take them I give to Mrs. Fell all my English Books of Husbandry one excepted

to her Daughter Mrs. Catherine Fell my Six Pieces of Silver Plate and six Silver spoons to Mrs. Iles my *Gerards Herball* To Mrs. Morris my *Country Farme* Translated out of French 4.⁽ᵗᵒ⁾ and all my English Physick Books to Mr. Whistler the Recorder of Oxford I give twenty Shillings to all my fellow Students Mʳˢ of Arts a Book in fol. or two a piece as Master Morris Treasurer or Mr. Dean shall appoint whom I request to be the Overseer of this Appendix and give him for his pains *Atlas Geografer* and *Ortelius Theatrum Mondi* I give to John

Fell the Deans Son Student my Mathematical Instruments except my two Crosse Staves which I give to my Lord of Doune, if he be then of the House To Thomas Iles Doctor Iles his Son Student *Salmuths Pancirolli* and *Lucians Works* in 4 Tomes If any books be left let my Executors dispose of them with all such Books as are written with my own hands and half my *Melancholy* Copy for Crips hath the other half To Mr. Jones Chaplain and Chanter my Surveying Books and Instruments To the Servants of the House Forty Shillings ROBERT BURTON—Charles Russell Witness—John Pepper Witness—This Will was shewed to me by the Testator and acknowledged by him some few days before his death to be his last Will Ita Testor John Morris S. Th. D. Prebendarius Eccl: Christi. Oxon. Feb. 3. 1639.

Probatum fuit Testamentum suprascriptum, &c. 11° 1640 Juramento Willmi Burton Fris' et Executoris cui &c. de bene et fideliter administrand' &c. coram Mag'ris Nathanaele Stephens Rectore Eccl. de Drayton, et Edwardo Farmer, clericis, vigore commissionis, &c.

# APPENDIX

## WOOD'S ACCOUNT OF BURTON

[This sketch is from Anthony Wood's *Athenæ Oxonienses*, edition of 1721, pages 627–28. Excerpts have been cited from this account many times, but it is believed to be of sufficient interest to warrant its reprinting in full.]

ROBERT BURTON, known otherwise to Scholars by the name of Democritus Junior, younger Brother to Will. Burton, whom I shall mention under the year 1645, was born of an ancient and genteel Family at Lindley in Leicestershire, 8 Feb. 1576, and therefore in the titles of several of his choice Books which he gave to the public Library, he added to his Sir-name *Lindliacus* Leycestrensis. He was educated in Grammar learning in the Free-School of Sutton-Coldfield in Warwickshire, whence he was sent to Brasen-nose Coll. in the long vacation, *an.* 1593, where he made considerable progress in Logic and Philosophy in the condition of a Commoner. In 1599 he was elected *Student* of Christ Church, and, for form's sake, tho' he wanted not a Tutor, he was put under the tuition of Dr. John Bancroft, afterward Bishop of Oxford. In 1614 he was admitted to the reading of the Sentences, and on the 29th of Nov., 1616, he had the Vicarage of St. Thomas' Parish in the West Suburb of Oxford conferr'd on him by the Dean and Canons of Christ Church, (to the Parishoners whereof he always gave the Sacrament in Wafers) which, with the Rectory of Segrave in Leicestershire, given to him some years after by George Lord Berkeley, he kept with much ado to his dying day. He was an exact Mathematician, a curious Calculator of Nativities, a general read Scholar, a thro'-pac'd Philologist, and one that underſtood the surveying of Lands well. As he was by many accounted a severe ſtudent, a devourer of Authors, a melancholy and humerous Person; so by others, who knew him well, a Person of great honeſty, plain dealing and Charity. I have heard some of the Ancients of Chriſt Church often say that his Company was very merry, facete and juvenile, and no man did surpass him for his ready and dextrous interlarding his common discourses among them with Verses from the Poets or Sentences from classical Authors, which being then the fashion in the University, made his Company more acceptable. He hath written,

*The Anatomy of Melancholy*—Firſt printed in quarto and afterwards several times in folio, 1624, 1632, 38, and 1652, &c to the great profit of the Bookseller, who got an Eſtate by it. 'T is a Book so full of variety of reading that Gentlemen who have loſt their time and are put to a push for invention, may furnish themselves with matter for common or scholaſtic discourse and writing. Several Authors have unmercifully ſtolen matter from the said Book without any acknowledgement, particularly one Will Greenwood, in his Book entitled *A Description of the passion of Love*, &c., London, 1657, octavo. Who, as others of the like humour do, sometimes takes his quotations without the leaſt mention of Democritus Junior. He the said R. Burton, paid his laſt debt to nature, in his Chamber in Chriſt Church at, or very near that time which he had some years before foretold from the Calculation of his own nativity. Which being exaᶜt, several of the Students did not forbear to whisper among themselves that rather than there should be a miſtake in the Calculation, he sent up his Soul to Heaven thro' a slip about his Neck. His body was afterwards with due solemnity buried near that of Dr. Rob. Weſton, in the North Isle which joyns next to the Choir of the Cathedral of Chriſt Church, on the 27th of January in sixteen hundred thirty and nine. Over his Grave was soon after erected a comely Monument on the upper Pillar of the said Isle, with his Bust painted to the life: on the right hand of which is the Calculation of his Nativity, and under the Bust this inscription made by himself; all put up by the care of William Burton his Brother:

· *Paucis notus, paucioribus ignotus, hic jacet Democritus junior, cui vitam dedit, & mortem Melancholia. Obit viii. Id. Jan. A.C. MDCXXXIX.*

(Known to few, unknown to fewer, here lies Democritus Junior, to whom Melancholy gave life and death. Died the twenty-fifth of January, 1639.)

He left behind him a very choice library of Books, many of which he bequeathed to that of Bodley, and a hundred Pounds to buy five Pounds yearly for the supplying of Christ Church Library with Books.